Financial Speculation

Trading financial biases and behaviour

By Gerald Ashley

HARRIMAN HOUSE LTD

3A Penns Road
Petersfield
Hampshire
GU32 2EW
GREAT BRITAIN

Tel: +44 (0)1730 233870
Fax: +44 (0)1730 233880
Email: enquiries@harriman-house.com
Website: www.harriman-house.com

First published in Great Britain in 2009

ISBN 978-1-905641-99-4

British Library Cataloguing in Publication Data
A CIP catalogue record for this book can be obtained from the British Library.

Printed and bound In Great Britain by the MPG Books Group, Bodmin and King's Lynn.

To the memory of my father

Donald Ashley

Contents

About the author

Gerald Ashley has over thirty years experience in international financial markets, having worked for Baring Brothers in London and Hong Kong, and the Bank for International Settlements in Basel, Switzerland. His primary financial market experience is in foreign exchange, currency options, precious metals and money markets.

He is now Managing Director of St Mawgan & Co Limited, a London-based strategy and risk consulting firm. He is also a well-known speaker on the benefits and applications of behavioural economics in decision-making and risk taking, and is a regular columnist in the financial press.

Preface to the new edition

Napoleon's close advisor Talleyrand once remarked of the French peasantry that they had learned nothing and forgotten nothing; in a sense his observation also captures the underlying state of mind of financial markets and its actors. When studying the markets it quickly becomes apparent that the same factors, emotions and activities always drive financial trading. The markets go round and round the same track – there may be different players, new instruments, different regulations and taxes which can change the particular circumstances, but not the overall game.

This may be seen as both a puzzle (why do we repeat the same mistakes in finance?) and also an opportunity (study the past and perhaps profit in the future?)

For example, in the 1920s and 1930s we had a huge speculative bubble followed by economic collapse, frauds by Ponzi and Ivar Kreuger, spectacular trading fortunes won and lost by Livermore, Cutten et al. Now, as the new millennium is well established we have Enron, the Madoff saga, the collapse of Bear Stearns and Lehman Brothers, and the huge fortunes won and sometimes lost by hedge funds. Not to mention the current fear that we might be entering a second Great Depression.

When the first edition of this book came out in the spring of 2003 the hot topics were the fallout from the dotcom crash, the telecom debt fiasco, how gold would struggle to stay above $300 an ounce and would sterling join the euro? Now at the time of this edition some six years later the big stories are all about the credit crunch, the imminent death of investment banking, why gold is cheap under $1,000 an ounce and why sterling is doomed, and perhaps we should join the euro!

I have kept the original preface in this edition because what was true then is just as true today. The lessons of markets in the past will serve us well for markets in the future, but will we learn? Somehow I very much doubt it.

Finally, throughout my thirty-plus years in the financial markets, I have had the good fortune to meet many interesting, wise and shrewd characters. Some of my closest market friends have been good enough to offer me suggestions, comments and advice regarding this book. In particular I would like to thank Chris Charlton, Richard Knight, John Norris, Alan Vear, Jim Sharpe, Alla Lapidus, Rosy Chesterman and in particular give special thanks to Juliette Clark and Terry Lloyd for their insights and thoughtful comments.

In addition to the above I would like to also thank both David Furlonger and Henrik Holleufer for their additional comments and observations that I have tried to incorporate in this edition.

As ever any mistakes, omissions or complete stupidities remain entirely my own responsibility.

London, February 2009

Preface to the 2003 edition

'Uncertainty and Expectation are the Joys of Life.'
William Congreve

It may seem simple, but it's not easy – how can we make money from financial trading? This book sets out to examine various aspects of financial speculation and possible routes to success and profits; but if you expect an easy answer, you can look forward to disappointment. The iron law of financial markets is that there is no quick, simple and definitive answer. This is because finance is not static, and any attempt to totally capture its defining characteristics is fruitless. If we are to achieve anything in markets we have to first understand this basic fact.

An enormous amount has been written on this topic already, but I hope to try and examine the subject from a number of different and interesting angles. In particular I want to concentrate on three key elements involved in financial trading: first, the concept of dynamism, not just in terms of price changes and frantic trading rooms, but through the mechanism of positive feedback; second, the importance of looking at financial markets as a whole and not just within narrow asset classes; and third, to question the importance of much of today's use of computers and bandwidth technology.

Financial markets seem to dominate our lives as never before. Whether one works in the industry or not, it is hard to avoid the constant bombardment of information, news and comment about markets. At times the markets seem all powerful, passing instant judgements on politicians, business leaders and policy makers – and forcing even democratic governments to take heed of their opinions, and sometimes change the policies that they were elected to advance. It is perhaps ironic that in an age when governments have anguished about a reduction in nation state sovereignty and the growth of supra-national organisations, it is the financial markets that have steadily grown in importance, and on occasions threatened to become the global masters.

In addition to these worries about the power of global capitalism, there has also grown a tendency to believe that markets have steadily become more sophisticated and cleverer than in the past. In truth there is little evidence to support this assertion. Technology has certainly added a gloss of sophistication to many financial operations, but in many ways the markets remain very conservative, and traditional in their operations. Indeed I think this book will amply show that, in virtually all respects, the characteristics of markets have changed very little with the passage of time.

Obviously methods of transacting business have changed – since the end of the Second World War, the markets have moved from the telegraph, to the international phone call, the telex machine and through to email and high security intranets, but the basic business is still the same. Still buying and selling, and still borrowing and lending.

The names of the players have changed as well, indeed the last decade has seen many famous and eminent financial houses wither away or swallowed up by the new global factories that dominate so much of today's business. Here again, there is little that is truly new – the current crop of behemoths will no doubt change in time and some will fall, only to be replaced by yet others; but the markets will plough ever onwards.

Let's begin with a brief outline of the first major theme. In recent years there has been a growing interest in the idea of behavioural finance – this rejects the received wisdom that markets are purely driven by financial numbers, valuations and statistics. Instead it tries to examine the motives and aims of the market players themselves – to analyse and understand their behaviour. As such it is really an alternative to the competing views of economics and accounting valuations, and the well-worn and somewhat facile path trumpeted by technical analysts. To my mind the behavioural approach has significant merit, and this book will look at some of these ideas, and in particular concentrate on the inner fears of the individual, and also the positive feedback loop of information that seems to influence markets. In other words one should not only concentrate on the asset values and price movements in the market, but equally follow the reaction and activities of the participants. Such activity is not always rational in the economic sense and one major factor in markets is that many, if not all, players have a flawed sense of value and risk-reward odds. This is a complicated but worthwhile area of study, and hopefully will help to underline two facts that are sometimes discarded; financial markets are not a precise orderly machine with predictable outcomes, and that to pursue a trading approach with that belief is to fall into the trap that can be labelled the fallacy of control. Markets are much more subtle and complex than we often think.

Allied to this behavioural view of the market is the interesting academic work that has been done on risk assessment. Today huge reliance is placed upon risk management and monitoring systems, but they contain a serious weakness in that humans are not very good at making correct risk judgements. So, however good the data, or indeed the computational prowess of the organisation, the weakest link in the chain still remains human judgement. Once again one can observe that despite all the advances in risk management, basic age old problems still lurk. Research work on group behaviour has some interesting insights into how groups assess information and this has much to tell us about the dynamics of market participants. This may seem rather arcane and removed from the business of trading and speculation, but in fact the fickle nature of groups and crowds can be broadly categorised and assessed – and this in many ways is a critical and relevant way to think about financial markets.

The second key factor to my mind is the idea that markets should be viewed and analysed as a whole, not just in terms of separate asset classes, industry groupings or individual instruments. Traditional analysis has tended to look at financial markets in this vertical manner. For example, the equity participant has usually concentrated purely on the stock markets, with the only real decision being whether to use top down analysis or its alternative, the individual stock picking approach of bottom-up analysis. This is a woefully myopic view of how things really operate and I hope to show that one is operating in the dark without understanding the ebbs and flows in the relationships between different asset classes. It is relatively simple to see the various relationships between stocks, bonds, commodities and currencies and these can be easily tied into giving a wider and deeper picture about the business cycle and the potential path of future prices. Time after time many of these relationships work astonishingly well, and can help both the individual and the institutional player to improve their performance. This is a dangerous claim – and some of the book looks at the fraught subject of price prediction, an area where most soothsayers fail in their forecasts, but still prosper because of the insatiable demand for wanting to know the future. A subsidiary area of interest is the great store set by technical models, and the fluctuating fortunes of so-called black box creators. In recent years massive computing power has given this area a significant boost – and we will take a look at the whole idea of computers beating the market.

The third theme that will weave in and out is the collapse in the price of computer processing power, and the explosive growth in bandwidth availability. The much fabled Moore's Law about the continuous fall in production costs and the rapid increase in the power of micro-processors seems to be acting here with a vengeance. It is these twin forces that have done so much to re-enforce our view of the marketplace. The growth of television alone has been astounding; in Britain it is as recent as 1982 that the country got a fourth terrestrial channel, and research in the US shows that the average household now has access to over 120 TV channels. Bandwidth and hard disk capacity is flooding the world with information. The serried ranks of traders in dealing rooms with endless monitors, the wall to wall television coverage of markets, and the avalanche of research material are all only possible because of these two factors. Arguably these two advances have been amongst the most important and lasting influences on modern day finance. However there is precious little evidence that they have made the markets any easier to interpret – indeed one could forcefully argue they have made trading life more difficult.

Other secondary, but still important, themes that the book looks at include the regulatory cycle, the critical importance of time (market timing is something of a cliché, but nevertheless merits serious attention) and the unbending financial fact that the successful few feed off the unsuccessful many.

Whether financial markets will continue to dominate life as they currently do is a moot point. The current set up is very much driven by cheap computing and global communications, but also by financial de-regulation. Clearly there is a cycle of regulation, de-regulation and then once more re-regulation. Viewed in retrospect it will be clear that the late 1990s marked a high water mark in terms of global financial de-regulation and that in fact now the cycle has turned. The tide has now started to turn back towards regulation and tighter controls and supervision. This may well tame some of the wilder excesses of the markets, and they may slip from their current place in the limelight, but such developments come with attached costs, most of which will, as usual, be borne by the smaller players. Although on occasions some of the market's bigger players have complained about the burden of regulation, it is in fact often a protective shield for the larger and richer participants, and in today's environment of cheap and available technologies, a useful barrier to entry to restrict the smaller fry.

This regulatory cycle is almost clockwork in its manifestations, and it is relatively straightforward to see the various parts of the cycle move in and out of fashion. Indeed the current stage of the cycle, in which news has been dominated by scandals about false accounting and huge leveraged risk, is one that has been seen many times before and doubtless will afflict future generations. What is less clear is the precise nature of the results of regulation; one only has to see the calamitous outcome of the botched regulation of the California electricity market to see that the law of unintended consequences has a large part to play in this area.

Another strong theme in the book is about time, and more precisely timing. Time is the constant imponderable in financial markets. Should I buy now? Can I wait until tomorrow? Do I wait until the stock trades at 100? I wish I had done it yesterday. Time is the nagging doubt, sometimes the inflexible master and then sometimes the painfully slow servant that haunts the speculator. Never enough time, or far too much when it's least required. This whole area again links back into the snake oil zone of prediction, but also more importantly is a key determinant in behavioural ideas. It is clear that market timing is not just about one's own thoughts and actions but intricately tied up with the actions and motives of others – a simple example being the placing and execution of stop loss orders. More money is lost in misunderstanding time within a market than almost any other factor.

For the individual, whether trading on his own account or on behalf of a financial institution, it is important to understand all these elements if one is to trade profitably. It is an indisputable fact of financial markets that few speculators truly succeed – most players lose money or fail to maximise their opportunities. It is a Darwinian process in which the successful few feed off the rest of the market. As a result it is hardly surprising that large parts of the market choose to be intermediaries – market makers, advisors, commentators – all with relatively limited risk and a profit source that is generally fairly stable and activity driven, rather than volatile and results orientated. This is why so much financial advice is entirely worthless. At the end of the day most of the market is more interested in your activity as a customer than if you are actually successful in your trading.

The final chapter of this book is called Signposts – these are some of my own ideas and thoughts on various approaches that seem to work in the market. They may well be flawed, first they are my view of the marketplace and seem to suit my trading style though they may not suit others, and second, the fact that I write and publicise them could diminish their value, as the positive feedback element kicks in once again. Though one could also argue that if enough players do follow them, they will in fact become a self-fulfilling system. Herein lies one of the conundrums at the heart of market analysis. As a result perhaps all they will illustrate is that it is a constant battle to stay ahead in the marketplace. That said I hope they will stimulate some thought and ideas and perhaps alternatives for the reader.

London, January 2003

1

Losers Anonymous

'It is not the knowing that is difficult, but the doing.'

Chinese Proverb

Woody Allen once famously defined a stockbroker as someone who invests your money until it's all gone. Amusing and probably dangerously close to the truth, but the interesting thing is that Allen used the term 'invests', which makes the barbed outcome all the sharper and somehow more shocking. We all are conditioned to believe that investment is safe and sensible; prudence and considered judgement are the implied virtues within the investment process. The wise man is an investor, who shuns wild speculation and abhors foolish gambling, and follows the steady path of carefully placing his money in sound enterprises. Is all of this received wisdom true?

The "S" Word

In beginning to look at the whole process of financial markets, perhaps we should start with some basic questions. When we deal in the markets, is it investment, speculation or gambling? Do we see ourselves as investors with all those underlying inferences of caution, prudence and informed decision making? Or perhaps as speculators, fearless plungers who are brave and ruthless at exploiting hitherto unseen opportunities in the marketplace? Perhaps, though less likely, some might admit that they are gamblers, out-and-out "chancers" who are hopeless addicts of the rollercoaster of betting, gripped by hope and often wracked by fear, but always confidently expecting the "Big One".

So does it matter what we call financial trading? What's in a name? After all surely it is success and profits that draw us to the business, not philosophical debates about what we call it? In many ways any name or title we give to financial activity can be dismissed as trivial and unimportant, but almost inevitably the three basic definitions of investment, speculation and gambling have a habit of pushing themselves forward.

Frequently these terms get mixed up and often have a political edge to them. Stock markets are nothing but gambling dens according to many left-leaning types. Carefully worded warnings (usually in fine print) to investors often refer to the speculative nature of the instrument (short option positions, and margin trading for example) and the financial rating agencies use the term speculative to act as a dire warning about the likely credit worthiness of an institution. Also, investment fund marketing front men stress how their fund is safe and conservative in its decisions, and seeking 'favourable investment opportunities' will dismiss speculative ventures. The financial world is full of blurred distinctions and definitions.

Without wanting to dwell on this subject of categorising for too long, let's try and make some attempt to define the situation. What really separates investment from speculation is nearly always a subjective measure of risk, and what marks out gambling as really quite a separate activity is pure mathematics and probability. Gambling and games of chance require no skill. It may be a tiresome cliché, but gambling is really about losing money – it's a rigged market if you like, with all the games having a negative expectation of return. You may win occasionally but in the end the iron rules of gambling games are carefully constructed to part you from your cash. Perhaps the only useful contribution that gambling has made to finance was to act as the spur to understanding probability. A number of famous mathematicians addressed questions of probabilities raised by games of chance, and in particular Jakob Benoulli and Pierre de Laplace stand out as having made important breakthroughs in our understanding of such matters. Probability has become a cornerstone of much of finance and the pricing of risk and weaves in and out of virtually any study of the subject.

We will examine gambling a little further on, but for the moment let's strip it away from the main body of financial activity and concentrate on the close cousins of investment and speculation. (Some readers may be protesting already – surely the exponential rise in spread betting in the UK is a classic example of gambling on the stock market? No – for in truth it's really a speculative activity packaged up to look like a straightforward bet to avoid capital gains taxation.) Many people seem to be uncomfortable with the notion that investment and speculation are virtually the same activity. It seems to offend their sensibilities, not least of all academics and regulators. No doubt cynics will note that these two groups often have the least direct experience of financial markets.

Academics have certainly tried to firmly separate these two activities, and from the point of view of regulators and law makers the distinctions seem to matter. Again there is an overwhelming belief that investment is good, and that speculation is at best dubious; though there is at least a strong body of thought amongst economists that has been generally supportive of speculators, suggesting that they are major providers of liquidity for other participants that wish to hedge future risks.

A number of distinguished economists and even some market operators (one thinks of Benjamin Graham) have sought to explain how to differentiate between investment and speculation. In particular it was John Maynard Keynes, of whom more later, who famously declared in his seminal work *The General Theory of Employment, Interest and Capital* that speculation was 'the activity of forecasting the psychology of the market', and defined the speculative motive as 'the object of securing profit from knowing better than the market what the future will bring'. And that as such, speculation was quite different from investment and the running of a business enterprise.

All of this has suited the marketing arms of the financial industry who have pretty much banished the term speculation as a taboo word; fund managers see themselves as custodians and careful managers of others' assets, certainly not as hired speculators! Even many of the buccaneering hedge funds have shied away from such a description, preferring to hide behind bland phrases such as absolute returns objectives, seeking positive alpha and employing strategic macro analysis. So, speculation is often seen as a pejorative term, conjuring up images of 19th century robber barons, wild unregulated markets and sharp practice. Of course, such disturbing images must be kept away from the nervous customer; soothing marketing phrases and impressive (though often woefully misleading) performance statistics are the order of the day, and under no circumstances should there be any mention of the dreaded "S" word.

However, there is an almost endless supply of cases where seemingly solid investments have turned out to be wild speculations, and equally there is a school of thought that says it is sensible and wise to take certain risks. Then there is the rather trite piece of advice that says the biggest risk in life is taking no risk at all. More subtly it can be very difficult to define what financial risk really is, and so whether you have an investment risk, a trading risk or a speculative risk can be an exercise in fruitless taxonomy. It really doesn't matter what we call market activity, either investment or speculation will do. Throughout this book there will be references to both investing and speculating and to my mind they are pretty interchangeable – the only variable is the risk appetite. Though as will be examined later, the initial risk appetite – or what we might term the willingness to take the known risk at inception – is often subsequently changed by circumstances outside the control of the participant. Certainly risk is not static.

Chance Not Skill

Returning to gambling, it's certainly a different animal from financial market operations, and is in fact a rather dull and ultimately depressing affair. It is curious that such a lacklustre and crushing experience can be so successfully marketed as entertainment, surely Las Vegas must be one of the most depressing places on earth – it's full of losers. After all, that's what makes the place exist.

We must remember that gambling is about chance and not skill, and as such offers no real long-term way to win. In contrast financial markets are far more challenging, demanding and potentially much more rewarding, but they demand – and then reward – a degree of skill and mastery. It is quite wrong to term most financial operations as gambling, however speculative they may be. What is equally dangerous is to somehow ring-fence apparently safe investments from so-called speculative adventures. This mind set can be catastrophic if circumstances change. Markets are dynamic in their activity and various financial ventures slide up and down the scale of risk – nothing is risk free. Indeed one could say that risk is in the eye of the beholder, and that it is dynamic and rarely entirely predictable. To master and profit from such conditions is the true challenge of financial markets – terms such as solid and safe, or speculative, are basically misleading and worthless.

Life, Luck and Lotteries

Many believe that life is a gamble, that some of us are just lucky and that the stock market is a casino that favours those of a gambling nature. Much of this thinking is romanticised, or just plainly ill informed. Nevertheless before we can get down to the real business of examining financial trading, perhaps we need to spend a little time looking at gambling.

Luck is a favourite topic in life. The Roman philosopher Terence declared that fortune favours the brave, Mark Twain opined that the harder he worked the luckier he became, and perhaps most famously Napoleon always flatly refused to promote anyone to a senior command unless they were deemed to be lucky.

Although luck and chance are a part of life, they are really a small part in any successful investment strategy. In a sense such terms are just our attempt to rationalise randomness; human nature seems to abhor random events, it seems to be in our nature to want to exercise control, even if this can lead to endless self-delusion. Luck is often invoked in operations that are doomed from the start – in particular, gambling. If a situation has a mathematically negative expectation then no amount of luck can save you in the long run. This conditional phrase, in the long run, is in fact rather important. One of the most difficult things for gamblers to understand, surely if they did they wouldn't bother, is that chance has no memory. Randomness can seem to throw up imaginary short-term patterns that can fool the gambler into believing there is a lucky streak or that next time heads is bound to come up. But in the long run they will be crushed by the negative mathematics of the game. In this sort of atmosphere of muddled thinking and down right innumeracy it is small wonder that lady luck is often invoked.

It Could Be You!

Perhaps a good way to look at gambling and to compare it with investment is to examine lotteries, and their close mathematical brethren, life insurance policies.

Although the mathematical arguments against lotteries are overwhelming, that is to say taking part not running one, there is a twist in the story – the concept of utility.

First, the bare maths is quite striking. In the UK the National Lottery ('Lotto') involves correctly picking the six balls that are randomly selected out of a total draw of forty-nine. Most games around the world have a very similar set up, with the overwhelming amount of prize money going to the lucky (that word again!) winner(s) who make the right prediction. Usually there is a lot of razzamatazz about how the drawing of the balls is scrupulously fair, and in many countries including the UK the whole business is a major light entertainment TV show. For all the show business, in bald terms there is a 1 in 13,983,816 chance of making the correct prediction!

To calculate this is very simple: there is a 1 in 49 chance of predicting the first ball correctly, to get the second ball correct there is a 1 in 48 chance (as the first ball is no longer in the draw). One repeats this process for the six balls and then you multiply the odds to get the overall probability, so:

6/49 x 5/48 x 4/47 x 3/46 x 2/45 x 1/44 = 13, 983,816

This is stunningly awful, in fact a cursory glance at crime statistics suggest all manner of horrible things including being murdered by a close family relative are much more likely than being able to predict which six little balls will come up. (Recent statistics show that in the UK you are more than four times more likely to be murdered than win the lottery jackpot.)

Another, perhaps even more revealing, way to look at the odds is to say there is actually less chance of winning the lottery than rolling the same number on a dice nine times in a row. In fact, for that probability the number is just over ten million to one. (Basically it is six, being the number of sides on a dice, to the power of nine, being the number of throws.) Put in those terms how many people would still believe the promoter's catch phrase that 'It could be you'.

There are gambling tactics that can help at the margin, for example a large number of people select lottery numbers on the basis of family birthdays (good grief!) and so people's selections are skewed towards the numbers between 1 and 31. Although this activity doesn't change the overall odds, it does mean that if winning numbers are not within this biased sub-group you stand a better chance of not having to share the prize with anyone else. No doubt those poor souls who believe thirteen to be an unlucky number, triskaidekaphobics is the impossible label they live under, are also slightly skewing the distribution of number selections. In an activity where the odds are more balanced and not so impossible, such activity could be very important, but in the no hopers game called the lottery it is pretty much impossible to gain much advantage from such tactics. As a point of interest though, the idea of trying to read what other players are doing rather than just concentrate on the game itself is in fact a critical part of winning in investment strategies – but in gambling the house rules always allow enough profit margin to swallow any such marginal advantages. Remember the rules are constructed to help you lose money.

Clearly the marketing of such games is crucial; the trick is to appeal to the gambler's hope that he stands a chance of winning – whilst avoiding any reference to what a forlorn hope it really is. Also, the prize allocation is structured in such a way that a very large number of players can win a very nominal prize relatively easily. In the UK the minimum win of £10 is often won by around half a million players at each draw, but their chance of the top prize of anywhere between £5 million and £10 million is well protected by the almost 14 million to one odds explained above. This creates the illusion that the player was close to winning, and therefore should carry on playing the game at each successive draw.

Enter Utility

So are all the buyers of lottery tickets foolish – don't they realise the miniscule likelihood that they will win? Well, little in life is purely determined by statistics and probability theory. Another element to consider is that the players are well aware of the appalling odds, but that the small gamble of £1 is well worth the chance to win the huge first prize. This means viewing the gamble in terms of both the probabilities and the consequences of winning – known by economists as utility theory. The first prize would have such a huge impact on the winner's life that it's worth paying out for that opportunity. This is often seen as being the motive of why the relatively poorer members of society are often the most avid players – the lottery ticket becomes a chance to escape their circumstances. Odds and probabilities, even if understood, have little part in such a calculation. Many have pointed out that this is precisely why such lotteries are immoral as they tend to be a flat rate tax on society's lowest earners.

Perhaps one of the most extraordinary, if not depressing, elements of the lottery is the way people study the past form! The oily voice-over on the television show never forgets to remind viewers when a number last came up (this must be the most public example of the gambler's fallacy) and other inane observations including, 'all the numbers this week are even!' Some enterprising characters have even produced software packages that can be used to track previous numbers, and if the punter can't decide on his next choice, a random number generator to help. This repackaging of simple spreadsheets is a triumph of the entrepreneurial spirit over the foolishness of the average gambler.

One final thought on lotteries – over time interest in them tends to fade and often they are eventually scrapped. In fact the popularity of lotteries is not always universal but tends to ebb and flow with social mores of the time, and the financial needs of governments looking to raise easy money. Indeed one of the first recorded lotteries in England in 1569 was organised by an Italian banker, Piero Grimaldi, to help the extremely cash-strapped government of Elizabeth I. Such was the scepticism about buying tickets, which were extremely expensive at ten shillings each, and targeted at the merchant class, that a degree of friendly persuasion was required by government officials, which included all sorts of promises including an offer of amnesty for criminal convictions. Clearly the prospective purchasers saw the lottery as a crude tax-raising measure and being in the business of trading in goods and commodities, saw the obvious flaws in such an "investment".

The UK Lotto is now nearly fifteen years old, with jackpots being reduced as overall ticket sales have drifted lower. In recent years, re-branding, TV advertising and new twists have been tried to boost sales, but the odds remain the same. Perhaps eventually the punters will learn after all.

Let's Hope It's A Losing Ticket

Curiously the maths that makes lotteries such a rotten deal is precisely why it is good value to take out a life insurance policy. In essence, the insurance company grants an insurance policy, payable on the death of the policyholder, that the holder hopes doesn't come to fruition. So in this case the policyholder is really like someone buying a lottery ticket and praying that it isn't a winning combination! Interestingly both parties benefit in this transaction as the holder of the policy "wins" (or at least the beneficiaries of his estate do) if his number does come up; and the insurance company writes the policies with much the same maths in mind as a lottery company – only a certain number of policies will be exercised in a given period of time, and the rest is a simple matter of managing costs, and the income from the policy revenue to cover the claims and return a healthy profit. This may all sound rather macabre, but here at least is a gamble in life you will be pleased not to win.

The Wrong Box

Whilst on the topic of life insurance, gambling and investment ideas it is worth mentioning an interesting curiosity, the investment concept of the Tontine, which once popular is now outlawed in most countries, though lives on in a truncated form as a tax avoidance vehicle in France. It also happens to be central to the plot of a 1960s film starring Peter Cook and Dudley Moore called *The Wrong Box*.

Named after the 17th century Neapolitan banker Lorenzo Tonti, the Tontine is a simple investment fund with an unusual sting in the tail. Every subscriber pays an initial fixed sum into the investment fund, and in return receives annual dividend payments from the capital invested. Then, over the life of the fund, as each subscriber dies his share is divided among all the others until literally the last man standing is paid out the capital in the fund, and the scheme is closed. Such a vehicle is a curious mix of pure investment, in fact a form of annuity scheme, with the added spice of a side bet that you will outlive your fellow investors – and win the capital in the fund. Needless to say such schemes are open to obvious abuse, in particular foul play amongst the members, and have been deemed illegal in many countries. Before readers wonder if such dark undertakings are a major part of the French investment scene, it should be pointed out that the so-called Tontine schemes in place these days are a way of pooling property ownership rights to avoid or at least manage inheritance tax liabilities. So for example a husband and wife may own a house via a Tontine arrangement, and when one partner dies the other need not pay inheritance tax, as the house is deemed have been in a tax-free joint ownership scheme.

Before we leave the topic of gambling, one final thought. If gambling schemes, betting systems and ways to beat the odds were really worthwhile why is the market unwilling to lend money to finance such ideas? In contrast, casinos and gaming operations have no trouble raising finance; after all they are a positive cash flow business, with a very predictable profit margin, an ideal client for any lending banker or bond issuing house. Indeed such is the consistency of many gaming operations they literally make more money in January than February simply because there are 3 more days in the month for gamblers to chase after the "Big One". The answer to the question is plain – gambling cannot be consistently profitable (remembering the long run effect) for the participants; in this vital respect it is totally different from financial trading. In the parlance of stockbrokers, clearly it is one to avoid.

Just A Game?

Having considered various definitions for financial trading and settling on the idea that investment and speculation are really the same activity but probably describe different rates of risk, perhaps we can consider another angle on how to understand the markets. Could they be described as a game, an activity with set rules and known inputs that if understood would give us the output, i.e. the market price? Could we study and accurately monitor these factors and somehow start to be able to understand what really drives the price, and perhaps even predict future outcomes?

This looks like being an extremely tall order, for example what are all the factors that govern, say, the price of gold? Obviously there is global mining data, then there is information about the demand for industrial and commercial uses for gold, the overall economic climate, and then the actual activity in the trading of gold both in physical and futures markets; all of which then culminates in a single bid-offer price for bullion. One could add even more factors such as politics, central banks' activities, taxation and regulation. How on earth do we decide what factors are important and what influence they have on that final outcome, the gold price?

Before trying to answer this very difficult conundrum let's wind back slightly and imagine how we would set up such a monitoring and assessment system for a well defined game we already know – for example, chess (we could equally choose bridge or perhaps the Japanese strategy game Go). In basic terms the game of chess is straightforward; it has precisely defined rules, and takes place in a linear time frame where each action (or your move) is directly countered by a counter reaction (your opponent's response). But it is quite apparent very quickly the number of possible moves and different lines of play grows exponentially as the game unfolds. Initially there are only twelve possible chess opening moves, either moving one of the eight pawns or one of the two knights which each have two potential moves. Actually even this is a simplification, as the pawns may move one or two spaces on their initial move, so in fact the correct number is already twenty opening variations. Very quickly after each player has moved even a few times the variations, the lines of play, and potential complexity has gone through the roof. No doubt, this complexity is one of the reasons why chess is such a popular pastime – but imagine trying to develop a series of rules that can predict future moves in the game. Well, after years of trying it looks now that computing power is starting to have some serious success.

The first attempts to program computers to play chess were developed by scientists at Bell Labs in the 1960s where a celebrated team led by Claude Shannon (a leading pioneer of information theory) collaborated with the then world champion Mikhail Botvinnik to create the first serious chess-playing software. Nowadays the latest generation of computers, most notably the Deep Blue series from IBM, is considered a credible threat to human players. Indeed in a very short series in May 1997 an IBM machine did beat the world champion Gary Kasparov, winning three games, losing two, and with one drawn. (Though apparently the machine did commit one or two very weak moves, and did miss some obvious lines of play.) Whilst extremely impressive, it was hardly an overwhelming victory. In late 2002 the then world champion Vladimir Kramnik held the Deep Fritz computer to a four-all draw, but it now appears that computer software is starting to overtake the human game.

Others have tried to develop fool-proof systems to conquer gambling games but this is a waste of effort unless you can manage to persuade people to buy your supposed secrets. A step away from pure gambling games of chance are those that involve some measure of skill, such as football pools and horse race betting. Attempts to develop systems here have had some limited success, with some examples of professional gamblers being able to live off horse race betting, but there have also been some spectacular failures. One such disaster centred on the attempt of Charles Babbage (the inventor of the difference engine and a mechanical forerunner of calculators and computers) to win a large sum of money on the 1851 Derby. His system was funded by Ada Byron, the daughter of the famous poet Lord Byron, who hoped to win enough to cover her existing gambling debts. Unfortunately Babbage's mathematical model failed to make the correct prediction at Epsom Downs, and only compounded his backer's financial woes.

Of course the game of trying to understand and then predict our market example of the gold bullion price is even more massively complex than chess, or betting on horses. There is no fixed number of players, their activity is certainly not neatly arranged in time order, and an almost innumerable set of external factors can come into play. So there seems little hope that we can solve the price of gold with computers and cunning mathematics. This hasn't stopped people trying and the advent of massively cheaper computing power has been a significant boost to the variety of methods tried. So far the landscape has been littered with false dawns, but the insatiable demand to see the future is a powerful incentive to crack the problem.

There are a number of well-known games that can be solved by logic, but understanding the games can still cause difficulties. Puzzles such as the prisoner's dilemma, Morra and the Japanese game of scissors-paper-stone all have optimal strategies that can be used to maximise advantage, but many people still come up with the wrong answer, or more subtly adopt the wrong strategy. In such games choosing a wrong strategy is just that – wrong.

In financial markets, however, there seems to be another level of complexity, as every market participant watches everyone else like a hawk, even plainly stupid strategies are sometimes adopted by the crowd. The chess player doesn't have to contend with rumours, whereas the investor is bombarded by half truths and misunderstood comments in what often resembles a gigantic global version of Chinese Whispers. There is huge pressure to cluster around the right strategy, to follow the current fashion, above all not to be left behind, to follow the current trend, however hare-brained. (Never was this more true than during the extraordinary dotcom bubble of the late 1990s.) Economists and believers in fundamental analysis label this behaviour as over-shooting and explain that eventually markets correct. Of course they do, but the key word is eventually. In this respect, things do have a curious parallel with the gambler's fallacy about short-term runs of luck. Once again the human mind is quite happy to rationalise mathematically irrational arguments. It is an interesting point that during periods of investment madness such as The South Sea Bubble or the UK railway stocks mania in the 1850s, it may be possible to justify the madness on economic utility grounds – in that the investors knew the price they were paying was too high, but still felt compelled to enter the market. Many contrary investors have lost a fortune trying to counter a market's irrational valuation, which is often driven by "the greater fool theory", in that the holder of an over-valued asset always fondly believes someone else will pay even more.

So plainly financial markets are not just about statistics and probabilities, utility is just as important as cash or monetary values; and success means different things to different people – markets are far more subtle than just a game of logic.

Top Of The Market

An event at the beginning of March 2000 close to the very peak of the US equity bull market, in fact it occurred just a couple of weeks before the absolute high in the NASDAQ Index, is probably one of the best examples of market irrationality in decades. The large American company 3Com Corp., partially floated off one of it's most successful ever developments, the Palm Pilot. This hand-held device had taken the world by storm in the previous couple of years, and was a must have purchase for every techno enthusiast. 3Com packaged the product into a separate company called Palm Inc. and a small block, in fact only 6%, of the stock was floated on the stock market. The issue price had originally been considered at around $14 per share, but in the frenzied days ahead of the launch the guide price was increased to the $30-$32 range. In the event it was actually launched at $38 a share, and in a bout of uncontained madness hit $165 at one point during the first day – settling back to finish the day at around $95, valuing the company at a staggering $54 billion. This for a company with its previous years profits of just under $30 million – a valuation of 1800 years earnings!

Even more extraordinary was the fact that the total market capitalisation of Palm Inc. was now greater than that of the parent 3Com (despite 3Com still holding 94% of Palm's shares). This wasn't just a slight mis-pricing but over-valuation on a colossal scale. Investors had driven the price of Palm Inc. through the roof, and ignored the valuation of the company that itself held the lion's share of the Palm stock. Clearly irrational exuberance had finally boiled over; indeed after the first days trading Palm Inc. was deemed to be worth more than either General Motors or the Ford Motor Company. Just as alarming is the fact that many who entered the market on the short side could have lost a lot of money – despite being ultimately correct in their view. No doubt as the stock sailed up through $100 on the first day there was ample evidence that the price was irrational and unsustainable, but who could have hung on as it rose another 65% before making its fleeting high?

Here was the greater fool theory demonstrated in full flood. What was going on? Why do people and markets seem to want to act in this manner? Well clearly the small amount of Palm stock on offer had helped induce the feeding frenzy for the new issue, but any sense of value and worth seems to have been totally forgotten. Certainly, the fact that 3Com was the biggest beneficiary – by virtue of holding 94% of the Palm stock – was totally lost in the blindness. As a result of this chaos, something was wrong; either 3Com was now grossly undervalued, or Palm was equally grossly over-valued. In time reality set in and there are no prizes for guessing the outcome. Needless to say Palm is no longer mentioned in the same group as General Motors and Ford (notwithstanding the recent woes of these motor companies). The share price soon plunged back to earth and, whilst still going, the company is a shadow of its glory days at the time of flotation.

This small episode is an ideal leitmotif for an important, if not the most important, element in financial markets – the intertwined factors of crowd behaviour and investor emotion. Whilst we tend to believe that finance is about statistics, valuation and economic theory, that is really only what is going on at the surface level. In addition the Palm/3Com episode calls into question efficient market theory when applied to stocks. The mis-pricing lasted some months after the initial offering. So are there other approaches and ideas that can explain this seemingly irrational behaviour?

The Financial Inner Game

Back in the early 1970s a book about tennis coaching called *The Inner Game of Tennis* by Timothy Gallwey became an unexpected bestseller. Its theme was simple yet revolutionary – to improve your tennis you had to train your mind equally as much as any work done on the practice court. There were two games going on – the outer game on the court and the inner game in your own mind. If you could convince yourself that you would beat your competitor you already had a huge advantage before the first ball was served. Perhaps, rather than look for external reference points to understand financial trading, we need to look within ourselves.

Clearly financial trading is different from tennis or any other competitive sport, but the importance of emotional control by the player in each is very important. As we have just examined, it is wrong to try and label trading as a game. The rules, such as they exist, are dynamic and fluid in their nature, not fixed as in sport. The human reaction to this fluidity – or, if you prefer, uncertainty – is to try and set guidelines and rules. It is through this method that we try to control ourselves and our trading. Unfortunately this human trait to set controls tends to expand so that we think we can control external events as well.

This is where trouble sets in. The internal rules we set ourselves are often changed to suit the external situation and we rationalise our own actions by believing that because things have changed we must change ourselves. After all, aren't we taught to be flexible in our thinking? So when our rules no longer fit the outside world, we change the rules but rationalise this behaviour by pretending that we are in fact being prudent and flexible in our attitudes. So, in a fit of muddled thinking and ill discipline any normal investing rules are junked and we go back to chasing the rainbow.

Curious Inefficiency

The Palm Pilot/3Com story is just an extreme example of these phenomena. It also frequently appears in the inability of investors, whether individuals or institutions, to cut their losses. We frequently rationalise away losses, and tell ourselves that it is right to hang on to losing positions. Clearly whatever games that are going on in the marketplace are also really going on inside our heads. Frequently one hears the term "they" in market conversations. "They" are completely wrong about this stock. Don't "they" realise that the gold bullion price should be lower? "They" are going to like the employment figures later today. Most participants see the market through the prism of an imaginary enemy or counterforce called "they". It's as if the market is secretly ranged against the individual investor or fund manager and that in some sort of Arthurian manner he has to overcome their dark forces to prevail in the marketplace.

Well if there is a battle and there is an enemy, it is within – a silent enemy that picks away at the individual's good judgement and investment plans. It is natural for humans to look for confirmation in their judgements; as a matter of course we swap ideas and opinions about everything in everyday life. We discuss endlessly with one another what TV programmes we like, what's the best value car or why a certain holiday destination is expensive. It is the same in financial markets – all the players are constantly discussing the various merits and de-merits of certain stocks, commodities and currencies. We also pontificate on economic data, company announcements, chart patterns, newspaper articles and a constant stream of research from economists, analysts and general market pundits.

Joining The Crowd

All of this activity has an influence over our investment judgements, in fact more than we probably realise. It is not just our own judgements that finally decide whether we make an investment decision; we need to cluster around others' opinions for confirmation. In fact we are very influenced by those around us. It is easier to join the crowd than fight it – and after all doesn't it make sense to follow a trend anyway?

In his fascinating book *Butterfly Economics* Paul Ormerod draws attention to some extremely interesting research that shows the importance of such information systems. In particular it appears that insect communities swap information constantly about food sources, and that the information received from other insects is just as important as any primary evidence collected by any individual insect itself. This may seem somewhat removed from financial markets, but as Dr Ormerod demonstrates, it has important lessons for all economic activity, including financial markets.

Essentially the individual actions by investors in the marketplace, or for that matter the actions of insects looking for food, can assume greater importance as they influence others in their actions. This is how trends appear to form. It's not just that we decide ourselves to buy the stock, but we carefully watch our fellow investors to see what they do. This activity can be termed a positive feedback model, as the initial activities get magnified and extended over time. In marketing speak one might say that the early adopters tend be very influential. The fact that they start to buy a stock can soon be spotted by other me-too investors and then a trend gets underway.

As an historical aside, a good example of this crowd following behaviour is found in the landmark English battle of Bosworth in 1485. King Richard's supposed ally, his stepfather Lord Stanley, kept his men to one side as Richard's forces battled those of Henry Tudor. With the King in trouble and Henry's men getting the upper hand, Stanley finally ordered his men to swoop down the hill, join the winning side and help defeat the Tudor forces. The noble Lord was clearly a trend follower!

So a complex mosaic is starting to unfold; the market is not an easily defined game, glib labels about investment and speculation don't really help us, and the actions, however seemingly irrational, of all the participants can have disproportionate effects at certain times. On top of this, how individuals act in their inner selves, or how they apply their own set of risk and reward values, is absolutely crucial. One could add a further layer of complication for the poor fund manager, who has peer pressure from his own colleagues plus the dreaded comparison with competitors via publicly available league tables. No wonder the investment community seems to huddle together like penguins in an Antarctic ice storm. It may be that being with the crowd is the safest place to be, with the issue of being right rather secondary.

With all of these factors it is little wonder that financial markets are the ultimate test in staying centred and calm in decision-making.

Who Cares Who Wins?

There is no evidence that there is a master plan of the universe that includes the idea that any of us should be rich. Market players may dream, strive and plan endlessly for this happy event, but no one else cares, least of all the market itself.

The nightly stock market round-up on the business TV news often announces that winning stocks beat losers by a ratio of whatever and that big gains or losses were made by investors in XYZ stock, or that players were surprised by a sudden currency devaluation or political crisis. Pundits and analysts are wheeled out to comment on the news and are always asked 'What does the market think?' They nearly always reply by repeating that what has happened was a surprise, and that the market will be very wary in the coming sessions. But the market doesn't think anything, it gyrates around whatever the latest story or rumour may be.

So what, and who cares? Do I care if you made or lost money today? Of course not. But curiously in the back of my mind I think that the market is interested in me. Here is another fallacy that helps fool the individual or institutional player. Most market players develop a sense of paranoia; how often is a losing position cut at the very extremity of the adverse move – it's as if the dreaded enemy "they" were watching and planning the humiliating loss and failure.

Nonsense of course, because the market doesn't know or care about you and your position; but we fret that it might. Almost like someone who has happened upon a secret and is afraid to breathe a word about it, the individual investor hopes to have uncovered a bargain or at least stolen a march on the rest of the market. Of course having established the position we trumpet our cause, and busily tell our friends and anyone that will listen that XYZ stock is going to fly, only fools would be short and the coming results look like being great. All of this is known in the trade as "talking your book". Do the regulators consider this inappropriate or illegal behaviour? Is it wrong to talk up a stock that you are long of? Why would you do anything else? This is all part and parcel of the positive feedback model touched upon earlier.

One complication in this description of events is liquidity. The market will latch onto players if it is known that they have a very large position. Suddenly that information becomes important and the limelight beckons. This is nearly always extremely bad news. Imagine you are very short in a commodity that has been gently drifting down. Suddenly the news of your large position will almost certainly drive the market higher as other participants attempt to squeeze you out of your position. Liquidity tends to dry up in such a situation (after all, why should any other players help you cover your trade?) and suddenly the paranoiac concept of "they" becomes a horrible reality. We will examine liquidity and its unpredictability in much greater depth later on.

Perhaps what drives the feelings of paranoia and the obsession with "they" in the marketplace is fear of failure. The simple fact is that many more people fail in financial speculation than succeed; as mentioned earlier it is truly a Darwinian model where the successful few feed off the losing majority. We could term the losers as anonymous, because as with most things in life, more time and space is given to success than failure. Of course, if the failure is of sufficiently spectacular proportions then we hear about it, but in general failed investments and their investors suffer in silence.

Obvious But Hard Advice

It was the successful 19th century English stockbroker, and subsequently highly regarded economist, David Riccardo who was credited with giving the investment advice to run your profits and cut your losses. This is obviously good and sensible advice, but common sense is at a premium in finance. Of course, one would expect to find that investors will seek to maximise their profits and minimise their losses, but in fact it appears people are more worried about minimising their pain than anything else. Losses are painful, so we should expect to see a rush to exit losing positions. But in fact a lot of market activity involves avoiding taking losses, by deciding to simply let them run. This so-called loss aversion, or sunk loss bias, can have the paradoxical effect of actually increasing losses. It's as if the mark to market loss doesn't really matter – it's only a loss when you close the position, and if you avoid closing the position, well you have avoided taking the loss and the accompanying pain. In a way this folds back nicely into Gallwey ideas on the inner game, except the investor thinks he can shield himself from pain in the real world by retreating to the world of the inner game in his head. It's as if the tennis game is never actually lost until the player admits it is.

This whole area has spawned the new industry of risk management. In financial institutions armies of staff gather statistics about the company's investment and trading positions and carefully calculate a series of measures of risk – all designed to give managements warning signs and levels at which it would be prudent to take a loss. Individuals sometimes use so-called stop loss strategies (surely they should be called take loss strategies?) to try and achieve the same discipline. As we shall examine later, these ideas, whilst worthy, often fall victim to the law of unintended consequences and the actual outcomes can be somewhat unexpected.

So many market players have an almost schizophrenic relationship with the market; wanting to know all that is going on, alternating between secrecy and publicity over their own positions and being constantly influenced by the opinions and actions of those around them. Now we can start to see why trading is a hard way to make money.

2

Past Masters

Perhaps if we are to better understand how to operate in financial markets we should also take a look at some trading stories from the past. The history of markets over the last two hundred and fifty years has thrown up a myriad of fascinating stories, and some equally larger than life characters. Although modern markets are generally thought to be more sophisticated and complicated than their predecessors, even a cursory study throws up many more similarities than differences. For this reason it is worth reviewing some of the activities of past greats from the financial markets; the challenges, opportunities and even the scale of risks were often similar to today's financial landscape.

Four very different people are examined in this chapter, and though all of them are now long dead, their trading activities and methods still hold lessons for today. Indeed, it is an iron law of financial markets that little alters with time, as one of the four, Jesse Livermore, once remarked:

> *'Wall Street never changes, the pockets change, the suckers change; but Wall Street never changes, because human nature never changes.'*

Clever Uncle Russell

Financier Russell Sage was widely regarded to be crooked – but he was also undoubtedly a master of financial markets, making his mark in money markets, stocks and the latest fad in the 1870s, stock options.

On the morning of 4 December 1891 a young man claiming to have a bomb burst into the New York banking offices of Sage. He demanded US$1,200,000 in cash and threatened to blow himself up, and blow up Sage into the bargain. Sage retreated behind a clerk, and on being refused the money the bomber – by the name of Henry Norcross – duly detonated a parcel of dynamite killing himself. The bank clerk was badly injured and Sage suffered thereafter from permanent hearing damage. So shaken was he by this incident that the 75-year-old Sage immediately announced his retirement and so ended the career of one of Wall Street's greatest options traders.

Whilst this somewhat alarming exit from active speculation certainly makes for a colourful and interesting story, it is not why Russell Sage merits our attention. It is estimated that at his death in 1906 he had amassed a fortune of some US$80 million, a vast sum in today's currency. Indeed, after his death his wife established a charitable foundation bearing his name that is still active to this day. Whilst a great deal of that fortune had come from slick inter-bank money market operations, much of the basis for his wealth and success had been Sage's brilliant trading of stock options. He demonstrated that it was possible to be successful in options trading long before cheap computers, the arrival of the Black-Scholes formula or the concept of financial "rocket scientists". He appeared to have an inherent ability to understand the risk and rewards of options trading, although he had never had anything but the most elementary schooling. Such was his mastery of the options market he was known as the "Father of Puts and Calls" and is often cited as the creator of the first straddle options. (The simultaneous holding of both a call and a put in a stock, with the same strike price and expiration.)

Sage had started life as a farm boy before joining his elder brother's dry goods and wholesale grocery business in Troy, New York. He also spent some time in local politics, and progressed to become a member of the US Congress for four years in the 1850s. It was during this time that he became friendly with various business promoters and industrialists, all of whom were keen to gain political support for their schemes. In particular Sage struck up a close relationship with the celebrated financial operator Jay Gould. Together with Gould he was heavily involved in the financing of the early US railroad network. Much of this early financial career was very dubious indeed, and his association with Gould, one of the most notorious characters in Wall Street history, was bound to taint his reputation. In addition to speculating in various rail takeovers, Sage made a great deal of money from short-term money market operations with various Wall Street broking firms. His supposedly kindly and helpful actions in lending to various brokerage houses earned him the soubriquet "Uncle", though in truth he was hard headed about credit risk and was extremely shrewd at avoiding poor risks. Also, there is little doubt that some Wall Street firms gave Sage valuable information in return for his help – nowadays we would label such assistance as insider dealing.

Early Options Trading

In 1871 Sage turned his mind to the sale of privileges, the term then used for stock options. Similar to today's products these so-called privileges consisted of calls and puts on an underlying stock, with a fixed time period. However, they were not traded instruments, in the sense that there was little or no secondary market, as the legal title of the instrument remained with the initial counter-party. So they were really buy and hold bets, with the usual appeal of looking cheap and with limited risk. It is a recurring theme of almost depressing regularity that investors still consider buying options an often cheap and low-risk way to play the markets – never was Oscar Wilde's jibe about understanding the price and not the value of things so apposite.

In those post-civil war days, the New York options market was in its infancy and was pretty much restricted to the big players on the exchange. Like all new and emerging markets it was an extremely opaque set up, with little independent information and pricing. The main stock market itself was burgeoning with optimism and new industries were appearing at almost breakneck speed; in particular oil and steel were growing apace. As usual with such bullish conditions, common sense was at a very high premium, and opportunities for the cool approach of Uncle Russell were almost overwhelming.

Value And Odds

It was these market characteristics that Russell Sage so expertly exploited. He realised that people often have a poor sense of value, and little idea of odds. This was equally true of the supposedly hardened professionals that were his main customers – there were just as many suckers on the exchange floor as hopefuls from the public who crowded the brokerage offices. Sage also took advantage of the favourable position a big player could command in such a situation. By being the largest market maker in privileges he gained a much better insight into market conditions, and had the natural protection afforded from spreading his risk. (All of this was some eighty years before either Markowitz or the Black-Scholes formula.) Being right at the centre of the market and seeing a substantial proportion of the overall turnover Sage had valuable flow information that was not available to smaller players, and certainly not to the occasional plunger who often as not, bought on a whim or a wild investment tip. As pricing information (implied and historic volatilities in today's terms) was non-existent, the best source of pricing intelligence came from observing supply and demand from investors.

It is interesting to note that there is a large fashion for flow information in today's over-the-counter markets where there is no exchange-based information. This is particularly true in the spot foreign exchange market, where the very largest market-making banks now package up such information and seek to re-sell it to their most favoured customers as a premium service – Uncle Russell would be proud of them.

So Sage's chief options trading weapons were not complicated formulas and computers, but the simple gauging of supply and demand plus what appears to be a good sense of probability. This portfolio risk approach is exactly the same as that of the life insurance companies' strategy that we discussed earlier. These simple tools were more than enough to sell options to punters at "wrong prices" or perhaps more elegantly at rich levels. To those that say the world has moved on, and that investors are far more aware these days, one only has to point to the boom in

Japanese equity warrants in the late 1980s as a more recent example of poor investor understanding in a relatively opaque market, clouded even further by insane stock market bullishness. Once again it would seem that human nature never changes.

Also, in an interesting co-incidence, Sage began his options trading business at almost exactly the same time that the English scientist Francis Galton was using new ideas in statistics to analyse genetic probability. We will spend some time on Galton's ideas later, but it is one of those quirks of history that important real-life applications for statistical theory were being demonstrated by a leading scientist for little or no reward, at the same time as a poorly educated trader was unwittingly using similar ideas to make millions of dollars!

From Sage we can learn two simple facts: first, that new markets are usually very profitable for market-makers or those willing to put their capital at risk to aid liquidity, and second, option trades need not be complicated, and that simple rules will help us gain relatively accurate approximations of their value and pricing. A new emerging market, with ill-informed investors and a lack of price transparency is almost a perfect environment in which to make money. What was true for Uncle Russell a hundred and thirty years ago, is just as true today. This is why emerging markets in telephone and data time, environmental pollution and emission certificates, and weather derivatives offer the chance to make good profits. Also, there is unlikely to be any special skill being used – in new markets investors take poor information on trust, and always end up paying the price.

The Bear And The Bull

In the period immediately after the beginning of the 20th century, right through until the financial crash of 1929, two of the leading lights of financial speculation in the New York and Chicago markets were Arthur Cutten and Jesse Livermore.

Other big names at the time included Bernard Baruch, who went on to become an important political figure right up until the Eisenhower Presidency, and E.F. Hutton who created the eponymous brokerage house, but it is the names of Cutten and Livermore that tower above all others.

But today it is only Livermore's name that lives on, immortalised in the semi-biographical *Reminiscences of a Stock Operator* and still remembered, and even revered by some, for a very colourful life and career. In contrast the rather dour, if not dull, Cutten has been virtually forgotten, but their parallel careers and their activities in the 1929 crash make a fascinating read, and also provide some interesting lessons.

Speculator King

The nicknames tell us all we need to know about Livermore; The Boy Plunger, The King of Cotton, the more reverential moniker JL, all culminating in the title Speculator King. He has been described as the greatest stock trader ever, and long after his death, books continue to be written about his eventful career. Livermore is big box office, but why?

Livermore lived his life on an epic scale, huge stock market coups, 300 foot yachts, high living and a succession of glamorous wives and girlfriends. All his life he was a serial attention seeker, becoming a full-time speculator in his teens, and never had a proper job in the normal sense of the word. He graduated from the corrupt and dangerous world of bucket shops (essentially illegal gambling dens where one could bet on stock price movements) to become a fully fledged member of Wall Street. He was a master of "pools", these were the then quite legal groupings that tried to corner and manipulate stock prices. He was also the Great Bear, the man who never feared to be short, comfortable with the pressures of financing and borrowing stock to run his positions.

Livermore first caught the eye of the press and the public after a celebrated short trading position in Union Pacific, the west coast railroad company that saw its stock price collapse after the 1906 San

Francisco earthquake. After this success, which reputably netted him some US$300,000, he moved his attention to the commodities markets – in particular cotton – and showed consummate trading skill by virtually controlling the world price of cotton for a period during 1908.

However, with the successes – and just as sudden – came the failures. Indeed, during his career he was declared bankrupt three times, but always bounced back with the help of brokerage companies willing to advance him credit. He had a reputation for always repaying his debtors and so he always found it relatively easy to re-join the game. His career see-sawed between unbelievable success and total ruin. Eventually it all ended with him taking his life in the washroom of one of New York's smartest hotels. One could be forgiven for asking, where the useful lessons are that can be learned from such a character. Surely his self-control and risk management must have been flawed? The answer is yes – but his career does merit attention.

Amazingly, for a man who really traded on gut feel and reading the tape, Livermore – admittedly driven by desperate financial straits – once wrote a book to try and explain his trading methods and approach to the markets. Much of what he wrote was some pure nonsense that he ran up quickly to raise money for a publisher's advance, in particular he fell back on that old favourite – the 'secrets of my trading system'. In amongst his writings though are one or two very useful and timeless pieces of advice.

Chief amongst these was his innate understanding of timing; Livermore understood that anticipation was the most dangerous factor in financial markets. Trying to be first on a market move is dangerous because one cannot tell the market when it should move – we have to wait for the market to tell us. In this respect Livermore was the master, always able to hold back, to lounge on his yacht moored off the Atlantic shoreline, or linger endlessly in brokers' offices without ever dealing. His downfalls were also linked to this personality trait; he often clung on too long, hoped against hope. In fact this is an extremely common flaw in trading, and probably the single most difficult problem to conquer; how can we contain our losses?

In many ways he was the master of the entry of a position, but found timing his exits and knowing when to give up far harder. In an age before the computer and the consequent reams of data created by technical analysts, Livermore was able to read the tape and sense when the underlying momentum in a market was changing. Rather like feeling that the tide is slowly changing, he was able to sense the coming changes in the current – but also had the self-control to wait. Nobody makes money in financial markets by being too early. He expressed this most brilliantly in the way he executed entry into new positions; and we must remember that such a colourful and public figure was often carefully watched by his competitors on the street. Here he was up against another key problem, liquidity. The marketplace is characterised by the price, but in reality the market is quite different for a large operator like Livermore compared to the ordinary investor who plays with just a small parcel of shares. In fact, every player sees the market from a slightly different vantage point – and being a famous and presupposed successful operator doesn't necessarily make it easier because a lack of liquidity can make big positions nightmarish. It was also Livermore's attempts to manage and control great blocks of stock that make him worthy of study – though in many ways his was a totally flawed career.

The Wheat King

Whilst Livermore built his reputation as the great stock bear (although he often played the market from the long side) his great rival, the Canadian Arthur Cutten, was universally known as the Great Bull. From a similar background of humble beginnings and hard lessons in his early days in Guelph, Ontario, Cutten emerged as the great long-term player, the man who could run with a trend. It is said it took him three years to save his first $500 and all his life he had a reputation for meanness and caution.

By his early twenties he had purchased a seat on the Chicago exchange and became a dominant figure in the wheat futures market. Cutten concentrated almost exclusively on this one market, and thereby only monitored approximately half a dozen futures contracts. Somewhat like Sage he put himself right at the centre of a market and, a little like being at the axis of a spinning disc, he was able to keep his head whilst smaller fry were sent whirling around.

In the early 1920s Cutten's grip on the wheat market became almost total, with a fit of bull market mania breaking out in 1924 as the price soared through the hitherto unheard of level of US$2 a bushel. Cutten was massively long during this bull run and for the first time clashed with Livermore who – sensing a sea change coming – put on a large short position. A huge battle enraged with newspapers, brokers and tipsters all trying to second guess the outcome. In the end the price held, Livermore was badly beaten and Cutten held his nerve and banked massive profits. Ironically though, this ability to hang tough was to be the fatal weakness in Cutten's trading style. (It is a curious fact in trading that the quality of persistence which is so admired and encouraged in general life can be a serious flaw. Persistence can be a quick route to penury.)

In the late 1920s flush with his huge earnings in wheat, Cutten moved his attention to the stock market. He had played around in stocks before, but now turned away from commodities and concentrated full-time on Wall Street. Basically, he invested in a number of growth stocks and sat on his gentlemen's farm in Illinois and just rode the trend. The twenties were the boom period for stocks, and he became the ultimate example of the buy and hold investor. All of his career had been about holding on for the long run, and his success in the 1924 wheat market had justified his beliefs. He was reputedly worth tens of millions at the height of his game in the summer of 1929, and such was his prominence on Wall Street he had featured on the cover of *Time* magazine the previous December.

1929

There are endless myths and stories about who did what leading up to and during the crash of October 1929, and most are impossible to prove or disprove. It does seem fairly certain though that Livermore was extremely short of stocks ahead of the great disaster, and that Cutten, the eternal bull, was definitely extremely long. After the crash and the resultant fallout Cutten was close to disaster. Various observers put his losses at close to US$50 million, but he limped on into the 1930s, though now dogged by endless government and tax investigations as the authorities sought scapegoats. (This "Something must be done!" reaction by governments is regular as clockwork after such events.) But by then he was a spent force and never made any further market impact. Livermore is supposed to have made upwards of US$100 million, a sum of staggering proportions, but in typical style JL seems to have blown the lot by 1934 and was once again bankrupt.

All good knock about stuff, but what are these two past masters telling us? Well, certainly timing is an obvious element in speculation, but more subtly it is the issue of activity and patience. Stop losses were something they both seemed to wilfully ignore, and this is long before the age of risk management, VaR techniques and today's more clinical and quantitative approach. Both Livermore and Cutten had a stubborn streak that caused them difficulty in exiting positions, or more precisely cutting losses. It is an age-old market saying that 'The first cut is the cheapest cut,' but it is always very hard to take a small loss. Vanity, ego and sometimes misguided hope often cloud one's judgement. This is a perennial problem for all players in financial markets, and will be a recurring theme as we examine speculation in greater detail.

The Extremely Irritating Mr Keynes

John Maynard Keynes was an economics genius, and during his lifetime he was widely considered the expert on financial markets.

Such a bold statement seems almost calculated to upset some market types – after all trading isn't about academic high flyers is it? Surely it's about gut feel, having a nose for the business, knowing the right people and keeping close to the big movers and shakers? Who ever knew an economist who made any money trading? Well, Mr Keynes certainly did.

Keynes was a man of many parts, as well as an academic, a highly respected international economist, a director of the Bank of England, a key member of the management of the Cambridge Arts Theatre and a close associate of the fabled Bloomsbury literary set; he was also a highly successful speculator. Contemporary photographs show a rather dull looking academic, but beneath the surface Keynes was a much more bohemian character, married to a famous Russian ballet dancer, keenly interested in the arts, and rumoured to have had a homosexual affair with the Post-Impressionist artist Duncan Grant. He was certainly no ordinary academic economist. Indeed, he was probably one of the most successful speculators in Britain during the first half of the 20th century.

Furthermore, he appears to have made the money by applying a small number of simple rules that were all grounded in his economic training and observation. No wonder he can be described as extremely irritating – a demonstrably successful speculating economist must seem an anathema to the hordes of simpler souls that haunt financial markets.

Keynes' Simple Approach

So how did he do it? Or perhaps to start with, where and when did he operate with such success? After the First World War Keynes returned to his Cambridge College, King's, to continue his academic work, and in 1927 he was appointed bursar of the Chest Endowment Fund. In this position he had discretion over the fund's investments. This fund was the main accumulated capital of the college, and the income was supposed to help with the college running costs.

Keynes had spent much of the 1920s speculating in the currency and commodity markets on his own account, often with pretty dismal results. On a number of occasions he had been close to financial ruin, and he seemed to lack any definitive style. Much of his activity was very short term and highly speculative. But with time he seemed to develop a better trading method, and by the time he took over responsibility for the college fund he was starting to develop a real talent for making money. In fact over the twenty year period he had stewardship of the Chest Fund, he increased the fund by around fifteen fold – an annualised rate of return of close to 15%. This was all achieved, of course, during a period of extreme market conditions with the commodity market collapse of 1928, the great stock market crash of 1929 and the following worldwide depression that blighted the entire 1930s.

When he took over responsibility for the Chest Fund, he not only invested in stocks but also continued to actively play in the currency and commodity markets. Even today such markets are often regarded with disdain by many fund managers, and are usually viewed as unsuitable for conservative investors – in the 1920s they were considered even wilder animals.

There has been much debate as to whether Keynes' academic work drove his trading style, or that in fact his experiences in the market were key in forming some of his economic views. What is certain is that his style changed and simplified with time, and as he grew more experienced he became rather more cautious and sceptical about short-term speculation. He does appear to have learned some of his economic theory from his experience as an investor, and this theory in turn reflected back to influence and reinforce his activities as an investor. In time he turned away from currency speculation, and came to the consider that it was a fool's game, believing that no one in the long run ever made any money in it. This is a slightly odd conclusion as, of all the markets, the currency market often appears to demonstrate the highest incidence of market inefficiency. Though it is a curious fact that many economists today still consider currency prediction, and by implication currency speculation, as a fruitless and impossible task.

However, Keynes went on speculating in commodities, but gradually his investment style became more cautious, and he made his big money by investing in American utilities during the recovery from the Great Depression. Over time Keynes completely rejected short-term speculation and in his later years became convinced that longer-term value investing was the only sound methodology. Probably most importantly, he developed a successful style that seemed to suit his personality – this in many ways is the key to successful speculation.

Keynes' Rules

Keynes' approach to markets may be outlined as follows:

- Deal in a relatively small number of undervalued shares. Stock picking rather than building a large portfolio seems to have been his style. He most successfully practiced this idea by investing in a number of bombed out American utility stocks after the 1929 crash, at a time when they were very under-priced.

- Stick to a buy and hold strategy. Whilst Keynes believed the market to be inefficient, he felt it was impossible to gain consistent results with a short-term investment horizon. Certainly his experiences in the more volatile and illiquid world of commodities markets of the 1920s may have coloured his views.

- He advocated a diversified portfolio – this is somewhat at odds with the first point, and the records suggest that his spread of stocks was not that great. Though investing in other asset classes such as commodities and currencies improved the balance of the overall portfolio.

- He claimed to shun market timing techniques. Again this is slightly odd as his trading certainly improved as he began to time his investments better (perhaps like the brilliant US Rail Stocks trader E.H. Harriman he had an innate ability to spot opportunities).

Animal Spirits and Beauty Contests

Perhaps as a final observation on Keynes activities we should consider the fact that he never published any work on his secret investment techniques, though his views and attitudes are well documented. In particular Keynes wrote interestingly about speculation and what he called "animal spirits". He noted that most market players are driven by optimism rather than mathematical expectation, and he was an early observer of one of the most corrosive of market practices – excessive activity or overtrading. He correctly realised that when under stress people often adopt active roles for the sake of it. Such is usually a substitute or a displacement activity, or as a way of trying to shake off the stress. Many people feel stress when involved in financial markets and they often alleviate this with quite manic trading activity. Bizarrely they trade even more ferociously when in fact they should calm down and draw back. Though in fact this is only one side of the behavioural coin in market psychology, the other big problem is curiously the exact opposite, freezing and being unable to act to stop losses from running out of control. Trading, like so many things, requires a happy medium of activity – few of us seem to be able to do this on a consistent basis.

Keynes also saw the problem of market speculation and prediction as akin to trying to guess who would win a beauty contest. He compared speculation to a newspaper beauty contest, where one is asked to pick out the prettiest faces among hundreds of photographs; and also most crucially to predict which is the most popular choice of all the entrants in the competition. So, for example, you may pick contestant number 54 but sense that girl number 23 is the most popular. This is akin to looking at the FTSE 100 list of stocks and deciding that you really like BP but realising that the market really likes Vodafone.

Keynes held that to be successful in investment we have to choose not the ones we think are the "prettiest", but the ones that we think everyone else will select. This piece of market thinking demolishes much of the supposed value of market analysts and commentators – what's the point in knowing the best oil company in the market if all the price action is in, say, transport stocks? When Keynes first postulated this idea in the 1930s it was considered somewhat radical and certainly didn't conform to the standard views of rationality and assessing financial markets and assets in terms of fair value. Over time, though, this idea has been developed further, now with a lot of interest being shown in market behaviour and psychology – though many market players and intermediaries seem to ignore it.

Finally, once again Keynes seems to prove the rule that successful market operators let their results speak for themselves. Only the also-rans and hopefuls promote their secret investment theories and systems, while the successful just do it.

Lessons From The Masters?

So can the past masters tell us anything? Well certainly the basics of financial markets remain the same, and so their experiences still have value today. In particular the following points seem timeless.

New and emerging markets are ideal for intermediaries – the profits for speculators, however, can be stunning but the timing and exit from such markets is particularly critical. This is very hard for the speculator to finesse; in addition all players in the market can suffer from asymmetric liquidity. Almost by definition these are easy markets to enter, but can be impossible to exit. (The ugly head of liquidity rears itself once again.) Information is at a high premium and market-makers are much better placed to gather and exploit such information.

Nothing is truly new – not even in derivatives. Also, derivatives trading is not really that complicated. The jargon and the intricacy of such instruments can appear very sophisticated and difficult to penetrate but at their heart derivatives are really quite simple. However, it is an iron market rule that if as a buyer or seller of such instruments you cannot see through the fog of jargon you should leave well alone. (Cynics will point out that it is in many people's interests to keep such markets opaque and impenetrable – it is in this fog that their profit margin lays!) Of course the pricing and fine tuning of risk has become more sophisticated thanks to cheap and available computing power, but remember that the key determinant for option and related derivative prices still is, and always will remain, supply and demand.

Finally, don't be overly impressed by big market names, titans like Livermore, Cutten et al. come and go – the vast majority seem to be like fireworks, burning brightly and ultimately withering into the gloom. Both the biggest and the best and small players alike have great difficulty in containing speculative losses – there is no guarantee that the star names will always perform. In fact as one becomes bigger the problem becomes greater, market liquidity takes on greater importance, and the dangerous fallacy that one can move the market often overtakes successful players.

Contrary to popular belief amongst many traders, some economists have been brilliant financial speculators, though in truth Keynes stands way above any others. At a stretch one could include the economist David Riccardo, but in fact he had a successful stock-broking career before giving it up to become an academic – though undoubtedly his market experiences influenced his work.

3

Basic Building Blocks

'Not everything that can be counted counts,

And not everything that counts can be counted.'

Albert Einstein

It is commonplace to believe that finance is complicated, that a huge understanding of mathematics and complex equations is a prerequisite to mastering the topic. This is not true; there is nothing in finance that should intimidate anyone. In fact, financial markets are remarkably straightforward; every type of transaction and scheme can be broken down into one of a small series of very simple basic principles. These principles – the basic building blocks of finance – never change and the drivers that cause change in finance are really marketing, government regulation and taxation.

Knowledge of these building blocks and how they can be fitted together with one another can serve as an excellent basis with which to understand all financial instruments, whether simple or complicated. It is vital to understand the nature of any financial instrument you trade in, how it performs in the marketplace and what its risks and potential rewards are.

Gentlemen Versus Rocket Scientists

In any financial transaction there can only be two types of player; the end user and the intermediary. Of course many transactions have no intermediary and just involve two end users transacting between one another. The two types of player essentially make their money from different sources; the intermediary typically charges a commission for a service (stockbrokers or merger and acquisition advisors for example), whilst the end user has no guaranteed income stream as such, but either seeks to gain from taking and off-laying risk (stock option writing by market makers for example) or to gain from acquiring an asset or liability that they can sell on for a profit. This is all very simple stuff.

The world after 1945 saw wholesale finance settle into a very straightforward business model. Brokerage commissions were fixed, bank lending commissions and margins were also broadly fixed, and both were controlled by government-supported or even sponsored cartels that strictly limited membership to these exclusive clubs. Earnings from businesses in the marketplace were sheltered from outside competition and almost took the form of a guaranteed rental income. The atmosphere amongst market intermediaries was risk-averse and in a system of fixed commissions, business planning centred around maintaining existing client relationships and controlling costs. This was to be the last fanfare of the so-called gentlemen financiers.

This cosy world lay undisturbed until the abolition of fixed commissions on the New York Stock Exchange in 1975. This was the first crack in the fixed price regime, the London stock market followed suit in 1986, and in a similar move to freer markets, a couple of years earlier the world of banking had discovered the world of interest rate derivatives, and the new era of off-balance-sheet finance was born. Well, to be more precise, the banking sector re-discovered the world of derivatives, because option, futures and the other types of derivative were anything but new. Cash settled financial futures also arrived in the mid-1970s, firstly in the Chicago trading pits with London following soon afterwards by opening its first futures exchange called LIFFE in 1981 – a tectonic shift in international finance was occurring.

The gentlemen bankers and brokers were on their way out – the new masters were the exciting fresh breed of "rocket scientists". Suddenly two-hour lunch breaks with tame and compliant clients were a thing of the past, and a new language of Greek letters, heavy duty maths and software programs to run on personal computers were the new in thing. Trading rooms grew from small gatherings around a few clumsy monitors into huge rooms with vast numbers of screens, keyboards, phone lines and the accompanying massive egos. The scale of these changes can be illustrated by looking at bank lending margins in London. Until the early 1980s 1% was the norm, this rapidly shrunk to under ¼% and in some cases below ⅛%. In those days, nobody had any idea what a basis point was (one-hundredth of a per cent) let alone did they envisage the cut-throat world of the 1990s that would see margins slashed to 5 basis points and lower. Clearly the financial world had totally changed – or had it?

The Promise of the New

New instruments and complicated terminology came cascading out of these shiny new trading rooms – forward rate agreements, Interest Rate Swaps, Floating Rate Notes, Barrier Options, Digital Options, Dual Currency Bonds, Zeros and Coupon Strips, Look Backs, Collateralised Mortgage Obligations, Asset Backed Securities etc. etc., the list seemed endless. The arrival of cheap computing power, the roll back of stifling regulation and a general atmosphere of free market global capitalism saw an explosion in activity from the mid-1980s onwards. These new instruments were predicated on complex calculations that needed computers, and the breakdown of the fixed commission regime forced fat and lazy intermediaries to embrace competition and swallow the lower margins of the new business landscape. These lower margins meant higher turnover was needed to compensate, and intermediaries adjusted their businesses accordingly. Mergers between pure intermediary firms (primarily brokers) and mixed end user/intermediaries (banks and fund managers) took place at breakneck speed. For example in London, ahead of the de-regulation of the London stock market – the "Big Bang" – there was a headlong rush by banks to buy brokers. The business rationale was for integrated houses, and the newly opened up stock market looked like a prime area for business growth, though the market crash in the following year of 1987 revealed that broking wasn't always such a one-way bet. However, the rather trite and tiresome "Martini" business strategy of anytime, anyplace, anywhere was the dominant mantra as the newly deregulated markets started to expand and participants looked to a much expanded future full of money-making opportunities.

The Illusion Of Sophistication

The new products were now designed and created by teams of specialist financiers often with a maths or physics background, with a much larger group of sales people chattering away to an increasingly bemused client base about the wonderful new products that had suddenly arrived. All this activity and innovation created an illusion of sophistication and creativity, whereas in fact the basis for all these ideas were just old (often Newtonian) maths, with some old products jazzed up and recycled to look new and interesting. This was carefully hidden from the buyers and customers, who were frequently sold products they neither needed nor fully understood. Complex and multi-layered products were much favoured by the issuers as these allowed for skilful camouflage of their profit margins. The game was to take a number of plain vanilla ingredients and make a complex end structure that appeared to be cheap or even free, but in fact had a host of profit margins neatly embedded within it.

This era also ushered in the idea that finance was complex and difficult to understand. At one level this may be true, certainly computer programming skills, ability at higher maths and such like are important to construct some of the more complicated products. But equally at a basic level it most certainly is not true – the base components of finance remain remarkably simple and there are only so many combinations that can be packaged together. It is not within the scope of this book to delve into the mathematics behind structured finance products, but that said everyone can and should have a basic understanding of financial instruments. This can be achieved quite easily and is a necessary step for anyone hoping to understand financial markets.

Risk Failure

Probably, most large and often financially fatal losses are caused not so much by misreading the market as by having taken completely inappropriate risk on board without fully understanding the consequences. One hears so much about risk and how to control and monitor it these days, but still one of the largest sources of risk in markets remain players who don't fully understand the commitments they have undertaken. The last twenty years are littered with cases of investors having been surprised when certain instruments have "blown up". This seems particularly true where short option positions have been embedded or even superficially hidden within a product. Often there are warning signs at the start – the most obvious being when a form of risk protection or market participation is said to be free. For example, many Japanese companies in the mid-1980s borrowed money for "free" via bond issues with embedded warrants. In fact all that had happened was that the premium income (less a fat profit margin for the intermediary) from the short warrant position was used to pay the interest element due on the bond. So in pure cash flow terms the borrowing was free but came with huge contingent risks in the form of naked short options positions with no hedging in place. Many such bond issuers had unpleasant surprises when they found their short option positions had gone massively in the money, and they had made no hedging provisions. Needless to say the free borrowing was often catastrophically expensive, if not ruinous.

Far too many investors have either not bothered to study or do not understand the underlying principles of the product they have taken a position in. The surface complexity and strange jargon surrounding many financial structures often obscures clear thinking. It is not necessary to have a higher degree in physics or mathematics to understand what is entailed in any financial instrument – a clear understanding of the basics will help us all steer away from any danger zones, or – as the market often colourfully calls some of the more volatile and dangerous products – toxic waste.

Time And Money

In probably one of the most famous quotations about money, the American diplomat, inventor and philosopher Benjamin Franklin, as long ago as 1748, offered the following advice in a letter entitled To a Young Tradesman, 'Remember that time is money'. These days such advice seems rather trite, but in fact Franklin was focussing on one of the immutable laws of finance. Time and money are indeed intricately linked, and in fact make two out of three of the core elements in a financial instrument. To be more accurate and precise in our examination of finance, we need to change Franklin's advice slightly and to add a third element. Restated, we can say that the three keys to finance are price, time and volatility.

All financial instruments and transactions, however simple or complex, have these components and in today's world of so-called global high finance it is easy to forget this simple fact. Whether it's an individual's home mortgage, retirement savings, credit card bill or a large company's forward foreign exchange positions, interest rate hedging or pension fund investments, the three primary elements of price, time and volatility are always present.

Looking at any financial product it becomes obvious that these three factors drive its valuation and future path. Complications arise because price and value are not necessarily the same. Furthermore, whilst time may be linear in the world of interest rate maths and calculations, it is certainly different in the markets. What we may call market time is more subtle, for example there are at least three forms of volatility – historic, implied and future (seekers of more exotic forms will be interested to hear there is some market interest in trading the volatility of implied volatility!) The various components also differ in their importance, but from these basic elements we can start to build any financial product.

Three Core Transactions

As well as these basic starting blocks there are in fact only three core transaction types in financial markets; we can buy or sell, borrow or lend, and transact for settlement now or in the future. As with the three components of price, time and volatility, these three transactions are often combined to create instruments, indeed it's impossible to think of a financial asset or liability that doesn't incorporate some or all of these basic transaction types. With the three elements of price, time and volatility coupled together with these three main types of transactions we have all the components necessary for understanding financial instruments and the markets they trade in. Now let's look at how these all fit together.

Three Triangles

Given that all financial transactions can be broken down into simple constituents perhaps we can illustrate the various relationships with a few diagrams. Below are three diagrams that outline the basics.

Figure 3.1: The Price/Time/Volatility triangle

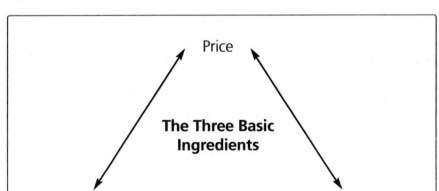

First, in Figure 3.1, we have the three building blocks of Price, Time and Volatility. It is interesting that most financial charts and diagrams concentrate on the first two and that volatility often gets ignored or forgotten about. For simple transactions this doesn't matter, but for anything remotely complex volatility is nearly always a component, in such cases we forget it at our peril.

Figure 3.2: The Buy-Sell/Borrow-Lend/Now-Later triangle

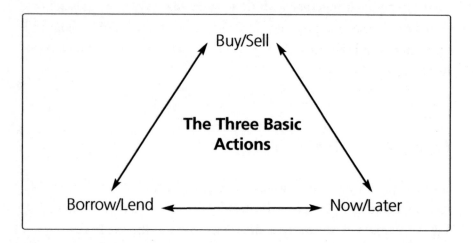

Figure 3.2 shows the three main transaction types. As we have already seen most financial deals or instruments usually involve more than one of these elements, and can comprise of all three. At one level this may seem rather facile but does help remind us that everything can be broken down into parts that are easy to understand and assess.

Finally, Figure 3.3 shows the three valuation outcomes, capital value, yield or interest cost, and implied volatility valuation. These three prices determine all financial instrument valuations, and we have to be certain that when we transact in the market we understand how these three drivers will affect the price.

Figure 3.3: The Capital Value/Yield/Volatility Value triangle

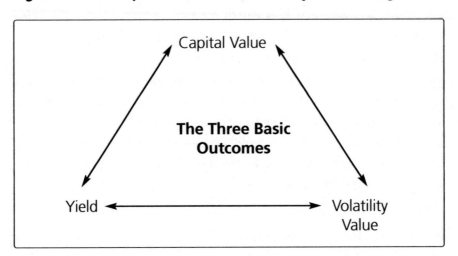

To give some idea of how all these factors come together let's take a look at a series of transactions with differing complexity – first, the plain vanilla example of buying or selling an equity.

Probably the simplest business transaction is where we buy or sell something, usually in return for cash, though if you want to go back to absolute basics one could consider the primitive use of barter as the very first type of transaction undertaken. There is very little complication in terms of risk and settlement, the counterparties swap cash for goods in person.

In the modern financial world it is pretty much the same; if you buy securities the stock is credited to your account and the cost is debited. Thereafter any movements in the share price are reflected as simple changes in your capital valuation. One additional factor is of course that the stock may pay a dividend or – increasingly fashionable in the United States in recent years – grant bonus shares in lieu of money. So the simple purchase has probably got a yield and you now have a capital asset (units can go down as well as up!) together with an income stream.

Instead of buying the stock though let's consider what happens if you went short, i.e. sold securities you don't own. In this case the securities would be debited from your account and the cash credited. However, you are unable to deliver something you don't have so the securities house or your broker will arrange to borrow the stock on your behalf so that you can fulfil the transaction. In this case things are a shade more complicated. There is a cost of borrowing the stock (stock lending is a big business for long-term holders of equities such as pension funds and insurance companies), depending on the size of the trade, and how long you run the short, this may be within the brokerage charge, or a separate on going charge.

Both these relatively simple deals involve price, some small exposure to time (in the case of the short, because of the cost of borrowing the stock; and the long may have an income yield) and also there is the more subtle influence of market volatility. It may be that the stock was selected as a long-term steady investment, but it is possible that liquidity and consequent volatility in the stock will change. Some of these exposures are pretty light, obviously the biggest risk to the investor (or should we call the short position holder a speculator?) is likely to be any future move in the price. The time or interest yield/cost is relatively marginal, and exposure to future price volatility is ungeared and consequently negligible (unlike say an options or warrant position) so the price is the dominant consideration for the investor.

Now let's turn to a slightly more complicated product – the bond with equity market participation. These instruments come under a variety of guises, but tend to be very popular after the end of an equity bull market. Essentially the bond issuer promises that the investor's capital is guaranteed, the bond may even pay a very small interest rate and give the investor the chance to participate in any upward price movement in the stock market. A sort of all things to all men type of structure you might say. The appeal is pretty straightforward. In an equity bear market people are fearful of straight equity purchases, they want the safety of a guaranteed capital instrument preferably with some income and also don't want to miss out if their fears are misplaced and the stock market starts to go up again. So what is this animal really?

For the seller of such an instrument the construction is simple. They receive an amount of capital from the investors, which has to be fixed or locked into the instrument for a period of time – three years seems to be about as much illiquidity that most investors will accept. The issuing house buys a zero coupon bond with a three-year life – these are priced at a discount and gradually increase in value to reach par value at maturity. This takes care of the "guaranteed" element; there will be enough capital at the end to pay everyone out. The difference between the cost of this zero bond and the total capital is then used in three ways, a three-year call option is bought on the stock market; usually somewhat out of the money to reduce costs, an amount is set aside for the issuing house's profit margin, and there may be enough to allow a very small almost nominal running income payable to the investors. There is often one further twist as well; because the out-of-the-money call option doesn't kick in straightaway, plus a certain amount will amortise with declining time value, it is not normally possible to give the investor equity gains from the market level at which they invest. The marketing gets around this by offering a percentage of gains – so instead of your bond participating in gains above a certain threshold on the equity index, you get a fixed percentage of any gains from the time you buy the instrument. This is simpler to market and seems to appeal to investors more.

So the final blurb on the instrument may say something like this: "Invest for three years in our guaranteed stock market bond. Your capital is guaranteed at maturity; you participate in 60% of any gains on the index and even receive a small interest yield of XYZ%." Of course the issuer has managed to hide their profit margin in the product and to push home the marketing message, which often trumpets that no commissions or fees are payable.

All of this is quite legitimate and in fact may be a good product for the small player who doesn't have access to the wholesale market, and so cannot take advantage of size to obtain good prices on the individual ingredients. For the big player these things make no sense at all – they should always be able to create a better deal themselves as they can dis-intermediate the issuer's profit margin.

Going back to our three triangles we can see where the investor has the following exposures. They bought an instrument with an out-of-the-money call (so they have locked in a volatility price, and will pay out time value – all of this is effectively crystallised at the start as the instrument has to be held to maturity), they may receive a small yield and they have potential capital gains if the stock market moves their way.

Asymmetric Risk

One thing should be very clear at this stage; risks are asymmetric in trading. If you are long of an asset your maximum loss will occur if the value of the asset falls to zero, in that sense it is quantifiable, you can only lose 100% of your investment. If you are short, however, in theory the sky is the limit, there is no maximum loss. This is true in spades in any derivative strategy – hence why most people buy options (you can only lose your premium paid) rather than run a short position. We have to be careful here – just because the potential risk of loss is greater with a particular trading strategy it does not necessarily make it the most dangerous strategy, but we have to be certain we understand the potential for losses. To repeat what was said earlier, the weakest link in the chain regarding risk management is understanding the risk you have undertaken. No amount of software and fancy maths with probabilities of risk of ruin, or any other statistics, will save you if you have failed to understand the risk you have on your books. This is what happened to the Japanese companies who thought they could borrow money for nothing.

We could go through literally hundreds of different instruments and break down the components, but hopefully the idea is pretty clear now. Perhaps to finish this approach we could take a look at more high level wholesale structure and see how this can also be broken down. A fashionable example these days might be the asset backed securities market – it also neatly illustrates one of the major driving forces of finance these days – securitisation.

With the breakdown of the fixed commission era and the drive for new products, a whole new industry was born, the securitisation of hitherto untraded assets. Typically these were assets sitting on banks' balance sheets that they were unable to trade or easily liquidate. For example, when a bank grants a loan, the loan stays on their books until it is repaid, or until it is written off in the case of a bad debt. With securitisation they can release the value in this loan, in plain terms they can sell it to someone else and realise the cash. This is achieved by the so called packaging up of the assets into special securities that are usually only traded on an over-the-counter basis amongst wholesale counterparties. In one stroke the originator, often a bank, has moved from the borrow/lend part of our equation to the buy/sell segment, and has also telescoped the future cash flows and capital repayments into a "now money" equivalent. (This is merely the present value of the future cash flows.) In fact, parcelling up loans is just one example, now many companies manage their borrowings through similar devices. They assign designated future cash flows from part of their business into separate and distinct legal entities that then issue bonds to raise debt.

Perhaps one of the more exotic versions of this has been the Bowie Bond – in this case the singer David Bowie, in March 1997, assigned a whole stream of future royalty earnings from his back catalogue of recordings to a specialist corporate vehicle that has then issued bonds with a par value of US$55 million. David Bowie gets his future money now, the bond-holders assume the risk that his record sales will be sustained and have first call on the stream of royalties. But as it is a bond issue they can sell on the paper to other investors, so they have gained potential liquidity. Though it should be remembered that the transparency of a securities price, as opposed to a loan, makes it more susceptible to price changes. This operation has pretty much moved around all of our triangles, but is actually extremely simple.

Credit Where It's Due

An important factor in asset backed securities is creditworthiness. The rise in securitisation has seen a parallel rise in the growth and importance of credit rating agencies as their skills have been called upon to assess all sorts of instruments. Credit ratings are now vital for investors as they try to sift through the plethora of securities offerings. Bonds linked to mortgage loans, car loans, and credit card receipts are all commonplace these days, but despite their fancy titles and often quite complex legal structures the financial principles remain stunningly simple.

To conclude then, whilst certain products and structures in finance have highly complicated computational maths driving their initial pricing and valuation, the underlying elements remain straightforward. There is really no excuse for an investor, borrower, lender or whoever being unable to understand the major characteristics of any financial instrument.

Critical Questions

When faced with a new complex hybrid instrument, we must set to work to break it down into the basic elements:

- Am I borrowing or lending here?
- Am I buying or selling? Do I have exposure to implied volatility?
- Does the passage of time bring me a yield or is there a running cost in holding the instrument?
- What happens if X happens? Am I covered or exposed?

Being able to answer these questions will go a long way to protecting the investor from disasters, perhaps more than just the grinding maths of the actual pricing.

The Trouble With Time

One of the basic elements of finance is time, and we need to examine this more closely as it is so deeply embedded in so much of finance and investing.

Scientists tells us that time can be accurately measured by calibrating the oscillations of the rare and slightly odd, silvery blue metal caesium. (Like mercury, it is in liquid form at room temperature.) Their success in encompassing time is now measured in nano-seconds, with the latest atomic clocks boasting an accuracy of within two nano-seconds per year; scaling that up, that is like saying accurate to within one second every 1.4 million years. Clearly the problem of accurate time has been cracked. In the physical world with its natural laws – yes; but in financial markets where time seems to often have strange characteristics the jury is still out.

We have already touched upon Franklin's aphorism about time and money, which really looks at time as a chargeable commodity, but time can also be seen as a cost, in fact almost a tax on life. George Bernard Shaw in his book *Everybody's Political What's What* identifies that we are all economic animals (or his term Economic Men – this being written in 1944, long before any concerns over gender labels), by which he meant life isn't free, there is an economic cost of survival. In Abraham Maslow's hierarchy of needs, food and shelter are at the core of our needs to survive – these things cost money. So we all, rich or poor, have a burn rate of costs, an economic cost of staying alive. In biological terms we could use calories as the accounting currency – every living being needs a minimum number of daily calories either consumed or burnt from fat reserves to stay alive. Failure isn't bankruptcy in this case – but death.

In the financial world this relationship between time and money can flow in both directions; some investments carry a naturally positive cash flow, such as interest bearing deposit accounts or the yield on government bonds. Other instruments have their own in-built burn rate – the classic example being time value on a long option position. This description needs to be expanded slightly; for the professional fund manager, the concept of carry is usually the net gain or cost after deducting short-term interest rates. So, for example, a bond investment is said to have a negative carry if the running yield is less than the short-term funding rate. The investor could have a higher yield by putting his funds on deposit, rather than choosing to buy and hold the bond; and so gives up some potential time-based income in the hope the underlying capital value of the bond will appreciate to more than compensate. Or if the investor had borrowed funds to buy the bond, the yield on the investment would not be covering the interest cost of the borrowing.

One could call this negative carry the cost of betting on higher bond prices in the future, or perhaps more subtly locking-in the current long-term yield in the expectation that interest rates will fall in the near future. Obviously if short-term yields are higher than long-term rates, investors believe that interest rates will be lower in the future, and so giving up the current higher short-term rate is worth it to lock in what may well be relatively favourable longer-term yields. Whether or not a bond investment has a positive or negative carry is a function of interest rate returns across time. This relationship between yields across future investment time horizons can easily be drawn – it's a yield curve.

The Yield Curve

The following diagram shows two yield curves; first, the classic positive yield curve (the solid line), with yield rates higher the further out one invests. This is logical, in that we would expect to receive a higher return for the risk of investing over a longer time horizon. Also it is possible for yield curves to be negative (the dotted line in the diagram).

Figure 3.4: Yield Curve Diagram

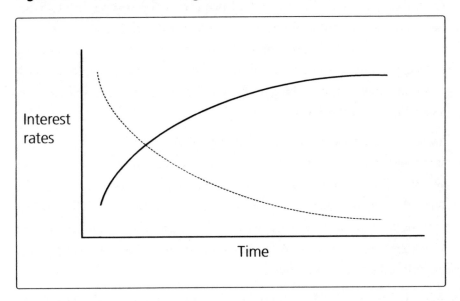

At first this may seem strange. Why should you get less return for assuming a longer risk and investment horizon? Anticipation and future expectation provide the answer.

The yield curve is not just about current conditions; it also shows the market's current expectation of the future. In this sense it is not just a snapshot about today's money market but also a window on the possible (one cannot push as far as even the probable, let alone the definite) future outcome of interest rates. So a negative yield curve merely reflects that the market expects lower short-term interest rates in the future, and so discounts that possibility by lowering the appropriate longer-term yields now. Markets rarely wait for actual events; much of their price action is about anticipation and perception of future events. In market events current time means more than just now, it is also a distillation of what the here and now believes will be the future.

The action and reaction of the yield curve is an extremely important function in finance. It determines the long-term rate at which governments and companies can borrow money, it acts as a yardstick for judging the viability of capital projects, it represents the balance between supply and demand for capital funds, and it also acts as a beacon for those trying to predict future interest rates. It is also only a partial picture of the marketplace – whilst it does provide a useful shorthand method of looking at the interest rate markets it is not always a good guide to the future.

Yield curves are usually an incomplete picture because yields are not static and time never stops gently ticking by, so in fact the curves try to adjust to account for these factors. The way yield curves flex and shift their shape is of course a major investment opportunity. The interest rate markets are full of strategies called "steepeners", "flatteners" and "barbells" that seek to exploit either an accentuation in the curve or a diminished slope of the curve.

What we have looked at so far may be called the classical relationship between price and time as represented by interest rates. As such it presents a perfectly straightforward linear world where most of the issues can be resolved through mathematics that provides us with fair value models etc. However, there are other time elements in financial markets that are nowhere near as linear in their relationships. By this I don't mean to plunge headlong into the debate about Chaos Theory and whether or not financial time series' can or should be viewed in terms of non-linear analysis techniques. Instead, just to make a more simple observation, some time periods in financial markets are vastly more important than others. 'So what?' you might exclaim. This is equally true in some sports games where extra time and sudden death penalties are clearly more important slices of time than the opening ten minutes of the game. True. In finance though, the market seems to repeat the same process of certain times of the day and even certain days being more important than others; it's as if the whole financial world is caught up in a version of the film *Groundhog Day*. For example, every first Friday of the month the United States government publishes employment data, and always at 8.30 am New York time.

Such is the perceived importance of this data (this is a fashion thing – some twenty years ago nobody bothered with such data – the killer stats were then deemed to be trade data) that major financial markets become comatose ahead of the announcement and then burst into often extreme volatility for a few hours after the publication of the statistics, before calming down. The clocks on the trading room wall are still ticking away in a nice linear fashion, but trading seems to be stretching and compressing the X axis almost at will. Is 'so what?' still the right response? No, because such intra-day volatility cannot be easily ignored.

"Now" Time

The greatest lesson about time in the markets is that we live in the now. One of the most common investment fallacies is the long view. Some investors claim that they are in for the long term, they ignore daily spikes, they never look at intra-day prices. Maybe – but at the end of the day the price you enter or exit a market is the "now" price, which may well be an intra-day spike or volatility driven move. Stop loss orders often fall prey to such movements. However, high up a mountain we hide ourselves it's impossible to be totally divorced from these effects. Of course we may have a long-term position in the marketplace, but risk management, Value at Risk, margin calls, stop loss orders, etc. are all fixed in the present. So we often find our long-term view is compressed into where the market is now.

Market Time

This is why market time is slightly strange. It is this element that gives rise to capitulation sell offs, and buying climaxes. The whole theory of delta hedging also falls prey to these intra-day moves and spikes. In the long term things may be smoothed out and damped down, but it is hard for the investor to keep his investment locked on to his investment horizon. Even pension funds with duration benchmarks measured in years rather than months or days are not immune to this effect. It may also explain the slightly maniac market view about news and information, even the long-term investor seems to want to know the latest news; although their sights are fixed on a distant time objective they remain gripped with now, and more importantly what we might term now + 1, i.e. trying to know what's next.

Pressure points in the marketplace where time seems to dictate price are everywhere, along with government statistical releases, option expiries and often the opening few minutes of stock markets are well known as pockets of volatility. In the case of opening prices on stocks, there is still a legion of investors who leave Buy at Open orders with their brokers, a practice that is particularly prevalent on Monday mornings after everyone has decided to react to the weekend press. The triple witching hour of quarterly option expiries is now an international event and the growing desire to hit daily currency hedging benchmarks has thrown up a new phenomenon in the currency markets, where large orders all vie to hit the exact price at 4pm London time. As you can imagine the market activity ahead of this aptly named fixing price can be quite bizarre, institutions armed with customer orders dance around various price levels trying to fulfil their customer orders, ensuring their own positions are correctly aligned and actually getting the trade done. Somewhat bizarrely much of this activity has developed in response to customers who wish to avoid volatility – the net effect has been to push a whole series of unstable dominoes ever closer together and actually concentrate volatility. Once again the law of unintended consequences, which is a frequent visitor in financial decisions, rears its head.

Before leaving the issue of market time we should just note there are at least one group of analysts who actually ignore time, indeed they filter it out of their work. A small but significant minority of chartists use a very old technique called point and figure charts, that seeks to only study and interpret price data, with no reference at all to the time frame. This very purist approach to price analysis cannot dismiss time entirely, for soon as a trade is entered, time comes flooding back into the investment process. Like many chartists they may have some modest success, but there is little evidence that this price only approach has led to any great investment fortunes.

More recently some non-linear maths types have drawn attention to the seemingly fractal quality of market price action. Draw a bar graph of any time period of market prices and it seems to produce the same patterns, whether the time increment is minute by minute, hourly or even weekly data. All well and good but this misses the point – we can plot and map past data as much as we like, and we can dream of future price movements, but the price now remains the only price that counts.

So time has many faces in financial markets; at one level being very straightforward and anchored in the world of interest rates and returns, but equally it plays tricks with investors, who often unwittingly fall prey to its caprices.

The Third Element

After time and price, the most important component in financial markets is volatility. We can describe volatility as the measure of the rate of change in the price of an asset over a specified period of time. It is usual to calculate this in terms of the standard deviation from the mean price of the asset. Fair enough, but what does that actually tell us? For one thing such a result is clearly backward-facing, the volatility measure will tell us how volatile the asset has been, but will that be much help in telling us about its future path?

The financial markets use two types of volatility in their calculations. The first, historic volatility, is what was just described above – it merely measures the past volatility of a stock, commodity or whatever, and gives a measure of that asset's past rate of change. As such it is of limited value, but has some use for investors engaged in asset allocation decisions. For example, a range of stocks may be analysed for their past historic volatility and then either selected or rejected for a portfolio on the basis of their previous price action. Risk-averse investors naturally plump for lower volatility items, and the more adventurous look for higher volatility, and by inference more risky stocks.

Whilst past behaviour patterns may be repeated, the historic volatility measure is not a certain guide to future volatility outcomes. That said, this stock picking technique has been formalised into the so-called beta valuation of a stock. Rather than just looking at the individual volatility of a stock, the beta valuation compares a stock against a basket (typically one of the large well known indices) of stocks. The index is usually calibrated as having a beta of 1, and so any stock that has a beta greater than 1 is deemed to be more volatile and is very likely to rise faster than the index on an up day, and also fall further on a down day. Risk-averse investors pick sub 1 beta portfolios and those willing to be more adventurous accumulate stocks with a beta of greater than 1. Beta is much used by large portfolio managers as a way of setting the overall risk in their holdings – it is a far from perfect tool, and strays into the dangerous and often misleading waters of investment benchmarks.

The second and much more interesting type of volatility is implied variety. Implied volatility is really the markets' estimate (perhaps we should say guess) of what future volatility will be. As such it is the central component in pricing options. Implied volatility is not a calculation using past data, it is the statistical measure that shows how the market (whether correctly or not) sees volatility over a future investment horizon. This makes it an extremely important and valuable source of information about market sentiment and future expectations.

It is the key to options pricing as it measures the all important supply and demand element within option pricing. The other ingredients in pricing an option are derived from other markets, principally the price of the underlying asset, and the funding cost factored into the duration of the life of the option. Implied volatility can in fact be seen as a very simple supply/demand measure for options.

It is this supply/demand characteristic of implied volatility that is its most useful facet. When looking at our triangle of time/price/volatility there is an unusual relationship with volatility. As we have seen, time and price are locked together in a close relationship, delineated by interest rates, rates of investment return, present value of future cash flows, etc; but volatility has a different role to play. Volatility, by this we have to be careful to mean implied volatility, seems to suggest that it has a predictive quality – it sometimes appears to lead price.

Indeed there is a school of thought that gives volatility an important role in future price prediction. The argument runs as follows. Implied volatility measures the market's future expectations for price volatility and it also records the supply and demand for options. So if the demand for options increases obviously their price is higher, or more expensive to be more accurate, and this is reflected in a higher rate of implied volatility. That in itself wouldn't fully explain why implied volatilities may be an early warning of price movements though. What we have to remember are the motives behind buying options; in general there seem to be two main strands of thinking behind buying options, hedging and speculation. Both of these activities often happen at the very earliest part of a new trend or market phase.

For the investor with, say, a long position in a stock index, rather than choosing to sell out or even reduce his position he may choose to buy a put option to give himself downside protection. The judgement being that it is worth holding on to the long position but a degree of uncertainty makes buying some down side price protection prudent and worthwhile. This is particularly true for the large institutional players who may face liquidity issues in liquidating a large part of a portfolio, and may find it easier to buy put options. In addition, many such funds have a naturally long bias and so rather than trying to finesse the selling of their holdings and then trying to time their repurchase, they find the options route simpler and more efficient.

Equally, uncertainty about the future trend or an inkling that a new trend is under way often stimulates options activity from the more adventurous investors, or speculators if you prefer. In this case it may be that they don't want to commit too much capital to the chance of a market move, or that they only have limited means – options created through their gearing may give a good way of increasing the potential rewards.

So the buying activities of both groups can be a powerful stimulant to demand at the beginning of a new trend. This may seem fanciful or at least unproven, but there have been a number of instances of large market trend changes being heralded by a prior and simultaneous increase in implied volatility values. A case in point was the activity in the currency markets during the summer of 1992 when interest in put options for sterling steadily increased well ahead of the subsequent blow up caused by the currency crashing out of the European Exchange Rate Mechanism. Throughout the early part of 1992 the implied volatilities quoted for sterling/Deutschmark options were extremely low, sometimes hitting 2%. As speculative demand emerged, and nervous investors seeking protection bought options, these levels ticked up to around 4% plus before the fateful Black Wednesday. Even those levels were still low. Typically, currency volatilities trade between 8% and 15% in usual market conditions, but given the fact sterling was supposed to be trading within a fairly tight trading band they were an important sign that the market didn't believe the system could hold.

Also, such options buying forced the writers to delta hedge themselves in the underlying currency market – which in this example meant selling sterling in the marketplace. This was undoubtedly a contributory pressure on the exchange rate and the "floor" for sterling in the ERM. This also neatly illustrates how the price volatility axis on our triangle is a two-way flow. Past price activity obviously creates historic volatility, but also implied volatility directly impacts on the current market price.

Unfortunately the potential for implied volatility as a definitive tool for predicting future price movements is not proven. Movements in implied volatility only appear to lead price, careful statistical analysis shows that implied volatilities are normally a co-incident indicator when looking at future price movements. That said there have been important occasions when the options market has priced risk differently from the spot market (as per the sterling example above). When this has happened an impending market explosion is nearly always at hand. So in fact, although the occasions are rare, when implied volatility gives a different risk assessment from the current price, then a serious price re-adjustment is usually in the works; and they are extremely violent when they happen. For this reason any diverse move by implied volatilities should be taken extremely seriously.

Time And Volatility

There is also a close relationship between time and volatility. First, there is the fairly simple observation that over longer periods of time volatility has a lower impact. For the investor this means that they can ride out short-term market movements if they have a long enough investment horizon (a pension fund for example). Equally, as time shrinks the final date of an investment, the best example here probably being approaching the expiry of an option, volatility can have an increasing and often explosive effect. Also, as we have seen, volatility has an inherent time element; with historic volatility measuring the past and known volatility values, and implied volatility representing the markets' best attempt at pricing the future values of volatility. The implied volatility market also offers a number of trading opportunities; clearly, volatility expectations are not the same across a range of different time periods. Three-month volatility may well differ from six month, which in turn may well be different from one year volatility. It is possible to plot these various values and create a form of yield curve that shows the shape of an asset's expected implied volatility. These curves can be positive (rising with time) or negative (declining with time), and just like interest yield curves flex around, flatten or steepen. Advantage can be taken of these changes by building a series of option positions across the curve, the most obvious example being a calendar spread.

Given that volatility is as important as the other two elements of time and price, it is somewhat surprising that it is still often overlooked, and volatility information in most markets is still extremely patchy. Amongst wholesale players implied volatility levels are well known, and relatively transparent. But at the retail level there seems to be little or no information. Newspapers often carry price data about traded options, but rarely carry the implied volatility levels that underlie the price. It is still rare to see a chart of an equity's implied volatility in an article. Analysis of implied volatilities is essential if one is to have any chance in understanding when options offer good or bad value. It is still amazing to think that a large number of option purchases (which by the way are far more popular than running short positions) are executed without any reference whatsoever to implied volatility values. As we saw in the previous chapter, market-makers in options are very grateful for such ignorance!

To complete the picture there is the actual volatility of an instrument – this differs from the historic measure and the implied version; it is merely the outcome or what we may term the unfolding volatility. This can only be known at the time, but is important as it impacts directly on delta hedging of option positions. This "now" volatility is curiously somewhat hidden and forgotten, but still has an impact on market activity.

To conclude then, financial markets are really about very simple concepts, and can be understood and analysed by viewing them in terms of simple basic building blocks. However sophisticated an instrument, it should be possible to break it down into straightforward parts. An ability to do this and to understand the relevance of the various parts and operations of a supposedly complex financial instrument is essential before we should consider trading with it. However, knowledge of these building blocks is not the full story – we also have to understand risk, which is what we will look at next.

4

Mental Curves

'No one tests the depth of a river with both feet.'

Ashanti proverb

As we have just examined, even the most complicated financial structure or transaction can be broken down into very simple components. Whilst de-constructing everything to its basic building blocks is instructive and a good way of understanding what's going on, to be able to take advantage of opportunities in the financial markets we have to understand financial risk. So now let's try to build from the basic concepts and create a simple set of tools to understand risk. To do this we will examine a number of simple curves that can help us build a mental picture of financial risk.

The Geography Of Risk

Somewhat like sex, every generation thinks they are discovering risk for the first time.

For the latest generation of market players risk sometimes seems to be the only topic. The measurement and management of financial risk has been a growth industry for the last twenty years, much of it driven by the new ideas in regulation, and as a response to the increasing complexity and volume of instruments in the marketplace. As derivative and structured products have proliferated in the market, so has demand to quantify the risks being run as a consequence. As computers have allowed faster computational methods, so more areas of risk have been priced, and so the whole area has grown. With this growth has come the usual expansion of jargon and seeming complication. Can we cut through all of this to make sense of financial risk?

What exactly is financial risk? The standard modern answer is to break it down into a number of specific areas, normally market risk, credit risk and settlement risk. Added to these one should also include liquidity risk, legal risk and operational risk. These categories pretty much cover every aspect of activity within financial markets, and to these we can also add the more general risk that the whole financial system might blow up, normally referred to as systemic risk.

These various risks have greater importance for some market players than others. In general, professional firms that are acting as intermediaries are the most concerned with risk measurement and assessment, principally because they are required by law to meet certain regulatory standards and thresholds. End users probably have less interest in some of these risk measures, but the key risk metrics are in fact probably just as important to them as the intermediaries. Given that we are examining the markets from an end user viewpoint let's concentrate on the three most important areas for investors, these being market risk, credit risk and liquidity risk.

Hope, Mope And Dope

Market risk is pretty straightforward, it's the risk of loss on your investments, and how to measure and control such losses. For professional firms this has lead to the development of Value at Risk models, which look to quantify losses in terms of probability and their overall impact on the capital of the firm. In simple terms VaR models define investment horizons and set confidence levels which are used to set boundaries for acceptable risk and losses.

Such VaR modelling has lead to an enormous industry of risk managers, middle office services, software systems and such like. In recent years it has become an accepted benchmark, or at least a best first step for quantifying financial risk, by regulators and supervisory bodies. Whether this is a good idea or not is a very great debating point and VaR is examined in further detail later in this book.

For the individual investor or speculator, market risk is usually a very simple affair; it really is just about trying to avoid or at least contain your losses. Unfortunately many investors seem to believe that praying and guesswork are the best ways to tackle this issue. It appears that few individuals are prepared for the most common occurrence in financial markets – losses. Far too many follow the well worn path of hope, mope and dope. First, you hope that the trade will do well, then you mope when it starts to slip into the red, and then when you finally take the loss your confidence is shattered and you feel a real dope! Whether the professional measures such as VaR are really suitable for individual players is doubtful, but that most certainly doesn't mean the issue should be avoided. It is important to concentrate on exit plans for your trade. There are a host of approaches, but sitting and hoping is not the best way forward. Unfortunately inaction is one of the biggest killers in managing financial risk, and it is doubtful if there is anything that can protect the investor from himself.

Crunch

The events in financial markets that started in August 2007 have now demonstrated to everyone the importance of credit – and understanding one's exposure to credit risk.

This risk can be defined quite easily as the likelihood that a counterparty to a trade will fail to meet their obligations; for example, failing to repay a loan on a due date or not delivering securities that they have already been paid for. Attitudes to credit risk often follow the usual bull-bear cycle. In good times credit becomes easy, lending criteria become more generous and often overshot in terms of prudential exposures. The recent examples of so-called NINJA lending (to individuals with No Income, No Jobs or Assets) is a classic illustration of the problem. In bear market conditions lenders slam on the brakes, demand much higher criteria and security, and lend on low income multiples, etc. This is exactly the situation the financial and banking markets faced in 2009 as the vicious squeeze on credit and lending continued.

For large institutions credit risk is probably the most important and most well understood financial risk. Interestingly many professional investment houses and lending bankers effectively outsource their credit assessments by making use of the ratings available from the credit ratings agencies. There can be no guarantee about the future of a credit issue, but nevertheless the agency's analysis does provide a great deal of detail about an issuer's credit worthiness. Critics though have pointed out that almost by definition the information is backward-looking and using third party agencies' risks, replacing the benefits of a close relationship between lenders and borrowers with a clinical rating.

Such is the current power and influence of these agencies that the ability to borrow in the marketplace can be severely affected if they issue an unfavourable analysis. One problem with this system has been the way markets react when a credit issue is downgraded. Often when a bond issue is downgraded there is a rush to sell after the announcement. This is usually because of the dead hand of benchmarking – if a bond loses its coveted investment grade status certain investment funds are not allowed to hold it under the terms of their investment guidelines, and it will not feature in the major industry benchmarks, so forced sales hit the market after the downgrade.

This can have the effect of actually adding to market volatility and inefficiencies as everyone rushes for the same crowded exit door. Ironically whilst trying to escape from the dangers of credit risk those hitting the exit often run into the third major risk – liquidity.

Resilience Depth And Tightness

Liquidity risk is a potentially extremely dangerous risk for investors, mainly because it is often only recognised when it's too late. We can define it as the probability that an asset can be converted into an expected amount of value within an expected amount of time. (Or if you prefer – I want my money now!)

This risk usually comes in two forms; market liquidity risk that arises when one cannot execute a transaction (usually a large amount) at the expected market rate, and funding liquidity risk when it becomes impossible to borrow funds to cover cash flow requirements. For investment strategies clearly the first is the more important, but liquidity risk can be fatal for banks and other financial institutions during times of financial instability. The collapse of the British bank Northern Rock illustrated this perfectly.

In market liquidity three factors come together: resilience, depth and tightness of the market. The first is the speed at which prices find a new equilibrium after a large trade, the second the volume of an asset (shares, currency, bonds, or whatever) that can be converted without affecting the price, and the third factor represents the cost and speed of turning a position around, i.e. the bid-offer spread or the speed of matching trades on an electronic trading system.

Only the most naïve believe the bid-offer spread will always provide their market exit point. All bids and offers are circumscribed by restricted liquidity, no market-maker provides a bid or offer with limitless volume. Whilst this is obvious and indeed plain common sense, any number of market players have fallen foul of shrinking market liquidity. One of the most common traps is when a position is steadily built up over a period of time and then the holder wishes to exit in one go. Markets are extremely adept at sniffing out abnormally large positions, and are always keen to exploit the profit potential of forcing a large position to be liquidated under duress.

One may consider that liquidity issues only affect a very few of the largest traders, and that most players including institutions normally have no trouble in executing their trades in the marketplace. This is generally true, but in small markets, for example penny stocks or minor commodities, one doesn't have to be very large to be visible. A telltale sign of potential liquidity risk is a widening of the normal bid-offer spread. Again this is common sense as any market-maker will seek to protect themselves from poor liquidity by increasing their profit margins (the trading spread) when they quote. Increasingly, regulators and exchange authorities monitor very large positions in markets in an apparent effort to help any problems, but there can be no absolute guarantee of liquidity in any market.

The Herd

Paradoxically the current fashion for benchmarks, index tracking, credit ratings and fixings may well be adding to liquidity risk issues, as more and more risk-averse investors seek to trade at "known" levels and prices, and within certain defined asset groups. This can have the effect of bunching up supply and demand and may well be adding to market inefficiencies rather than mitigating them. The herd atmosphere amongst fund managers is so strong these days, and the fear of scrutiny from outsiders so great, that they seem to prefer to act together and be wrong, rather than risk being different, original and creative.

One side-effect of herding is the attempt by some players to bypass exchanges and indulge in so called Dark Liquidity trading. Exchanges help provide liquidity and also give valuable information on pricing and current market prices and spreads. Dark traders deal amongst themselves outside the exchange and do not report the trade and in so doing they deny the marketplace the relevant trade and price information. They are in effect making parasitic use of the exchange for the all important intelligence of price discovery but giving nothing in return. Indeed if everyone indulged in dark trading, overall liquidity would deteriorate and exchanges would dry up. In to this mix must be added the regulators and governments, who naturally want more transparency and openness, and wish to limit dark trading. These additional actors, dark traders versus regulators if you like, are naturally at odds with one another and the overall welfare of the marketplace is finely balanced.

It is clear that liquidity begets liquidity but interestingly it can also beget instability. Low liquidity will badly affect the efficiency of a market but how can we have too much liquidity? In modern markets a number of drivers have pushed up the availability of liquidity: the benefits of the dispersion of risk (market and credit risk in particular), interlinked markets, similar or even standardised risk models, and rating agencies can all contribute to excess liquidity and this inevitably leads to a bubble and then a crisis. This is really the back story of the 2007/08 credit crunch – it's not just about credit, it's really the bursting of an enormous overblown liquidity bubble.

All of this discussion about risk only really looks at one half of the investment or speculation equation; the other component being reward. Our aim must be to maximise rewards but to maintain a level of risk that we feel is appropriate and manageable. Almost by definition the relationship between risk and reward is different for every player in a market, but is there a sweet spot that can be hit?

This will depend on a number of factors, but as we have already seen in the previous chapter both volatility and time play a key role in this calculation. In broad terms, the more volatile your investments and the shorter your investment horizon the greater your risk of losing money. It would be natural then to avoid highly volatile and risky instruments in your portfolio, but of course less risky assets come with a lower return. So the trick is how to build a portfolio with a mix of higher and lower risk assets that give a superior return. The relationship between these factors can be nicely demonstrated with a curve called the Efficient Frontier; and indeed a number of other important market aspects also lend themselves to simple analogies using curves. It is these simple tools that we will examine next.

A Landscape Of Curves

Markets are not just about mathematics, probability theory and fancy equations, in fact a narrow reliance on these methods is often a sure path to disaster. That said a number of simple statistical tools make useful guides for navigating the risk geography of financial markets. In particular there are four curves, the efficient frontier, the "S" curve, the gamma curve and that old favourite the normal distribution curve, that are very useful as navigational aids.

In common parlance we sometimes hear the phrase "nothing ventured, nothing gained", which implies that every potential risk has a reward. In the Bible we read the parable of the man who buried his one gold talent coin; not much venturing there, and was subsequently chided for his timidity (and perhaps lack of entrepreneurial flair?) and given no reward. So it seems that potential rewards always involve some form of risk; and at this point we need to pause and note the word potential in this little equation. There is no guarantee of reward in the risk/reward equation, and it is important to understand that undertaking a risk is a guarantee of nothing. Greater risk taking should lead to greater reward, and indeed risks are normally priced in that manner, but the risk assumed can still more than wipe out the reward received. In such cases one may observe rather harshly that the risk was wrongly priced in that an overall loss was incurred on the deal. Most of us understand this problem, if not there is usually an expensive lesson ahead to make the point, but how can we learn to overcome it and correctly price risk, and protect ourselves from nasty financial shocks?

Interestingly there is some evidence that the Medici banking family in medieval Europe had some sound ideas regarding risk; they had branches of their bank in different countries each with its own bullion hoard as capital, and with their own separate loan books. They often switched bullion between branches to cover against local losses caused through credit default, political upheaval or perhaps to bolster the business of a particularly active branch – they were in effect running a crude but effective diversified risk portfolio.

On The Frontier

Bankers and investors ran their operations using those basic principles right into the 20th century, and it was only in the 1950s that a more formal theory of risk and reward emerged. In 1952 Harry Markowitz (who subsequently won a Nobel prize in 1990 for his work in this field), published a paper entitled 'Portfolio Selection' that demonstrated how investment diversification reduced risk, but not entirely at the expense of return – in more precise terms he showed how the volatilities of uncorrelated risks do not sum directly, whilst the expected returns of investments do. This theory, which is now known as Modern Portfolio Theory, demonstrated that the volatility of a diversified portfolio is less than the average of the volatilities of its component parts. So it should be possible to create a portfolio with stocks that are not closely correlated and that in effect damp down the overall risk whilst still giving a high average rate of return.

To demonstrate this, Markowitz plotted a large number of sample portfolios with different mixes of high and low risk stocks, and came up with The Efficient Frontier graph, as shown in Figure 4.1.

This graph shows the relationship between risk and reward, with the most efficient point – the investment sweet spot we are all striving for – being represented by the curved line. Any portfolio on this line provides the greatest expected return for a particular level of risk. Portfolios to the right of the line (the shaded area) are achievable combinations, but take unnecessary risks for that expected return.

The interesting part of this graph is the fact that the line is curved; this illustrates that in a portfolio, the individual stocks have all got slightly different characteristics, i.e. they don't all do well or badly at the same time, so don't totally correlate with one another. In statistical terms they have low covariance. This means there is an opportunity to push the envelope of possible portfolios to the left, hence the bulge in the line. We can gain higher returns without correspondingly higher risks if we select the right portfolio.

Figure 4.1: The Efficient Frontier

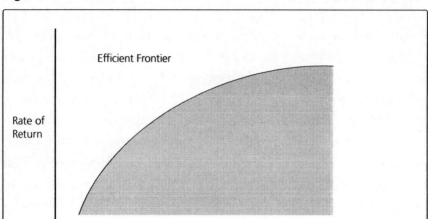

Of course this graph probably only confirms what we have always instinctively thought – just like the Medici bankers, we should spread our risks. That said, in the recent bull market culture this judgement was sadly lacking; whether it was day traders trying to snipe at individual shares, or company executives who had all their potential wealth (and often a significant part of their pay) tied up in options on one stock, there was precious little concern about the dangers of concentration. The case of the day trader is in fact doubly dangerous; not only do they tend to trade a small number of stocks, often just one or two at a time, but they also try to achieve profits in an amazingly short time frame. Pitting themselves against the short-term effects of volatility it is little wonder that few succeed on a long-term basis. Of course day trading is not for widows and orphans, but one wonders if it might not create a few!

Our second curve – shown in Fgure 4.2 – is the "S" curve, sometimes known as the logistic curve, and it is an excellent metaphor for many occurrences in financial markets, or indeed life in general for that matter.

Figure 4.2: The "S" Curve

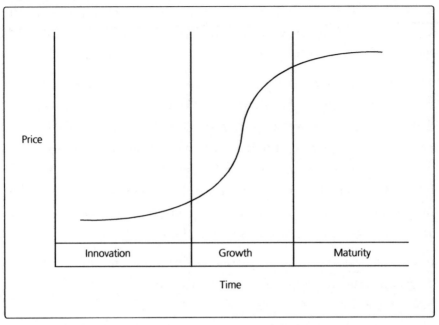

In the example above I have put price on the Y axis, though for some phenomena we could put a label that shows cumulative activity, and on the X axis is the passage of time. Some market types might recognise that this curve resembles the delta curve used to explain option price movement. This is correct, but this curve can also show us many other things. Business people will see how the curve represents the normal life cycle of a product (in this case sales data would be on the Y axis); in time virtually all products follow this path, though businesses seek to stretch the time line as long as possible. For those running large businesses that effectively have a portfolio of products the key is to produce a range of goods and services that have "S" curves that overlap one another, producing an underlying upward curve of growth. A good example of this has been the changes in the music industry over the last forty years; where vinyl discs saw enormous growth in the 1960s and 1970s only to give way to CDs in the mid to late 1980s, and now in turn CDs are being rapidly overtaken by downloads. Each product line has travelled along the "S" curve.

Basically the curve manifests, in a stylised manner, the usual pattern of growth – at first slow but steadily increasing expansion, then at the steepest part of the curve maximum growth, and then as the curve flattens still progress but a steadily reducing rate of increase.

This curve perfectly shows how momentum is the driving force behind many transient things in life, slow beginnings, explosive growth and then gradual slowdown back to zero growth. One can think of this curve as a good picture of bull or bear market sentiment for example; it most certainly describes the path many financial bubbles seem to follow. In the actual market we will rarely see a perfect "S" curve, but the point is that we should remember to consider where our investments are at any one time on this hypothetical line.

Interestingly market news and sentiment about any topic, stock or currency, seems to chime nicely with this curve. Many observers have pointed out that once something is well known it's too late to get on-board. It appears that at the steepest part of the curve the screaming and shouting about the merits of this or that are at their loudest, so indeed caution about being long is sensible. Equally, though, it's too soon to short the instrument, although the rate of change is falling away the underlying price is still going up. It is often in this part of the curve that contrarians fall into the trap of trading too soon.

The rate of change of the "S" curve charts the level of hysteria.

The following diagram – Figure 4.3 – is again familiar territory for option traders who will recognise the similarity to the Gamma curve. In more general usage it shows first the increase in interest and later the decreasing interest that is portrayed in the "S" curve. Using the analogy of movement, it represents momentum, or the tendency for a body to continue to travel at the same speed.

The peak of the momentum curve equates to the very steepest part of the "S" curve. Readers will recall that during bull markets the phrase momentum investing often comes to the fore, the idea being that you should buy strong stocks as they are the one's most likely to continue going up. In a flood every boat floats, and this makes perfect sense whilst the market price action is pushing up at an ever increasing rate, but once the momentum curve tips over we know any further advances will be slower and hard going.

Figure 4.3: The Momentum Curve

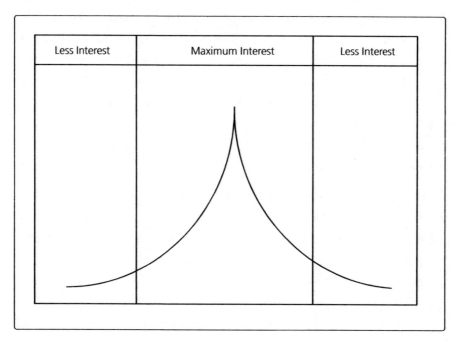

Less Interest	Maximum Interest	Less Interest

Again we should strive to decide where we are on this curve. In a perfect, and frankly impossible to achieve, investment world we would accumulate longs when the momentum is increasing, then as momentum rolls over, start selling our holdings into the still firming market and be out by the end of the piece. Equally, with perfect foresight we could then look to do the exact opposite during bear markets. Easy then! But of course we can have no certain idea where exactly the curve is or more importantly how long the duration of the move will be. Naturally there is no neat answer to that question – but we can try to protect ourselves from some of the more extreme market moves by using the last curve in our toolbox, the normal distribution curve.

Abnormal Ostriches

In 1995 British investors were targeted by a series of advertisements in the national press trumpeting the benefits of investing in ostrich farming. Over the next eighteen months the promoters raised over £21 million for their scheme with some 2800 investors rushing to invest. The scheme promised a guaranteed annual return of over 50% (in fact 51.6% – the boosters of this scheme rightly believed that potential investors are often fooled by such spurious accuracy) with the potential for even greater returns. It was claimed that the birds were so valuable that each one was to have a microchip implanted in it so that they could be protected from being stolen. Well naturally the whole thing was a ridiculous fraud, the scheme collapsed, the directors of the promoting company were charged, and in the autumn of 2000 they were jailed for periods ranging between two and four years.

All very amusing and entertaining stuff – but what on earth were those 2800 investors thinking when they clipped the coupon and then subsequently wrote the cheque? Common sense suggests that we should be cautious about an investment with a guaranteed return of over 50% per annum. After all, who is this guaranteed by? Clearly the investor's first mistake was to ignore basic credit risk. Also, a simple distribution curve rooted in over three hundred years of mathematical history would have raised a serious storm warning.

Originally investigated and created by a Belgian mathematician called DeMoivre in the early 18th century, the concept of normal distribution was the result of studying gambling and its possible returns (so perhaps the investment community can pay a small nod to the army of losers in casinos and gambling halls after all!) This curve shows the likely distribution of outcomes around a mean; the result is a bell curve around the mean value. The shape of the bell curve is perfectly symmetrical around the mean if the sample is perfectly distributed, or may be skewed one way or the other if there is any bias in the data sample. Extreme values appear in the tails of the curve and may create "fat" tails if an abnormal amount of them sit outside the normal result.

Figure 4.4: The Distribution Curve

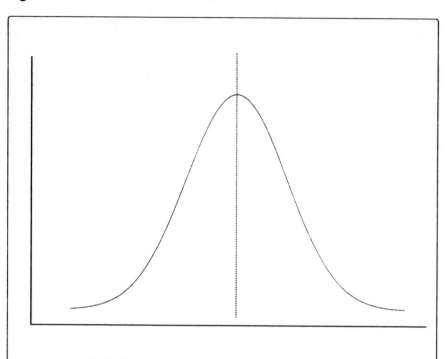

Now, going back to the wonderful ostrich investment opportunity, where would this sit on the distribution curve? Well we need to agree what the mean of possible returns is in the investment universe before we know where the fantastic 51.6% will exactly sit (though it shouldn't be too hard to guess). At any given time the investor can invest in deposits, bonds, equities, etc. all with some form of yield; from this we can create an average potential return. Of course we add in the spicy return from ostriches which will no doubt boost the average a bit, but nevertheless the return from the ostrich farming still stands out, in fact it is at the far end of the distribution curve, somewhat like the end of Southend Pier, miles away from the mass of land. This is an enormous warning – such returns are freakish and almost certainly unsustainable, and this result should have been enough to warn off potential ostrich farming investors. Indeed it is the lack of sustainability in the result that is the biggest warning. Occasionally one may receive an abnormally large return due to some good luck, but these are very much one-off events. It stretches credulity too far to think that 50% returns can be achieved regularly and steadily. Finally, it is impossible to resist the observation that the heads of the investors must have been in the sand!

Now to round up on this small tour of helpful curves, a few reminders and warnings. These curves are not the philosopher's stone; they cannot be used to protect every investor and speculator from every possible market mishap. Instead they should be viewed as useful aids in the difficult terrain of financial trading; perhaps they are best imagined as instruments on a risk dashboard. As with driving a car, these instruments are useful and often important, but don't tell the whole story, in investment as in driving we have to remember to look ahead and not just at the instruments.

Mr Galton's Machine

Francis Galton was the epitome of the wealthy upper class Englishman during the Victorian era, a polymath with a high degree of curiosity and a private income, he spent his entire life investigating and researching new ideas. His range of interests was diverse enough to encompass criminology, where he helped pioneer finger-printing techniques and weather patterns, where he devised the classification of cyclonic and anti-cyclonic weather systems, and he even conducted experiments to test the efficacy of prayer – though his results were not very encouraging on that front. Of more direct relevance to our interest in finance he spent a great deal of time looking at statistics and probability.

Whilst looking for ways to enliven his lectures on statistics Galton developed a simple mechanical device he named a quincunx in the mid-1870s. The apparatus, which he first demonstrated at the Royal Institution in London, comprised a wooden box with a glass front and a funnel at the top. Metal balls of equal size and weight are dropped via the funnel to fall through a number of rows of pins spaced equally in the box. Each row was offset from the previous row so that the pins sat between the gaps of the row above. These pins then deflect each falling metal ball to the left or right with equal probability and at the bottom of the box each metal ball finished by falling into one of a number of compartments. After a number of metal balls are dropped through this device a pattern in the compartments below starts to emerge. The balls start to describe a binomial distribution which with a large number of rows approximates to our previous curve – the normal distribution.

With this device Galton sought to demonstrate that seemingly random events or facts do in fact tend to arrange themselves into a distribution. So it would appear that the distribution curve we examined earlier is a natural occurrence that appears even when seemingly random events take place. Galton went on to do a large number of experiments that looked to see if distributions did in fact appear in natural life. His research conclusively proved that they do, and furthermore the outcomes were often quite close to the normal pattern described by the quincunx.

At this point we can depart from Francis Galton but use his ideas and clever box-like device to look at financial derivatives. Derivatives have been around since finance began, some claim there is a reference by Aristotle to an option like instrument, and certainly by the Middle Ages very crude option like transactions were being executed. As we saw earlier with the story of Russell Sage, by the second half of the 19th century stock options were starting to emerge as a recognised, although specialist and niche, financial market. Of course options really took off with the publication of the Black-Scholes formula in 1973, which for the first time sought to accurately value options. The financial de-regulation of the late 1970s and early 1980s really boosted derivative trading and nowadays the global market has expanded massively. It is estimated by the latest (June 2008) Bank for International Settlements report to have an outstanding nominal value in excess of US$680 trillion. This is a truly eye-watering number. To give you an idea of just how large, there are a trillion (being a million millions in modern usage) seconds in 31,710 years!

The Black-Scholes formula was just the start of a series of equations that sought to value and price options, and it still remains one of the best known in the business. To calculate it, we need the following inputs:

- The time to expiry of the instrument

- The asset price, i.e. the stock, commodity or currency price

- The strike price

- The implied volatility of the instrument

- The so-called risk free interest rate – typically the yield on low risk short maturity government securities, e.g. 90-Day Treasury Notes

From these basic inputs we can get an option valuation, but it comes with a number of conditions and caveats, namely:

- The asset price follows a log normal random walk

- The risk-free interest rate and volatility are known functions of time

- No transaction costs in hedging portfolio

- No dividends paid during the life of the option

- No arbitrage possibilities

- Continuous trading of underlying assets

- Underlying assets can be sold short

A number of important problems are raised by these conditions; first and foremost an enormous assumption is being made that the underlying instrument is continuously traded, this ignores that most dangerous of foes – lack of liquidity. Second, in the real world, brokerage, bid-offer spreads, slippage (effectively the monetary cost of less than perfect liquidity) and taxes all loom large. In fact as we will see these charges can be quite punishing. So whilst Black-Scholes gives us the first serious approximation for pricing options risk it is hemmed in by a number of limitations. In fact it is probably true to say that it is more important to understand these limitations than to worry about the underlying maths. Risk assessment is not just about cold equations, the judgements we make about the softer more fuzzy elements of the decision process are often much more important. It is unlikely the maths alone will protect us – we have to know the context in which the result was calculated.

But let us go back to Mr Galton's box with its pins and metal balls, as it can produce a useful mental picture with which to consider and understand option pricing. Consider Figure 4.5 on the following page. The position of the funnel represents the current price of the underlying instrument; move it to the left to decrease the price; move it to the right to increase the price. Every row of pins is an increment in time, for example one day, and the number of rows represents the time to maturity. The horizontal distance between neighbouring pins represents the volatility; moving the pins further apart increases volatility, moving them together decreases volatility. The figure shows the passage of one ball as it bumps down onto a pin and has to go either right or left, before falling to the next row. This represents the daily price movement of the underlying instrument and the movement of the option by one day towards maturity. At the bottom, the ball will drop into a box. The boxes are divided into two groups by the strike price. The boxes to the left hold winners for owners of put options; the boxes to the right hold winners for owners of call options. In each case, the boxes furthest from the strike price are the most valuable. Increase the strike price and there are more put winner boxes; decrease the strike price and there are more call winner boxes. When we drop a large number of balls, they finish up (expire) in the boxes distributed in the bell shaped curve that we met earlier. For the mathematically inclined, this requires us to deal in logarithms of prices, rather than the prices themselves, but ignoring this does not affect the overall picture.

Many aspects of option behaviour can be understood from this model. In the example in the figure, the put option is in-the-money, while the call option is out-of-the-money. You can see that adding more rows of pins (increasing the time to maturity) increases the number of winners that are far from the strike price, so generally increasing the value of the option. Increasing the distance between the pins (raising the volatility) has the same qualitative effect. The model also highlights the arbitrary nature of the underlying assumptions of the Black-Scholes formula. For example, why should all the pins be equidistant?

Figure 4.5: The Quincunx as a proxy for options pricing

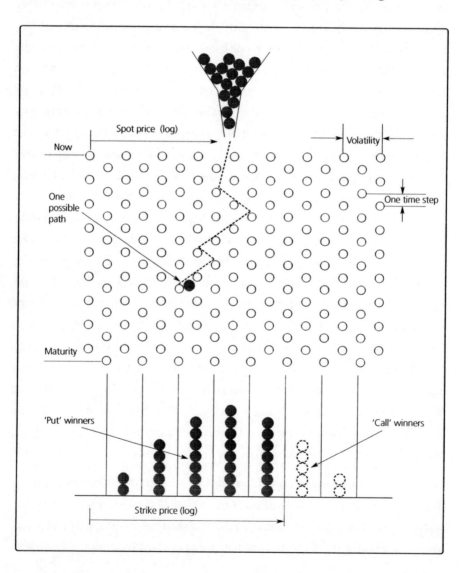

In a way this is all just a parlour game, and it's not meant to be a serious substitute for Black-Scholes or any of the myriad successor mathematical formulae for options and alike, but it does provide us once again with a quite vivid picture of option risk and a broad idea of how prices react in the three-dimensional landscape of derivatives risk.

These mental pictures as represented by the quincunx and the other curves described earlier can be a great help in understanding risk. Very few mathematical formulae are intuitive, and only the best and most astute mathematicians can look at a formula and gain a full insight into its market implications. However, a good general understanding of risk principles and when and where to consider the background mathematics is always going to be helpful and important. Risk, by definition, is everywhere in financial markets and we have to learn how to price and value it. These curves will hopefully give some straightforward insights into the correct way forward. It is clear that having a holistic approach to risk brings benefits; mathematics and probability represent only one facet of this complex mosaic. Risk is not a closed set problem that can just be solved because there are also non-mathematical elements in the overall mix that are frustratingly fuzzy, hard to quantify and often harder to master.

Instinctive Idiocy

There now only remains one factor left when discussing risk, and it's probably the biggest and hardest part of the whole business – human judgement. Earlier we touched on the problem of hidden demons within everyone's make up, and how hard it can be to stay objective when assessing risk and its consequences. Now we need to take a further step in to this inner world and try to understand what makes us repeat poor decisions and try to work out if we can overcome these failings. All the maths and computer models in the whole world will only help us so far. They may tell us what we should or should not do; but there can be a world of difference between this theory and the actual execution of these instructions. Why is it that we can be so bad at recognising risk and taking action when appropriate? Can we learn to overcome our own personal trading shortcomings?

Anthropology teaches us that we are far from our natural habitat; that man's origins were as hunter/gatherers, only truly at home in lush green savannah lands and hunting grounds. We are still somehow hard wired for this ancient environment, and still carry some of the responses and intellectual thought processes of our ancient forefathers. Unfortunately these mental processes are not always best suited to modern life, and this seems particularly true for operating in financial markets, and so can lead to us making poor investment decisions. It is somewhat of a cliché these days to talk of the fight or flight syndrome that makes up so much of our psychological profile, but it remains a basic truth. Without dwelling on this too much it is clear that humans are emotional beings, who often respond to unexpected situations (being attacked for example) by expressing fear, dread or even an overwhelming sense of doom. These emotions are the agents that can cloud our judgement – they may be fine for life as a wandering hunter deciding whether to stand and fight or make a run for it, but in the fast unrelenting real-time world of financial markets they can be disastrous.

Earlier we considered investment, speculation and gambling, and dismissed gambling as being a separate activity from the other two. This becomes even more apparent when we look at individuals and their risk assessment. Investment or speculation is decision-making under uncertainty – there is no precise set of odds that can describe a likelihood of loss on a financial investment, unlike gambling on a roulette table where the odds are exact and known in advance. As we have seen, the financial markets are not a game with fixed rules because both inputs and outcomes are frustratingly difficult to delineate and define. It appears that chaos rather than order is the dominant regime, and this both offends and confuses human intellect and reasoning.

This uncertainty is the basic truth of financial markets, and people react to it differently, and often emotionally. These feelings usually express themselves in a number of ways, a hunger for news and gossip, a desire to be part of the crowd (this is ancient man's genetic heritage kicking in again) and a tendency to search for and believe in the simple answer. As all followers and participants of markets know, these thoughts and feelings are on display every day.

Simple analogies for this market behaviour can be found in other risk situations where uncertainty is the prime mover. For example, the outbreak of a fire in a theatre, cinema or nightclub usually provokes mass panic. Clearly the rational response – and the response likely to save more lives – would be if everyone left in a calm and orderly manner. Certainly this is true at the macro level of the crowd, but at the micro level of the individual no such thought is usually considered, certainly not in the compressed time frame normally available. It is the natural human reaction to bolt wildly for an exit and disregard those around and about with, all too often, tragic consequences. So it is with financial decision-making. What may seem rational and sensible decision-making at the individual level often leads to market manias, asset bubbles or prolonged market depressions at the macro level. The nature of uncertainty in the market, and the lack of any indisputable right answers, means that the market is not like an examination where we can succeed by answering questions correctly to attain a certain number of marks. Needless to say this obvious point has been missed by financial regulators who persist in the fiction that examinations are a suitable method to judge individuals' market competency. Also, in this age of global communications, market activity is increasingly conducted on a 24-hour basis, with weekends providing the only periods of temporary truce in what otherwise is a constant and intense experience.

One approach to overcoming these demons is to try and de-personalise the trading experience by making use of models or trading systems; in essence train a computer to do your trading for you. Trading systems are useful, but even assuming you have the ability and the resources to mount such a project there is still the problem of pulling the trigger. It may be that one day computer models will create trading systems that make all the investment decisions and are directly linked into financial markets to facilitate the trade execution with no human override. But this seems pretty unlikely because a host of legal and regulatory issues would no doubt be raised, plus it is hard to see anyone truly trusting a computer model to that extent. However good the model, humans are bound to want to exercise some control, and it is here that the old issues will re-emerge.

Another technique that bites the dust in the face of these problems is so-called paper trading. It is standard advice to the newcomer learning about markets to start out by trying a number of dummy trades on paper, the idea being that you get used to the feel of the market without actually committing any of your funds. This is a seemingly sensible and prudent approach but totally flawed. It's simply not the same as real trading, just as playing poker for sweets or nuts is totally different from playing for meaningful amounts of money. One cannot learn entirely about war by firing blanks on a mock military exercise and so it is with financial markets. Our decisions and thinking are totally different when there are meaningful stakes at risk – it's only when we are trading with "live ammunition" that we start to understand the rollercoaster emotions of financial trading.

Traditional financial theory has not paid much attention to any of these decision-making issues; as we saw earlier with our curves and the quincunx, much of the theoretical work on markets has concentrated on statistical analysis, seeking to calculate fair value, and to point out when certain asset prices or events are outside these statistical norms. All of that is important and needs to be remembered, but it is only half the picture. Clearly even if we have the statistical information there is no guarantee that we will take note and act.

The relatively new science of behavioural finance, which first emerged in the 1970s, looks at these problems from a more psychological stand point and has taken up the challenge of trying to understand why we act as we do.

This exciting area has concentrated on looking at human motivations, the way we gather and assess information, and how we make decisions. In particular it breaks down these processes into a number of distinct problem areas where we seem to make bad or wrong decisions. If in fact individuals are making wrong investment decisions this should add up to a mis-pricing in the market, and as such presents a challenge to efficient market theory, which states markets are efficient because participants are rational and seek to maximise their own benefits. Of course EMT does make allowances for occasional and fleeting examples of irrational behaviour and labels these as noise, and then expects markets to quickly readjust back to a rational state. Unfortunately though, the problem has been that on many occasions markets seem to stay irrational for relatively long periods of time and sometimes in a spectacular manner (the 3Com/Palm example cited earlier being a classic instance). Behavioural finance thus challenges the standard orthodoxy and says that markets are not efficient in the way postulated by followers of EMT and that simple observation shows this to be the case. It argues that we need to look beyond the statistics and valuation models to other areas.

In essence behavioural finance looks at the psychological aspects of market participation rather than just the raw data and news, and categorises the relevant issues into two broad groupings; heuristic type decision-making, and framing, or what we might call investor perceived context and circumstances. Investor perception is important here, it may not be the actual context or true circumstance, but it is what we feel or decide is the right framework in which to set our investment decisions. First though, let's look at so called heuristic decision-making, by which we mean the simple fact that most of us base our decisions on past experiences, and that we use these past experiences to build a structure of general principles that guide our present and future behaviour. This seems pretty normal and sensible and at first glance not in the least likely to clash with the classical idea of the rational investor. However such thinking can have unintended consequences, and research has sought to identify a number of key factors that can cause problems, such as overconfidence, stereotyping, confirmation bias, and aversion to ambiguity and uncertainty, or what may be called the search for simplicity.

Overconfidence is pretty straightforward – investors and speculators seem to display an above average sense of their own abilities. This need not be arrogance but is in fact a hazard of the activity, given that most participants see themselves in a battle against others (the "they" element) it is natural that they believe they have more knowledge, or better intuitive ability, or perhaps better nerve than their competitors. If they didn't it's not very likely they would be involved in markets. Interestingly this isn't something that just afflicts individual investors, as a similar pattern seems to run through the mindset of professional fund managers, where if anything it's exacerbated by the fashion for star type rankings and sales-driven publicity. Fund managers often compare themselves to their peer group, and indeed are often singled out in press reports for praise and admiration (well at least in bull markets!) and this atmosphere doesn't lend itself to humility. The consequences of overconfidence are – as in all walks of life – pretty obvious; disaster or at least poor performance often follows such hubris. Allied to this is the general human trait that we tend to believe we are more successful than we actually are – thus reinforcing our confidence. This may seem hard to fake in the world of investment with its precise figures on returns and performance statistics, but it may be a sub-conscious reason why fund managers love benchmarks. Selective use of benchmarks, league tables and alike can often make the most modest performance look rather good – this can be the case when money mangers believe their own marketing a little too much.

Stereotyping is in many ways a more subtle trap; we constantly look for patterns in life as a form of shorthand that explains the cause and effect of events and circumstances around us. This is particularly true in finance, and very much so in our old bugbear – gambling. The gambler's fallacy of a hot streak, or a belief that tails must come up next time we toss the coin, is a classic example of this shorthand and how it can fool us. In financial markets the issue is somewhat more complex than gambling with its known odds and careful boundary of possible outcomes; in finance investors also search for patterns and apply stereotypes, which may induce them to act in the marketplace and reinforce this phenomenon. So the individual's actions in applying his past experience to a current situation through the prism of a stereotype or pattern can cause that pattern to develop and extend further. This is how the micro activity of the market participant becomes part of the bigger macro trend or event. It may well help to explain why markets become irrational. It also explains the self-reinforcing nature of many financial trends and how positive feedback mechanisms can thrive in markets.

Seeking confirmation through selective use of the facts is another frequent problem. Humans have a fantastic ability to only see and refer to facts that suit their beliefs; one might say – why let the facts get in the way of your prejudices? In a world that has tidal waves of information, most of it is missed, ignored or filtered out, we tend unfortunately to hold on most dearly to whatever bit of confirmation or reinforcement we can find that suits our current investments. Needless to say this factor is a major culprit in that most heinous of investment crimes, holding on to a losing position. Allied to this is the desire to find the simple answer – markets and their participants hate indecision or a lack of clarity, we all want answers to our investment questions and don't like to hear that there may not be a simple explanation. This is why financial forecasters and market gurus have such a fruitful career path, we want answers come what may and will listen to virtually anyone who can seemingly provide them.

An interesting twist on this confirmation bias was offered to me by a friend from the currency market. A junior dealer in the Far East has a position long of US$1 million in USD/yen and when asked by a colleague in London why, he replies that his immediate superior has a similar position in US$5 million, who it turns out has taken his position because the chief dealer has a long position of US$25 million in

USD/yen. So here we see a good example of everyone following their boss (after all there is little incentive to trade the other way round) and as a result an institution builds a big position all based on the boss's opinion. Nothing particularly wrong in that, provided overall risk controls are not breeched, but it does demonstrate the benefits of joining the crowd. After all for the junior dealer it's a no lose situation – if the trade is a winner his trading book made money, as did everyone else's; and if it is a loser, at least his losses were small compared to everyone else's and, hey, after all he was only taking the same route as his more senior and presumably more talented colleagues. Quite what shareholders of an institution that did this would think is another matter of course.

The second set of problems about our market behaviour centre around context and circumstance; framing is the more scientific term used by followers of behavioural finance. Chief amongst these issues is regret and sunk loss bias. It appears that when faced with a loss it is not just the monetary aspect that pains us, but it is the fact we have to acknowledge responsibility for the loss. This regret is a powerful block for many trying to control their losses; it can be an almost impossible hurdle for some, and is very debilitating in financial trading given that we have to control and cut our losses on a continuous basis. It is axiomatic that we have to keep our losses under control, but for many the pain and regret (perhaps even shame?) is just too great. This is how small losses get larger, why investors often try to average a loss by actually increasing their position in an adverse market, and how large company and government projects often spiral out of budgetary control. Perhaps the British government's experience with the Millennium Dome is an example *par excellence* of the sort of fiasco that can result from not getting out of bad decisions. This behaviour is sometimes called sunk-cost bias, and really refers to the problem of throwing good money after bad. We are often taught in life that persistence is a good quality, unfortunately in finance it can lead to ruin.

For readers who wish to examine this area further I would suggest some of the writings of Amos Tversky and Daniel Kahneman who accumulated a large body of evidence through careful surveying and research that overwhelmingly demonstrates many of the problems above. It looks as though this new psychological approach to markets and participants' actions and reactions is still in its infancy. We are still at the stage of recognising the problem, learning to overcome it is still a fairly distant prospect. In fact it may be that there is no definitive way to teach people to overcome these hurdles and that a large body of people are condemned to keep repeating the same psychological errors when deciding on their investment strategy. Investment groups might also like to consider that rather than select individuals to run funds in terms of their education in maths, statistics and economics, it might be better to pick those who can demonstrate a mastery in controlling their emotions and are aware of the pitfalls in the investment decision-making process.

This chapter has tried to look at understanding risk in simple terms, and to illustrate the problems we all have in understanding and interpreting risk, even when it has been properly calculated and delineated for us. Unfortunately, even if we manage to master all of this, there are other challenges ahead.

5

Assorted Killers

'Facts do not cease to exist because they are ignored.'
Aldous Huxley

Success in financial markets demands an enormous amount of skill and concentration, the factors that have to be weighed and assessed can be complex and unexpected. In addition events happen in real time, usually leaving little time to make important judgements. The constant stream of often useless advice and opinion can frequently drown even the most discriminating of players, added to which there are all the personal mental hurdles to overcome. If all of that wasn't enough, there are a number of real killers that can cause even more damage. Whilst these not exactly hidden, they are often ignored, which can be an expensive mistake.

The Sloping Pitch

There is a large amount of debate, usually by those that don't trade, about game theory and financial markets. In academic terms are financial markets a positive, negative or a zero sum game? This is a slippery topic; classical economics teaches us that the process of commercial trade has a positive outcome (Adam Smith et al.), but what about the merry-go-round of finance? For example, many argue that futures trading is at best a zero sum game, because all the players' positions cancel one another out, and that investing in stocks and bonds is an overall positive arena because of the income derived from interest and dividends. In fact the first example gets worse if one includes the vital element of trading costs, which are enough to turn the overall futures market into a negative sum game, and the second argument falls into the trap of merely looking at financial returns – it could be argued that there is possibly a utility element to the calculation as well. Fascinating stuff but what does this achieve? Can we turn any of this theory into profit? Well, in truth, probably not.

We could certainly get very distracted by this whole issue which soon becomes deeply complicated and academic, so we must remember that our primary aim is to make money, not worry about game theories. This is why it was necessary to junk gambling earlier on – it's simply a fruitless activity with an overall negative expectation of profit. Whether or not investment in stocks and futures, or any other financial asset class, is a positive, or a zero sum game, we are faced with three unpleasant costs; brokerage, spread and slippage. Whilst looking relatively tiny these three costs can easily turn success into failure. It is a tell-tale sign of the inexperienced market player that he or she believes these costs to be marginal – the costs are anything but marginal, and can easily tip profitable strategies into loss.

Anything But Trivial

These costs may look trivial, but they swallow up enormous amounts of money. The next time you look at the huge bank and brokerage offices in Manhattan, or Canary Wharf in London, remember they are temples of brokerage, spread and slippage. Those small little clippings off every trade add up to hundreds of millions of dollars every year – they pay for the huge (necessary?) costs of these intermediaries.

In general, brokerage has become much more competitive over the last thirty years or so, starting with the reforms on the NYSE in 1975 and then followed by the Big Bang in London in 1986, share trading costs have definitely fallen considerably. This is certainly one area where technology has been very beneficial, transaction costs have been reduced and the Victorian system of share certificates and the cumbersome nonsense of paper transfer forms etc. have largely been swept away. These reforms opened up competition, and meant that margins on pure broking quickly fell; as a result stockbrokers have had to merge to cut costs, and have also aggressively moved into other areas. In broad terms they have had to take principal risk to bolster earnings. Fortunately for nearly twenty years from the early 1980s, whilst technology was driving down the costs, there was also a huge bull market in stocks. With every boat floating nicely upwards on this tide there was little to worry about. Fierce competition, culminating in e-commerce, drove commissions through the floor but the larger and larger turnover figures more than compensated; and taking principal risk in a bull market is usually a lucrative endeavour with little pain on the way.

As investors first saw the abolition of fixed commissions, and then a twenty-year price war driven by technology and apparent de-regulation, they came to believe that commissions were so low that they couldn't hurt performance. (As an aside, it is worth recalling that in the 1970s you had to have a personal introduction to open an account at a stockbrokers; a far cry from the screaming newspaper ads and free offers on the internet that followed as the newly de-regulated stock markets experienced a massive bull run.) Indeed, the dealing and brokerage costs were deemed to be so insignificant that it became economic to day trade stocks from a PC at home. This is in fact very doubtful when you consider the following numbers. Let's assume there are 250 trading days a year (leaving out weekends and public holidays), and that the day trader just trades once a day. Say he has capital of US$25,000 and brokerage is the bargain basement flat fee of $8 a round turn. So in fact he spends $2000 a year on brokerage, some 8% of his capital! 'Oh chicken feed!' is the rejoinder; you can easily make that sort of money on a single trade. (Another small but financially important point: how many brokers pay interest on their customer account balances? Again this "trivial" matter can add up to a significant revenue stream for the broker.) You might make money, but the broker definitely gets his $2000 a year – nice business. Of course, over time, most day traders lose money and fall by the wayside – hence the screaming brokerage adverts. The brokers need new punters to keep paying those tiny $8 commissions everyday. It all adds up to pay for the marble atriums, the self-indulgent modern art collections and the all-important staff "performance" bonuses.

This happy scenario always stalls in a bear market. A classic example was the dotcom implosion in March 2000, when the wheels fell off the tech market. The bear market in "new economy" equities began (quite different and far worse than a mere crash), and then the broader markets also started to fall considerably. Of course, the more recent calamity in equities during 2008 (FTSE's worst year on record) is another re-run of the familiar fallout once stock prices start to drop. Bear markets are extremely bad news for brokers because turnover always falls dramatically for two reasons: investors get out of the markets and don't return, and in addition a large number of investors freeze, sitting on desperate positions and trading far less frequently.

Lower turnover means lower brokerage and so brokers have to react. This reaction will manifest itself in two ways: first small traders are suddenly deemed superfluous (perhaps you should stick to a post office savings account?), which unless they are constantly dealing is true, and second, the brokers try to charge for all sorts of added value products. With profits from principal risk, new issues etc., melting away, other revenue sources are quickly sought. So we can confidently expect to see attempts to sell all sorts of bells and whistles to clients, managed funds programmes (with nice front end management fees), supposedly high tech trading black boxes ("as developed by our own strategic risk desk, which is staffed with physics PhDs and experts in ballistics and fluid dynamics"); not to mention a slow but steady increase in brokerage fees. Brokers will invoke all sorts of reasons for re-introducing the concept of the full service (i.e. full commission paying) business model, and execution only types will find flat fees tick up.

Spread And Slippage

There is another angle to all of this of course. Are you still paying brokerage? 'No management fees, no front loading, no brokerage – why settle for anything less?' screams the appealing marketing blurb of some firms. Indeed – but there is a price to pay. It's in the bid-offer spread, which can be frighteningly large.

We have all seen the breathless advertising for penny stocks – see huge gains on your investments, buy a stock at 10 pennies, when it gets to twenty (hey only 10 pennies away) you have doubled your money! Hmmm... but what is the bid-offer spread on this stock? It's not unusual to find a quote of some 3 pennies (that's 30%!) on such a stock, so in fact you may be only able to buy at 12, after a quote of 9-12, and sell at 18 on a quote of 18-21. Okay so you have still made 6 pence on an initial in-rate of 12, giving a return of 50%, but already it's half the touted 100%. Of course in practice it is worse than that, particularly when exiting a position. When you ask for a quote on a stock, your broker checks his records to see if you have a position, so on the second quote he is likely to read you, knowing you are long. So in fact they may make you a price of 17-20 and now the return is down to just over 41%. 'So what?' goes the cry again, 'We're still making money.' Yes, this is true, but don't discount the costs of the spread – even in large liquid stocks a spread of between ½% and 1% is common, and this can be big bucks.

Going back to our imaginary day trader, let's assume he is trading in very big liquid stocks with relatively tight spreads – say ½%. With the starting capital of US$25,000, every day $125 goes out of the window in spread costs, and he would have spent his entire capital after 200 trading days. If we add in the generously cheap brokerage of $8 his capital is winnowed away in only 188 days. In practice as his capital goes down, so does his deal size, and consequentially so does the incremental cost of the spread, but destruction still awaits unless good and consistent profits are found fast. So, suddenly, that slight slope on the pitch is beginning to look like a cliff face. But there is still a third cost to be overcome – slippage.

Slippage seems to be the hardest for the newcomer to understand – it is in effect the difference between what you pay or receive in a market from what you thought you may get. It is in essence a liquidity charge. When you ask a broker a price you may get either an indication price, an idea of the current trading price or a firm dealing price. That firm dealing price will be for a maximum number of shares, futures contracts or whatever you are trading, and is often in good size. For most players most of the time the dealing size is large enough to accommodate their request – however in times of panic or sudden and unexpected news, liquidity melts away and dealing sizes can shrink alarmingly. So, particularly in a panic fall, it may not be possible to fill all of your order at the expected quote with the result that the balance has to be executed at a worse price. This difference is slippage. Slippages in panic moves can be a significant percentage (3% may be quite a lucky escape in some circumstances, there have certainly been cases of far worse).

By now it should be crystal clear just how hard the market makes it for you to make money – these three monetary killers affect everyone, from the private investor through to the biggest proprietary traders. They cannot be avoided or ignored, but must be part of the calculation of trading. Importantly these killers show the extreme danger and cost of high activity trading patterns; constantly diving in and out of the market is usually an extremely expensive strategy. (One is reminded of the market adage that day trading is like picking up pennies in front of a steamroller!) This is in addition to the extra exposure the short-term trader suffers, caused by volatility, from their short investment horizon. Many participants continue to discount or fail to understand the impact of these costs; one such example was perfectly illustrated by a detailed analysis in a public journal of a black box system that sought to trade perceived inefficiencies in base metal futures. The performance statistics, the testing methodology, the care taken in gathering accurate data all looked very impressive but then the author killed the whole thing by blithely announcing: 'No transaction costs have been included.' But trading comes with transaction costs – they are the three killers. One wonders whether the author is a broker?

Finally there can be no excuse for overlooking these issues; a classic book by Fred Schwed written in 1932 entitled *Where are the Customers' Yachts?* details the whole landscape in a witty and clear manner. (Encouragingly it is still in print so perhaps some market types are learning the lessons.) The familiar cry is that times have changed since then – well, no they haven't. Times don't change in financial markets and you can be sure the old pitfalls still baffle the new fools. We are all foolish to an extent, but much of our own ignorance can be eliminated by taking a look at what's gone before. The innocent looking and supposedly trivial costs of brokerage, spread and slippage are as old as markets and will always be with us.

Death By Numbers

The nasty trio of killers outlined above is unfortunately not the whole story. The would-be investor or speculator has another serious menace to deal with – numbers themselves. More precisely, humans get very muddled over figures and statistics and this can lead to bad mistakes and poor judgement. We have already seen from the science of behavioural finance how we find it hard to make value judgements about risk, and humans also have terrible trouble making judgements about figures and numeric values. The human mind has difficulty seeing numbers in cold reality, instead we seem to want to ascribe certain important characteristics to particular numbers (we can recognise this as often being part and parcel of confirmation bias). Hence the idea of using family birthdates for lottery numbers, or the idea that the number 13 is unlucky. This superstition seems linked to the massacre of the Knights Templar by the French King, Philip the Fair, in Paris in 1307! In China, people believe that the luckiest number is 8, but in the West there is an idea that 7 is lucky. This is especially curious considering that in Chinese culture the number 7 is *unlucky* – to the extent that people avoid having property on the 7th floor of an apartment block!

Humans invest numbers with a lot of meaning and even mysticism. The number 666, mentioned in the Bible as the number of the beast, still strikes fear into a few (though how many know it is supposedly originally a Hebrew reference to the Roman Emperor Nero?) Likewise Friday the 13th is deemed to be a bad day in the English-speaking world, whereas it's Tuesday the 17th you worry about if you are an Italian. (Readers will no doubt note that Tuesday 17th always follows Friday the 13th!) Chartists try to claim that numbers in markets are more than mere numerical notation, suggesting they are loaded with emotion and even some sort of memory from the past. Therefore, they argue, it is right that the market should concentrate on particularly important numbers that have become embedded into the market's thinking. Well, whatever the truth, the market is gripped by certain numbers.

Probably the best example of this is so-called round number-itis, or sometimes big figure-itis. For example, the foreign exchange market was gripped in 2000 by the idea that the euro/US dollar rate would fall below 1. The was seen as a crucial psychological level for the nascent European currency. However, needless to say, the myopic market gurus who claimed that disaster was at hand had conveniently forgotten that this wasn't really a new level at all because in old USD/DM terms we had been there before. But, as ever, why let the facts get in the way of a good market story? In 2008 the whole saga was reprised again, but this time it was concerned with GBP/EUR and whether it's a national disgrace if the pound hits parity. Stock indices habitually attract huge attention at round numbers, when the Dow Jones Index went up through 10,000 in 1998 even general news coverage was considerable.

The F Word

We can't avoid that old market favourite the Fibonacci series (how one's heart sinks at the appearance of this F word). In market mythology the Fibonacci series can apparently explain everything: it can help predict price moves, lapses of time between peaks and troughs in markets and needless to say it throws up any number of important numbers that we should all carefully heed when watching market price action. The series itself is perfectly innocuous, having been first postulated by an Italian mathematician from the 13th century called

Leonardo of Pisa. In simple terms if you start with 1 and sum the answer with the last term you get the following progression: 0+1 = 1, 1+1 = 2, 1+2 =3, 2+3 = 5, producing the series 1, 1, 2, 5, 8, 13, 21, and so on. Followers of this series have pointed out that such progressions appear in nature and also give us the underlying mathematics for the so-called golden section, which is considered nature's answer to perfection. Analysts and gurus constantly announce how a market has stopped at one of these important Fibonacci numbers, and how this demonstrates the powerful attributes of the series. Unfortunately these people are fooling themselves, and possibly others who listen to them. It is a classic behavioural fallacy to be selective in picking data, as we saw this is the curse of stereotyping and confirmation bias. We never hear of the endless occasions that markets didn't stop on one of these mythical price levels because such inconveniences are quietly forgotten.

Needless to say all sorts of pointless market games can be played with these numbers; perhaps we could develop an important market number of our own here? What about 144? It's a Fibonacci number, it's a square of 12 ("So what?" you might say and personally I would agree, but it helps build the spurious significance factor of the number), it's 40% of the degrees of a circle (even more obtuse, I agree) and if you split the day into blocks of 144 minutes you have blocks of 10% each. Meaningless of course, but no doubt all sorts of important events and strange market analysis could be attached to this number.

Apart from this surface curiosity value though, many in the market seem to play a double bluff with one another over such numbers. Hence certain numbers are deemed as very important, and because some people trade with this in mind these special numbers sometimes gain short-term market significance. This is possibly another example of the self-fulfilling aspect of so many market generated ideas. The rational course of action in such cases is to ignore such behaviour, or even take advantage of it, but powerful forces can sometimes be at work.

This Number Is Important

The use of important numbers is particularly prevalent in two market areas: stop loss limits and orders, and the placement of trigger levels in barrier options. The topic of stop loss orders could occupy a separate book, and no doubt books have already been written on the topic. A perennial game of cat and mouse takes place with these orders, which, whilst supposedly employed to just contain any unexpected losses, are often wrapped up in an enormous amount of mumbo-jumbo. Market wisdom states it's not sensible to place stop loss orders at round numbers or so-called big figures (e.g. a stock price at $10 or $15 exactly) as this placement is too obvious and the stop will be hunted down, executed and the market will then promptly reverse, with the order taker holding the now favourable position once held by the order giver. Clearly it is common sense for the order giver to avoid such outcomes, but markets still see huge amounts of orders placed at the magnetic attraction of the round number.

The picture is similar with barrier options. Readers unfamiliar with this area of financial exotica can find a host of information on the web, and can become imbued with knowledge about knock-ins, knock-outs, reverse knock-ins, double knock-ins, phoenix options et al. But briefly here, barrier options are like plain vanilla options with an additional barrier level, or if you prefer trigger point, that depending on the instrument either activates or extinguishes the underlying option. So the buyer of such an instrument has not only to decide on the strike price of his desired option, but has to nominate a level at which the trigger level is set. Pricing is an issue here, so the choice of barrier level is not without cost considerations. Once again round numbers seem to be a favourite. Such barriers can have huge market significance because if triggered they can unleash large amounts of trading by the issuer who may have to re-hedge their exposure. For example, if an option is knocked out when a barrier level is breached, then the option writer no longer has the liability on his books and needs to dump the accompanying hedge position that had been previously put in place.

In these situations with geared instruments the motivation to hunt down and trigger barrier levels can be enormous. Such instruments are particularly popular in the currency markets where on occasions a global battle over some days may ensue as barrier levels are defended and attacked by various parties. So the human propensity to use round numbers can be turned into a self-fulfilling prophecy of importance.

Number Blindness

In addition to an attraction towards certain numbers, the human brain can also show worrying signs of number blindness in other cases. Chief amongst these are percentages and the murky topic of investment performance. It is common to express investment success and failure in terms of percentage returns. People usually refer to the percentage gain on a particular success story rather than the actual amount of money made and the whole investment industry is constantly screaming performance percentages at one another, and any prospective clients who can be bothered to listen.

And here lies another seemingly innocuous killer. Let's imagine we have bought a stock at $100, and it falls to $80, we have made a loss of 20%. Now we only have remaining capital of $80, but to return to our existing pot of capital of $100 we need to make a 25% return. Again this is not trivial. Hidden away in these percentage differences, the pitch has just increased the upward slope a little bit more.

To illustrate this more vividly, imagine a rather strange situation where you invested in a series of stocks where you first lost 20% on an investment and then made 20% on the next trade. If this sequence was repeated a total of five times, your capital would have been reduced from $100 to $81.53. Percentages can fool the investor about his true state of performance. Add to this the fact that losses are far harder to cope with (as per our look at Tversky et al.) and the inherent dangers of rationalising away poor results. No wonder many players let losses mount, hoping against hope, or even worse trying to fool themselves about the true extent of the damage.

Another problem caused by percentages – which we might dub the falling knife syndrome – is a tendency in falling markets to buy simply because a stock or commodity has "fallen so far" or that it "can't go any lower". Of course there may be good reasons to buy, but just because a stock is lower in price there is no guarantee that it will start going up again. This problem was illustrated in spades with the calamitous fall in the share price of British company Marconi. This stock fell from £12.50 in September 2000 to less than 5p exactly two years later – a decline of over 99%. Many investors may have been tempted to buy after they fell by 50% or even by 75%, but such were the troubles of the company the share price kept plunging. Investors often seem to get number blind again, and think that after such a spectacular fall, of say 80%, the worst must be over, but it's never too late to lose 100% of your own investment stake, irrespective of what has happened to the share price before. Indeed there were stories of some speculators buying stock at round 20 pence (after a fall of some 98%) and treating their investment as effectively an option premium payment. This proved to be accurate for all the wrong reasons, as they lost virtually all their money even though they were only involved in the stock for the last 2% of its fall. Trying to catch a falling knife such as Marconi can be fatal, and being fooled by previous percentage falls is extremely dangerous. Buying a stock because of a great fall, or selling it because of a large rise, is not sufficient in itself to bring success – it can on occasions be financially painful.

Investment reality can often be bleak, the adventurer in the marketplace has to pay up for the costs of brokerage and spread, may well suffer considerable costs from slippage, and having overcome those trials is still faced with seemingly harmless issues of numbers and how to treat them. Needless to say there are yet more horsemen of the investment apocalypse to come.

The Monstrous Regiments

The final two horsemen we should also touch upon are the costly effects of taxation and market regulation. We can deal with taxation very simply – unless you fit into a small minority you will have to pay tax on your investment gains and income. (No doubt American readers will point out that Uncle Sam levies tax wherever they are resident – if you are an American citizen you pay federal tax irrespective of your domicile.) This taxation charge varies amongst administrations around the world, but in broad terms is usually between 25% and 40% on capital gains, and whatever the marginal rate of income tax is, for any dividend or interest income.

The 19th century American railroad tycoon Cornelius Vanderbilt once declared that compound interest was the eighth wonder of the world, which is undoubtedly true if you can sit around and wait for the benefit after the first fifty years or so, and if you can avoid paying tax. Taxation kills the ability to build up significant wealth easily and the crushing effect of 30% plus taxation should not be discounted by those dreaming of armchair riches from trading the markets successfully. Occasionally governments create tax sheltered schemes, one of the most prominent being the Personal Equity Plan (PEP) scheme in the 1980s in Britain, but in general tax cannot be avoided, particularly on any meaningful gains.

In the UK in the past twenty years or so a novel market development has been the growth of spread betting. In essence, the investor or speculator places a bet with the spread betting company that replicates the price actions of a particular stock, commodity or currency. In legal terms such a deal is a contract for differences (CFD), which had had a rather indistinct position in English Law – it was not clear if such a contract would be viewed as a wager and therefore not a legally enforceable contract.

In the mid 1980s the wholesale money markets also turned to contracts for difference (forward rate agreements and interest rate swaps for example) which could have fallen foul of the law at the time. If such contracts had been deemed to be wagers then clearly this market would have collapsed, and so the big financial institutions set about successfully lobbying the government using arguments about the benefits of deregulation and financial innovation, and as a result the law was clarified. Spread betting benefited from this clarification, and its further growth may have been a happy by-product of the rapidly evolving deregulation of wholesale markets. For the speculator any profit from such spread betting trading is deemed to be the proceeds of a wager, and therefore is not currently subject to taxation. This market has exploded in size as punters have sought to avoid taxation. It must be tempting to the government to tap this source of financial profits, but so far the industry has escaped.

So the misery continues. If the investor has managed to make a profit, having paid brokerage, and spread and having suffered from slippage and the mental demons of rationalising his performance, the dead hand of taxation relieves him of a portion of the gains, but still there are yet more costs.

"Something Must Be Done"

This is normally the screaming reaction that kick-starts financial regulation. It is generally held that the past twenty-five years have seen a significant collapse in financial regulation, and a blossoming of new techniques, instruments and markets. This is true in parts – clearly the markets have developed new products (or perhaps more accurately re-invented and re-labelled some old techniques) and initially there was a freeing of monopolies and regulation. But if viewed over a longer time horizon we can see that regulation ebbs and flows like everything else in markets, and as we move towards the end of the first decade of the new millennium, financial regulation (or you might prefer re-regulation) is once again back in fashion and about to be in full flood. After the perceived excesses of the 1990s, and the revelations that all was not well in the world of finance and accounting, the regulators were back in business, particularly in the corporate audit arena.

As a result a large army of lawyers, accountants and clerks now oversee a huge global business called financial regulation. In recent years their powers have started to increase considerably – this is a long way from the free market ethos of Thatcherism and Reaganomics – and needless to say the costs of this monitoring have also increased apace. Banking, insurance, fund management, securities and futures trading are all now feeling the flow tide of greater regulation, with a whole host of other areas attracting regulatory scrutiny, even including the selling of simple domestic housing loans and refrigerator insurance! Post-Enron US legislators passed a heap of laws and regulations in response to the corporate frauds uncovered when the dotcom fiasco hit the markets, chief amongst these being the wide ranging Sarbanes-Oxley Act that seeks to set down strict rules for corporate governance.

The current disaster zone, in the aftermath of the credit crunch of 2008, will spawn a lot more legislation, rulebooks and tighter controls – chief amongst these is the likely return of legislation that recreates the structures put in place by the Glass-Steagall Act in the US in 1933. All of this is entirely predictable, when bubbles burst (as they always do) there is an immediate call of "never again" and "something must be done". Often what is done is misguided and has the potential to inadvertently fuel the next disaster. There is a cycle in regulation like all human affairs, or perhaps it is more precise to call it a spiral.

The Regulatory Spiral

Currently the regulatory cycle seems to have an additional twist, which has its roots in computing and bandwidth once again. In fact rather than just a regulatory cycle, one could be tempted to describe it as a spiral, with each twist of the cycle the system grows more complex and pervasive.

Finance is now truly global, so naturally the regulators feel they have to operate on a supra-national basis as well. There is little point in having rules in one country if companies can easily move their place of business electronically to somewhere else. So regulators are building a network of legislation, rules and guidelines that can operate everywhere. Not only is the regulatory environment wider than ever, it is also deeper; for example with most market practitioners now having to be registered and required to take a variety of examinations. This last situation is really rather curious because of all occupations financial trading and investment is the least measurable and definable by examination, you cannot pass a test and then hope to automatically be a successful market player – the test is the market itself. But to the bureaucratic mind, testing of topics such as exchange opening hours, futures contract sizes, and double bluff multiple option questions about calculating interest makes perfect sense.

As with most things in finance, regulation seems to develop over the same cycle, and some observers have noted that it seems to follow a path that is around 30 years or so in length. In broad brush terms this may be true: first there is a decade of free unfettered market capitalism (the 1990s in the current evolution) which almost inevitably leads to excess and scandals, and results in the second phase, about a decade later, with new regulation being introduced (the first decade of the new millennium). Then after about ten years or so people eventually realise that this is choking competition and some of the machinery (though rarely all) is dismantled. In the last cycle this process of dismantling was very much the driving force of free market governments of the late 1980s and 1990s. Indeed, one could argue the high water mark for de-regulation was the repealing of Glass-Steagall in 1999, and those who doubt the necessity of the current round of regulation look like having to wait until at least 2020 before they will witness the ebbing away of the current cycle. Whilst no market cycle is precise it does appear that this 30-year evolution also worked quite well to describe the period after the Second World War. The late 1940s and 1950s saw both Europe and America emerge from the war with food rationing being abolished and industry and commerce generally forging ahead in a new freer market atmosphere. The 1960s brought further de-regulation, an economic boom and rising prosperity. This was characterised by the abolition of many price cartels in industry and more competition for banks from secondary banking institutions and savings groups. The 1970s saw the boom of the 1960s stall badly, government intervention and micro-management of the economy became the order of the day (wage freezes etc.), with further nationalisations in the UK, and trade protection by the US command economy paralysed much of the Western economy until the whole cycle re-started again in the 1980s.

At the time of writing the world looks like returning to a more government-led marketplace, free market ideas are on the back-foot and central control is back in vogue – after all with the seriousness of the credit crunch "something must be done". Defenders of regulation will point out, with some justification, that the proper policing of financial markets is needed to ensure fairness and to track criminal acts. This is undoubtedly true but the problem with regulators is always proportion – once in place it is very hard to get rid of regulation (regulators themselves never demand fewer powers), and if it fails to work, the answer is always more rules and paperwork. This comes with a considerable cost that is always borne by the end user – the investor.

These costs are in fact huge; the latest set of accounts of the UK's Financial Services Authority (for the financial year ended 31 March 2008) show their total costs at just over £330 million, but this is chickenfeed against the total costs for the industry. All financial regulation and legislation costs money – for example the rather arcane set of rules called MIFID which has sought to give greater transparency to equity markets has cost the London market alone over £1 billion. When one tots up the costs of banks compliance departments, endless legal advice, form filling and box ticking the figures must run into billions worldwide every year. These costs have to be paid by someone of course.

The end user of financial services is the one who pays eventually, and he or she has no say in the matter. This charge on the market is hidden though, as it is lost into the accounts of banks and securities which bear the initial costs. Of course these institutions pass the costs on, through charges etc., and they do occasionally rail about the situation but are careful to do or say nothing to upset the panjandrums that oversee the financial industry.

All the costs outlined in this chapter add up to a situation that is quite daunting. Clearly, making money in the markets is not easy, and importantly the investor or speculator must remember they are playing on a sloping pitch. The siren calls that suggest trading is an easy path to riches are false – getting the market right is only one part of the equation, and the accompanying costs are a major factor in the business.

Little is usually said about these costs, particularly by the next group we will examine, the forecasters and seers into the future who claim to be able to help us make easy money.

6

Chartists, Economists And Gurus

'One inch forward lies darkness.'

Japanese proverb

None of us know the future, but in financial markets little else is talked about. Will the latest economic figures be good? Is it true the central bank will intervene overnight? What are the chances of a take-over bid? Why is the market lower, when we expect good news next week? What will happen next? This insatiable demand for prognostication has led to a huge industry of analysts, commentators, pundits and experts. In every financial market there is a veritable travelling circus of performers that seek to persuade us they can guess, surmise and predict absolutely anything and everything – in return for a modest fee.

Much of what is said and written about financial markets is dreadful rubbish, but as we all know, the truth doesn't count in finance, but rather it's what everybody else believes that is important. As a result there are numerous amusing and bizarre stories about how rumours and misunderstandings sometimes grip markets. Efficient Market types usually label such behaviour as noise and assert that over time random and ill-judged market moves are soon corrected. Certainly much of the noise is created by market commentators themselves, who feed the never ending demand for information, opinion and that ultimate Grail – what will happen next? Once again we can see that the rise of cheap global communication is a major cause of this activity. The sheer omnipotence of computers, email and 24-hour business television, has caused avalanches of comment, analysis and opinion to rain down on the marketplace. The market is full of information – but knowledge is much more rarely seen.

It is against this background that the financial soothsayers operate. Theirs is a business with almost infinite demand, and a client base that is usually forgiving of their poor predictive records. There are many different groups to choose from, they have differing methods and techniques, and frequently they approach their work with almost religious fervour. Often however, the only thing that truly unites them is their barely concealed hostility towards one another. Again for the sake of good order and to try and maintain some sanity when discussing these would-be financial Merlins, let's just remind ourselves that none of us know the future.

Chartists – Selling Maps Of The Future

Charts have been around for ages – certainly since the days of Charles Dow, the American journalist and publisher who, in the late 19th century, was a co-founder of the Dow Jones Index and created the *Wall Street Journal*. Dow recorded closing prices of thirty major industrial stocks, created the world's first stock index and plotted various line graphs of industry sectors. In addition to this, over a period of time he created a predictive idea called Dow Theory. From this point on the chartists were in business with a vengeance. Bar charts, point and figure charts, market timing cycles, percentage moves, swing charts; a whole plethora of inventive ideas appeared, all long before the computer. In the Orient the Japanese can lay claim to their own system – Candlestick Charts – that has a history going back to the 17th century rice market. They have also created the Kagi, Ichimoku (a particularly bizarre format) and Renko charting systems.

If one thinks about it, charts are a curious investment tool because they can only perfectly map the past. Unlike naval charts or road maps they record a journey that cannot be revisited. Of course a stock can trade at a previous price again, but the time frame will have changed, and the precise price action is nearly always different. So financial charts cannot be used in the same way as road maps, perhaps in a way they are more like a diary of the past events that faithfully records where a share price, or commodity has been, but they can give no definitive answer as to the future. You cannot use a stock chart to plan your future investment journey in the same way as you might use a road map to plan a touring holiday of France, though many market players seem to adopt this approach. Many chartists would bridle at such a notion;

this is to misrepresent their craft, their skill they claim is in the interpretation of these past moves and postulating likely scenarios going forward. In one sense they do have history on their side because financial markets do seem to repeat the same cycles and the same general patterns of events, certainly at a macro level. But the key is can charts do the same on the micro level?

Nowadays, of course, charting is big business, and it has exploded in popularity with the advent of the personal computer. Every cheap and cheerful internet broking system offers free charts, and charting tools. Of course some market participants were hand-drawing charts long before computers, but only a dedicated band of players could be bothered to do all the donkey work. As a result most of the data that was plotted was daily information; usually the open, high, low and closing prices for the stock, index, commodity or currency that was being charted. Occasionally trading volumes were also included, and amongst futures traders the open interest data was also plotted. These days computing power and graphics allow almost limitless time slicing. Some people create one-minute bar charts, or perhaps divide the day up into unusual time periods, all as a way to try and reveal the coming moves in the market. Charts have also developed into technical analysis, which seeks to create and analyse essentially secondary or derivative information about the market price. This can range from simple moving averages, through a whole gamut of mathematical indicators, to some of the latest ideas involving fractals, artificial intelligence and Chaos Theory. In fact some have extended the art (could it be called a science?) to make predictions about time in the markets as well as prices. Not content with predicting the Y axis on the graph, many claim to know when on the X axis things will happen. This seems to be prediction on a heroic scale; and the punters are keen to hear these predictions. Imagine knowing where the price will move to, and when!

As a result of all this activity, chartists, or technical analysts – as they prefer to label themselves – have turned a once fringe activity into a global industry. Conferences, training courses, professional examinations and po-faced interviews by experts on business television are now all part of the circus. Chartists may well believe that all of this is proof enough of the validity of their trade, but in fact other simpler forces are really responsible for the exponential growth in this business.

"Free" Research

In essence, there are three approaches to chartists and their ilk; there are those who dismiss the whole activity as innumerate mumbo-jumbo (economists and statisticians are in the van of this view), there are the true believers who like latter day alchemists devote enormous time and effort to perfecting their analysis skills, and then finally and perhaps most importantly there are the cynics in banks and brokerage houses who pump out technical analysis as a way of generating more business.

This final group are the real drivers behind the popularity of charts. The most important skill for the banker, broker or indeed any intermediary is to retain, or if necessary feign, relevance. The most dreaded word in their lexicon is disintermediation – at all costs they must prove and demonstrate their worth to the fee paying client. This is where charts and technical analysis come into their own. Imagine you have a job as an institutional salesman at a stockbroking firm, or investment bank if you prefer the more grandiose title. What do you tell your client every day? You talk about the weather, the weekend, their golf handicap, but what is there that is new to talk about in the market? Fortunately there is a fair amount of economic and company data (more of this later) but if all else fails there are always the charts. Charts provide the hook to that daily conversation, a way to engage the customer and hopefully generate more business and commission. They are easily understood by customers and have the important virtues of being visually interesting, and easy to transmit to hosts of customers via email attachments. Unsurprisingly it is nearly always sell side institutions, i.e. brokers and banks, that employ technical analysts. The buy side, i.e. fund managers, corporate treasurers and pension funds, rarely bother; after all, their friendly banker or broker will provide that information for free. (Free is completely the wrong term to use here – all such bells and whistles come at a price – it's just that the cost is well hidden in the service provided by the intermediary.)

One aspect of charts and technical analysis that is particularly alarming is the incredibly shaky foundations that the whole edifice is grounded upon. Let's just think slowly and carefully about the proposition made by chartists. They suggest that by examining past price actions they are able to predict the future, that all the relevant information regarding an asset is contained in its last traded price, and that careful mathematical calculation of various indicators can predict and confirm future price trends. These are pretty bold claims. However, at least one piece of support for the view about the price containing all information comes from the 19th century French statistician, Louis Bachelier, who said: 'Clearly the price considered most likely by the market is the true current price. If the market judged otherwise, it would quote not this price, but another price higher or lower.' Bachelier was largely ignored during his own time, but nowadays is hailed as a very perceptive expert on financial markets. But other than his observations about market prices containing all known information, technical analysis is pretty bereft of serious academic support.

The work of technical analysts is innumerate according to most statisticians, indeed the statistical evidence that such ideas will work is very slim. A central tenet of modern day statistics states in any given series of numbers it is impossible to predict the next number in the series, and it follows from this that predicting tomorrow's share prices is impossible. The chart followers counter this by saying there is more to a share price than just its numerical value – we mustn't forget that the price holds a distillation of emotions that have made the price. The market is not just ruled by numbers and asset valuations, but by these emotions as well. (At this point the familiar hydra of investor fear and greed is normally wheeled out by the defence.) In fairness there may be something in their argument. Simple observation shows that some markets (foreign exchange is a prime example) seem to have a propensity to trend, but whether charts can successfully predict the future of such trends is at best a moot point. The statisticians and their close allies the economists will always dismiss chartists as no better than financial witch doctors, but something other than randomness is often seen to be going on in financial markets – though whether charts and technical analysis can capture and understand such underlying forces is unproven.

Occasionally some have defended this accusation by saying that this no different from weather forecasting, after all meteorologists use past data, run it through their models and come up with predictions for the future. Well, arguments rage about how accurate weather forecasts are (not surprisingly the forecasters themselves are pleased with their efforts) but there is one vital difference. When the weatherman says it will rain tonight, his prediction can either be right or wrong, he cannot influence the weather itself. With financial charts if the analyst makes a convincing enough story that stock XYZ will go up tomorrow enough market players may jump in to and cause the rise, but not before the market-maker has judiciously marked the price up anyway, to anticipate the demand.

The Rear View Mirror

Looking at charts is like driving a car by looking through the rear view mirror – albeit, these days it is a highly polished and computer enhanced mirror. Past data is the only source of information to feed into these charts and indicators, and everything else is a complex mix of extrapolation and sometimes wishful thinking. Indeed charts seem to feed a dangerous fallacy about markets – they appear to show future trends. Most of us have seen the obvious up and down trends on stock charts, all carefully overlaid with trend-lines, moving averages and other indicators. At first glance they do seem to be telling us something about the future, but all they provide is an accurate picture of the past. Trends always continue until they change, or as is often the case, just start to meander in a fairly directionless manner. However charts and their popularity won't go away, and are now a permanent part of the financial landscape.

A common jibe against the technical analyst is that he is the easy one to spot in the trading room – he's the guy with a hole in his shoes. By implication no one has ever made serious money following charts – though many seem to be doing very well selling training courses, magic systems, secret methods and other snake-oil. It is a curious fact that most market gurus are drawn from chartists and technical analysts – their particular brands of futurology are so compelling to the marketplace that I will cover their particular claims in more detail in a separate section. Overall there is little independent evidence of successful chartists dominating a marketplace. Somewhat like teachers they seem to be busy educating others rather than executing the ideas themselves.

Another criticism levelled against charts is that they are self-fulfilling. This in fairness is a rather curious line of attack by the critics. Surely if they are self-fulfilling it would be wonderful news, the truth is that charts are really very subjective, at best open to interpretation, at worst not much better than a guesstimate of future price movements. In fact one could argue that the problem is they're not self-fulfilling enough.

Certainly if enough market players believe in a chart pattern they may trigger enough market activity to influence the outcome. But this line of argument assumes that the chart prediction is that definite in the first place. In fact most chart predictions are very woolly and full of conditional statements and get out clauses. Chartists seem to prefer to surround their views with conditional statements and to call for endless further confirmations from their menu of indicators – it is rare for the charts to give a definitive view.

Perhaps slightly surprisingly, this seems to suit everyone. The analyst and the salesman always have an escape clause if the suggested strategy didn't work and the customer, the recipient of the advice, is just as satisfied. Why? Well it is naïve to believe that market players just want advice in financial markets – even when they ask for it. What they really want is confirmation of their own views and prejudices, a form of comfort blanket if you like. If the charts turn out to be wrong about the future but coincided with the investors' views at the time he is often still (relatively) happy – at least there is a scapegoat to kick when losing money. After all who ever really believed charts?

Bring Me Another Support – This One's Broken

One obvious problem with predicting the future is what do you do when you are wrong, after all analysts can't take the classic advice offered by the Hollywood movie mogul, Sam Goldwyn who proclaimed: 'Never predict anything – especially the future!'

Well the solution to overcoming one's bad predictions is actually very simple. The iron rule of forecasting is clear, the best approach is to make endless predictions and only refer to your successful ones. If this sounds unduly cynical lets look at how the trade in financial prediction seems to work. Given we accept that there is endless demand for views on the future, the methodology to supply this need is straightforward. First, no analyst ever makes one prediction in isolation, they essentially adopt a portfolio approach to the risk that their predictions by might be wrong. Analysts that have the luxury of ranging over many asset classes, as opposed to single stock groups for example, have the largest number of opportunities to create predictions. With around two hundred and fifty business days in a year (allowing for public holidays) it is relatively easy for an analyst to come up with five hundred predictions a year – if twenty are really good (a one in twenty five hit rate) they can soon put together a track record of success. The second extremely important aspect is to avoid referring to both time and price in a single prediction. The amateur tends to say things like 'Gold will be at least 10% higher by Christmas.' The professional analyst would be much more careful and say either, 'Gold is in a positive trend with a projected target 10% higher than current levels' or alternatively 'Gold will continue its advance until Christmas, the prospects for bullion are very positive'.

By only covering either price or the time horizon, and not both, the professional analyst has an escape route if the prediction is wrong. Either, 'The lack of movement up in the price is puzzling / disappointing / surprising but looking forward prospects remain sound' or perhaps if the price has fallen heavily, 'We continue to see improving prospects in the medium term'. Another subtle point here – and this is true throughout finance and probably in life in general – success is always personal, failure is hidden and dispersed over a group. The individual always saw the successful move coming, but it's the corporate "we" who are blamed when things go wrong. Another trick is to describe matters in relative rather than absolute terms. If an analyst says a given stock will outperform the market it could be that the stock declines by 10% whilst the main market as measured by an index falls by 12%. The investor loses money, but the prediction was correct. This method of hiding behind benchmarks and relative measures of success is endemic in financial analysis, and allows poor analysts to survive prediction mistakes, and prosper.

The unfolding bear market in stocks which has arisen since the credit crunch, has brought the activities of stockbrokers' analysts under terrific scrutiny. There has been a measure of public outrage that these analysts had been very bullish on virtually all stocks during the previous bull market but this should not be so surprising – it was a bull market after all – and importantly the critics forget that stockbrokers are always bullish. When stocks are going up they always say buy now before they go even higher and when stocks fall they often say buy now as the stock is at better levels (i.e. cheaper prices).

Clearly this is a slippery subject, and the following two examples illustrate how easily potentially fraudulent behaviour can creep up on the pundit. One quite well known prediction scam, and nowadays totally illegal, is recounted in John Allen Paulos's excellent book *Innumeracy*. There are a number of versions of the idea, with Paulos illustrating the principle with stock index prediction. The following version is similar, but with a slightly stronger marketing message as the punter is offered the products of supposed predictive genius across a number of stocks, rather than just a single index.

The would-be expert starts a stock market commentary business and sends out free predictions to an initial group of perhaps one thousand investors. The commentary tells one half of the investors that Stock A will rise in the next month, and the other half that it will fall. After a month the losing five hundred are dropped from the mail shot, and the process is repeated to the group that received last months' correct prediction. Now one half (two hundred and fifty potential punters) are told Stock B will go up and the other half are told that it will fall. After a few rounds of predictions you can demonstrate to a core number of potential subscribers that you have a 100% percent record across a number of totally different stocks, stretching across a number of months! In fact the initial mail shot could be to ten thousand recipients and then after six months, and six correct market calls in a row, you would have around one hundred and fifty souls who think you can see every stock market turn! Of course once subscribers pay up you are faced with trying to predict as successfully in the future (likely to be impossible) or making a run for South America.

Another similar idea, and equally fraudulent, is to set up a service predicting the sex of unborn children. Simply place an advertisement in the national press advertising your service, asking for a fee and (this is the rather unpleasant part of the idea) a small urine sample. In your marketing and advertising blurb you stress that the methods used are ground-breaking, and of course guaranteed. Everyone loves a guarantee and rarely stops to question its value. If for some inexplicable reason the system fails to predict the sex of the unborn child correctly the customer gets their money back. As all marketing men know, the two most powerful phrases in any business are "New" and "Free". So you have a new product, and whilst it's not free, it does have a money back guarantee if the service fails to make a correct prediction. So how do you make this work? Easy – just tell every customer that the child will be a boy. Around 50% of your predictions will be correct! The twist here is that you are only predicting a known outcome, but the marketing and packaging make it look like you are offering a genuine service.

Seeing What You Want To See

Now back to the charts. Whilst chartists have a natural advantage in promoting their story with graphs and coloured lines, they are equally exposed by these pictures when things go wrong. Charts and technical analysis are really about trend following – the only issue for the technical analyst is whether to predict a continuation of the trend, or a reversal of the trend's course. To do this, a typical technique is to offer a series of scenarios that allow for both outcomes – in fact this is like having a mini portfolio of sub-predictions to spread the risk – within the one overall prediction. For example, in traditional charting much use is made of retracements, that is to say how far a stock, commodity or currency may retreat from a recently made high. Much emphasis is also placed on accurately finding the last significant low and corresponding significant high (one can feel the wooliness creeping in already) then a number of percentages can be suggested as likely retracement levels. Perhaps the asset will fall back to half its previous up move, or perhaps about 25% or 75%? Another measurement is to divide the previous move into thirds, and then announce that the one-third and two-third levels are the key supports.

To add a degree of sophistication analysts sometimes use Fibonacci retracements – this is the practice of dividing the price action with reference to the golden mean, so now 38.2% and 61.8% are the levels to watch. There is presumably also scope for the use the Lucas series of numbers, developed by the French mathematician Eduard Lucas, for chart analysis. It is similar to the Fibonacci series, but different enough to give a completely different series. There could well be an opening for an enterprising analyst to try this on the investing masses. The whole use of Fibonacci as a label in technical analysis is usually a warning sign – numerous statements about how the Fibonacci series governs patterns in nature are often summoned up as evidence that the Fibonacci series is a central part of the natural law of life, and somehow is mystically embedded into financial markets. This does not seem to be an entirely rational argument.

Pursuing the idea that retracements can be predicted and calculated, lets just work this claim through – say a stock has moved from a low of 50 to a high of 120, and suddenly we have a host of possible supports created by these ideas; namely 25% is 67.5, 33% is 73.1, 38.2% equates to 76.74, 50% comes in at 85, 61.8% is 93.26, 66% is 96.69 and finally 75% equals 102.5. Seven levels that might or might not hold the price – is this really very useful? Needless to say there is a chance that the price will hold at one of these prices – and then we can claim that retracements work after all. Unfortunately we only know this after the event, but trading is not a rear view mirror activity. The hungry crowd want to know about tomorrow, but curiously gain comfort in seeing past events dressed up as predictions about the future.

So charts are a waste of time then? In themselves they may well be, though in fairness they are no worse than a lot of the other analysis foisted on investors, but because they are widely followed and examined they may have an indirect importance on market perceptions. This, in a way, comes back to the self-fulfilling argument. Occasionally a chart indicator becomes so embedded in market lore that it does indeed start to attract some activity – probably the best example of this is the unsophisticated idea of the 200-day simple moving average. Certainly amongst stock traders this indicator is widely followed, and one occasionally sees it on ordinary stock price charts in business newspapers – whether it is right or wrong is secondary, to investors all the media exposure and implied reputation suggests that it might be right.

Some of the behavioural aspects we looked at earlier are very prevalent in forecasting and prediction. Many market players seem to endlessly sift through systems, models and indicators to find something that works; no doubt the aim is to find by testing and empirical means something that will make money in the future. The risk is that confirmation bias will overtake their judgements, and they pick a chart or indicator that best suits their particular bias at the time.

So are we being too hard on chartists? It may be that chart following actually obeys the law of unintended consequences; it may be possible that those who use charts and trade successfully would do so without the charts, the computer print outs and the endless indicators, but they think they need this information. So technical analysis may help as an emotional comfort tool to give confidence and courage – perhaps in that way charts may work, if for the wrong reasons.

But in the slippery and uncertain world of financial market price prediction it is insane to claim that any indicator or method will definitely work consistently. What we can be certain of is that if enough people believe, it may work for a while. So once again the direct inputs into the market, be they traded prices, charts, news or outside events, are not really the issue – it is much more important to follow your fellow participant's reactions. Positive feedback remains the key to market price action and charts will from time-to-time be an input in that process, so whilst not a solution to the financial trading puzzle they remain another component and cannot be entirely dismissed.

Mine's Smaller than Yours

Time after time many so-called breakthroughs in finance have had little to do with genuine new ideas (once again we should remember the quote from Jesse Livermore), but are often the direct reaction to events external to the marketplace. In the past twenty years cheaper computing and bandwidth availability have been amongst the most prominent of such factors, and certainly the next group of analysts who work on the ideas of examining high density market data are a direct consequence of the advance in personal computers and global communications.

Somewhere around the mid- to late 1980s two interesting things happened: the general public, or least those moderately interested and educated, became aware of Chaos Theory. Suddenly it seemed everyone was talking about Mandelbrot Sets, Strange Attractors, Koch Curves,

Points of Singularity and the Butterfly Effect. A number of popular science books burst on the scene and one or two market players started to propose the idea that the financial markets were a perfect example of such phenomena. Indeed some of Benoit Mandelbrot's early research into fractals had looked at price patterns in the cotton market, so this was possibly an interesting line to be investigated.

Second, coupled with this, was the arrival of the PC in the brokerage house, the bank dealing room and the exchange floor trading booth. Any attempt to use the new non-linear maths in financial markets was clearly going to need serious computing power and suddenly traders and analysts using hand-held calculators to work out moving averages looked like dinosaurs. So here was a new area of market analysis that needed more computing, and fortuitously cheap and accessible computers had arrived right on cue.

In fact, Chaos Theory and non-linear maths had been around for some time, and the arrival of cheaper computers just opened up its possibilities to a wider audience, not just the pure maths academics with large computing resources on university campuses. Of course the market preferred to see it the other way round – the market had discovered this new tool to predict the future! Also we should quickly note here that relative to today's machines, these early personal computers were still very crude in their capabilities; machines with 286 Intel processors were probably the most widely used in the mid 1980s and they usually came with only 512k RAM and a hard disk capacity of 10Mb. So any high hopes for significant breakthroughs were probably misplaced, given the still relatively weak computing power on the analyst's desk. Nevertheless, opportunities were sensed by some, and the race was on to produce non-linear trading systems, charts and models based on Chaos Theory and a whole new area of new predictive software to sell to the customer.

Two different approaches were soon adopted: one group concentrated on the idea of examining massive amounts of market data – and applying the new maths to it – whilst another group advocated using the maths to create new software packages developing neural networks, using back propagation and genetic algorithms in relatively simple forms that could make use of existing market data series.'

The first group soon encountered a serious problem in obtaining accurate price data. As we touched upon earlier, in the pre-computer age people were quite satisfied with just obtaining the open, high, low and close data points for a stock price each day. In addition stock exchanges usually provided volume figures, though often a day late, and futures exchanges also gave out statistics on open interest (the total number of futures contracts outstanding). These fairly limited data sets still allowed the creative analyst to invent many trading ideas, plotting chart patterns, volume patterns and seasonality in commodities. But for the new breed of non-linear analyst large amounts of raw price data was essential. In fact, the new methods called for careful statistical analysis of every price change of a stock during the trading day. The emphasis was now on vast numbers of tiny price changes and the amount of data needed was truly awesome. For example, on average the five major currency pairs each change price quotes around 20 times a minute. So just one hours' data creates 6000 data points. Straightaway these new data demands threw up opportunities for some – the electronic information vendors quickly saw an opportunity to increase their sales of price information. The screen-based data that sat on dumb terminals in the past was now to be replaced by itemised data that could be manipulated and cut and pasted into computer software and specialist databases. Although it was not a problem to start storing all of this huge amount of tick data, none had been collected in the past, so it would take time to build up meaningful databases with which to back-test the new ideas.

In addition, a new and more subtle issue raised its head in the difference between indicative prices posted by banks and brokers and the actual prices that traded in the market. In markets with formalised exchange-based trading such as stocks, this was not a problem, for example the New York Stock Exchange provides a time stamped ticker of every trade in every stock throughout the day. But in a market such as foreign exchange where there is no centralised exchange, there is in fact no correct price for any currency pair at any single time. A number of market-making banks make prices in a currency, but there are often slight differences in the quote, and there is certainly no recognised official ticker price for currencies. In the normal course of events the differences are tiny and of little relevance, but in the world of Chaos Theory where supposedly tiny differences are the key to future changes, this struck at the heart of the philosophy. Nevertheless huge efforts were made by some, and clean and very detailed data was assembled and was ready to run through the new mathematical models.

Programmable Prediction?

Meanwhile advocates of the other approach launched an explosion of cheap software products, hitting the market by offering new and exciting ways to analyse market price action. Forget charts, moving averages and standard maths, now it was time to buy a neural network programme for your PC, or one that would run sophisticated genetic algorithms. These products were often priced at as little as US$500 and were accompanied by the usual extravagant claims that hitherto unseen structures and patterns would be revealed. (The temptation in marketing blurb to fall back on the old saw of revealing new trading secrets continues to be irresistible.) This was an arms race and no one could afford to be behind.

This group also found they had a small problem – the programmes didn't seem to work(!), or at least not in the hands of the average person in the trading room. Many traders seemed unable to successfully train the software, or at least to understand its outputs. In simple terms neural networks are given a series of inputs, then by an iterative process make an attempt to predict the output, and then compare their efforts to the actual output (the stock price in this case) in the real world. The system is trained by repeating this process over and over again, and ideally the software should become better at learning the relative importance of the inputs and thereby improve its results.

What became clear though was that financial markets seem to have a whole host of potential inputs that fluctuate wildly in relevance, so setting up the initial parameters was extremely difficult, if not impossible. Indeed this is an age old engineering problem: it's not just that you don't know, but it's that you don't know, that you don't know. This is far harder than looking for a needle in a haystack because with that problem at least you know you should be looking in a haystack! Just as serious was the rejection of such new fangled ideas by the institutional sales forces who spoke to customers. Such ideas were just too complicated and arcane to explain to the customer in between holiday plans and golf stories from the weekend. The sales types still preferred good old charts – the customers understood (well at least they thought they did) what charts were telling them – but this non-linear information was a black box that they couldn't fathom.

Where are we now, some twenty years after the initial burst of enthusiasm? Well, neural networks and genetic algorithms haven't died completely but are no longer in demand from the mainstream. They have had some successes, for example in being used in credit evaluation and rating models where the inputs are far fewer than the traded markets. In fact, neural networks seem very good at these relatively limited problems, though some have criticised them for just being gigantic data optimisation machines. Less is heard about genetic algorithms, though undoubtedly research and some trading model-building is going on. In time it might be that genetic algorithms do make progress, as the way their "agents" seek to find and develop dominant themes and patterns may be similar to the way markets really work. But currently the complexity of the markets does seem to be beyond their capabilities, and as a final damning verdict the software in the magazines is getting cheaper and cheaper – US$250 is often the going rate for the magic secrets of neural networks these days.

The first group, who have now tended to label themselves as high frequency data analysts, have had a better time of things. Huge efforts, not to mention significant sums of money, have gone into creating large price databases, with literally hundreds of millions of price increments, and there has been some mainstream interest in their activities. One or two commercial prediction services have been launched and have survived, and there are instances of some hedge funds using the techniques relatively successfully. That said, the technique has hardly taken the world by storm, and the initial early hopes of proving that markets can be predicted by non-linear maths are at best unproven. In truth, what the whole tick data and chaos episode demonstrated was the market's insatiable appetite for something that will foretell the future will always lead to all sorts of techniques being tried.

The whole idea of non-linear maths and the high level computing techniques to analyse high frequency data was yet another challenge to traditional statistical theory. Chartists have tried to argue that the information contained within a price is far more than just being a numerical value and that to apply purely statistical reasoning is both wrong and too narrow an approach. Now the high level computing types are trying to attack the same theories from exactly the other end of the argument. Effectively they are saying that traditional statistical theory is wrong, or perhaps more fairly incomplete, as it fails to spot the nuances and slight distortions found in the statistics generated in market price data. To date neither group has won the argument against the hard nosed statisticians; but equally they could argue they haven't been totally defeated in their attempts. Though, as far as traditional number crunchers are concerned, there is clearly more intellectual sympathy for the high frequency analysts than the chartists who remain beyond the pale.

So the battle to know about tomorrow rages on – with investors continuing to shell out endless amounts of money to all the analysts and pundits. It looks certain that more time and effort will be spent in hunting the hidden pattern within the maths generated by markets, but high frequency analysis has lost its fashion appeal in the marketplace. Currently some work is being done on an idea called Kernel Based Learning – with the latest technique called Support Vector Machines regarded as the next great breakthrough. Again this idea has seen most of its applications in comparatively simple environments, such as hand writing recognition, and text searching and analysis – the far greater tests in the marketplace are only just being examined.

Unfortunately though, the high tech promise of various maths theories in markets has worn thin – as ever the dedicated followers of fashion have moved on to the next idea, in search of tomorrow's news today. Of course the developers will keep trying, and we can be confident that new ideas will continue to emerge. One could even postulate that if quantum computers ever actually get off the drawing board their expected mega calculating capacities will be directed at market data almost straightaway – and equally it seems likely they won't quite be able to crack the puzzle of financial markets.

Economists – Re-Drawing Maps Of The Past

There ought to be some sort of law against writers who trundle out Carlyle's quote about economics being the dismal science because the followers of this discipline in the commercial sector are not having a dismal time at all. Although once dismissed as 'teenage scribblers' by the then Chancellor of the Exchequer Nigel Lawson, the fact is that in the world of commercial finance, economists are riding very high indeed, and their opinions and forecasts are avidly consumed by the market and broadcast high and wide. In many ways they are one of the biggest beneficiaries of the new age of cheap global communication.

For example, in recent years they have become a regular feature of business television – in fact some institutions have even fixed camera links in place so that any resident analyst or economist, when called upon, can make an immediate live link to the TV broadcast. (This is surely yet another sign that as bandwidth capacity has exploded the broadcasters have become ever more desperate for content – even the followers of government statistics are now deemed to be an interesting way to fill up airtime.) Some of the big names have syndicated newspaper columns, personalised websites and they are the backbone of their own institutions customer gatherings – often breathlessly described as special briefings by the internal marketing men.

The rise of the financial economist over the last twenty years has been spectacular – many large banks and broking firms now have whole economics and analysis departments with a star system to rival that of Hollywood. The big names glory under pompous titles such as Global Head of this or that, and are supported by an army of lesser analysts and a seemingly never ending stream of recently arrived academic achievers to bolster the cast – all trying to guess what will happen in the future!

Their areas of interest are far removed from the chartists and technical analysts who gaze endlessly at the market price action – the economists prefer to look at the raw data of the economy, the government statistics, the gnomic speeches of dull and boring central bankers (this is not meant to insult these worthy individuals – in central banking to be considered boring is a significant accolade), and the sometimes wild claims and promises of politicians. They then pull all of this together to formulate the all important forecast. It is always a forecast – rather like weathermen, economists rarely use the word prediction, forecast has a more solid and somehow reassuring ring to it – but they are only trying to guess and make estimates about the future, just like you and me.

In very simple terms the methodologies of these economists and their rivals who study charts, are in fact quite similar. This at first glance may seem astonishing, but in fact both groups gather past data and then run the data through various models or frameworks and hope to come up with predictions about the future.

What is even more fascinating is the essentially static approach both these groups adopt towards analysis and forecasting – their models are essentially deterministic set-ups where fixed rules are created that can explain the economy's inputs and outputs, and hopefully how the financial markets will react. This seems rather at odds with all the dynamic activity around them in the trading room. By this I don't mean the usual ego maniac nonsense one sees in trading rooms, but the fact that financial markets don't obey static rules, they are dynamic and flex and even flail around in a constant fog of rumour, truth and lies. How can a chart or an economic model capture such seemingly random behaviour? Well the standard response is to play around with the rules, and to adjust the model, but there is little evidence that any particular economic model has cracked the puzzle of predicting markets. Only a few economists seem to have spent time studying the behavioural aspects of financial markets, though it is encouraging to note the 2002 Nobel Prize for economics was awarded in this area.

Tribal Differences

Almost inevitably economists break up into their own sub-groups (again very similar to technical analysts who have a whole sub-strata of tribes with their own favoured methods and techniques). The result is that one is faced with Keynesians, Monetarists, believers in free markets, those who stress the social economy and a whole group who sit in the middle of all these views – these tend to be the financial economists. One is tempted to ask whether this matters or should we care? Of course not – but it just confirms an iron rule in financial forecasting that whatever your view you can find an expert who will agree with you, and no doubt another who will say your views are nonsense. Needless to say at any one time one of these groups will have a good run of forecasts as their particular approach coincides with market activity for a while. Almost inevitably things change and the predictions go off the boil, and another group take up the running. It's a curious and interesting parallel with the gambler's fallacy – just as the gambler can have a lucky streak and attribute it to luck and judgement, perhaps forecasters suffer the same cycle of good and bad times – believing it to be skill, but in fact it may just be closer to chance than they dare admit.

When studying economics, the topic of statistics looms pretty large. Virtually all economists have a statistical background in their training, and so must be fully aware of the pitfalls of predicting, and the sheer hopelessness of making future predictions about any statistical series. So we should expect them to be fairly circumspect about making any comments about the future; but of course, this is to forget their audience, the baying hounds of clients that feel it is their right to know the future.

However in fairness, most economists do seem to be quite canny in their approach. For anyone who has thought about the issue, precise forecasts may only work over a very short-term horizon, and even the evidence for that assertion is weak; and predictions have to be broader and vaguer as the time frame expands. And as we discussed earlier there is little merit in clarity, the client base is very forgiving of all but the most hopeless forecasters. (One is tempted to observe here that if someone had a truly dreadful record they would in fact be lionised by the market – after all, you could profit from them by following the exact opposite of their advice. Such is the mindset of the manic customer base.) Whereas technical analysts try to make a virtue of spurious preciseness ('the stock will rally to $20.45 and then hit resistance'), economists seem happiest with bland generalisations ('the fall in consumer confidence last month, whilst surprising, doesn't alter the overall modestly positive trend'). Fortunately the client base in the financial markets has an attention span that finds 24 hours a challenging time horizon. To paraphrase Harold Wilson, a day is a long time in the markets. So much of the research and output of these modern day wizards is directed to the very short term. Instant opinions about the latest government statistic are considered a primary function of the role.

There is also a specific practical reason why economists have to be vague – in their world of government statistics and economic indicators, the past keeps changing. Unlike chartists and followers of market data, economists have to contend with a database of economic and government statistics that are subject to enormous amounts of revision, readjustment, rebasing and Lord knows what else. Trying to keep a grip on the economic past is hard enough – let alone trying to make any sensible predictions (forecasts if you prefer) about the future. This should be a crippling flaw for economic forecasting, but in fact it allows for a useful expansion of the business. In the best traditions of turning an obstacle into an opportunity, economists now routinely forecast both future economic data, and likely revisions to past data. So they are now also in the business of predicting the past!

Needless to say the institutional salesman loves economists, just like chartists they are a good source of fresh news and commentary. A quick observation, or a rushed paper in response to a client request on the latest government statistic or market event, are all grist to the salesman's mill. Also importantly for the salesman, many clients who distrust, or have had bad experiences, with charts often turn to economists and analysts. After all they are dealing with real numbers, and bona fide official statistics, not the curious voodoo served up by the chartists and technical analysts. (No doubt chartists can counter that there is an equal flow of disillusioned souls moving from economists to their own ideas.) They also usually come with a strong academic background and many are first class speakers, writers and presenters; all valuable skills when trying to schmooze the all important customer. Needless to say, as with chartists, economists normally reside in the sell side institutions, with the buy side clients expecting to receive their service on tap via the salesmen. Some economists have formed independent research houses, but it is a hard life trying to sell such research when torrents of similar work are given away free. Current moves by the regulators to separate the research functions of banks and brokers from the trading and new issue side of the business, if carried through, could be a brake on the further growth of analysis and research. It would certainly be an acid test of who actually wants to pay for the information.

One advantage that financial economists have is that unlike stock analysts, they are never in and out of fashion; their careers are not tied to vagaries of bull and bear markets. The standard equity analyst usually rides the wave of a bull market very well, and then almost disappears when the market retreats. The bank or broking firm economist seems to always be in demand whatever the state of the market. So should we believe the research written by financial economists? The answer is no, but equally we would be very unwise to ignore it entirely.

Curiously the financial regulators (certainly in the UK) seem to consider economic research as outside their ambit, and presumably consider their work to be irrelevant to the market. Of course in the large financial institutions every research document comes plastered with longer and longer disclaimer clauses, but amongst the independent economic research houses there is no requirement to be registered with the regulators. This contrasts with those (again in the UK) who produce technical analysis and chart research that is subject to the full scrutiny of regulation. This may have something to do with economists' refusal to make direct forecasts, and that the regulators consider bland statements about the economy, as just that: bland.

Of course it's pretty irrelevant whether economists are right or wrong, but it is important to know if they have influence over the market at any given time. The regulators may be dismissive, but given their often huge market profile, and their access to almost endless publicity and information distribution channels (how long before a bank or broker launches a private clients only TV service to broadcast their research?) they can sometimes wield enormous short-term influence.

Perhaps as a final thought on economics we should take the advice of the 18th century politician Lord Chesterfield who advised never to open a letter until two weeks after it had arrived. It was his experience that most problems or indeed unexpected surprises would have played themselves out by the time you read the contents. Perhaps this is how we should approach analysts' and economists' research on financial markets?

Gurus – Secrets Available For All

Away from the major financial institutions, this is another group of seers into the future – in some ways the most exotic of the lot – the gurus. In general they operate outside the normal big firms, sometimes because they have found they can make a good living as independent analysts, often because their ideas are deemed too wild and woolly for the mainstream and occasionally because they are such maverick and difficult characters no traditional firm would give them a job.

The whole business proposal of a guru is, in the most precise meaning of the word, quite fantastic – they usually claim that they have invented, developed or can expound a theory or model that will predict the future movement of financial markets. Even at this early stage statistics types will either be laughing out loud or making their excuses and leaving early. The claim seems so unlikely that one would expect such hype to be instantly ignored – but we mustn't forget the hunger that the market has for the answer to the eternal question, what will happen next? The gurus feed that desire with their special brand of financial snake-oil.

There are a number of elements that are usually common to gurus. In general, they usually don't come from the fundamental or economics based end of the business, it is much more likely they promote chart systems. Many have a background completely outside the financial arena, and as with all true heroes the most acclaimed are dead. These luminaries from the grave often attract messianic supporters, who spend an enormous amount of time arguing with one another about who is following the true path to investment riches. As one can imagine this area is rich with what we may term colourful characters and membership of the Guru Club seems to be exclusively male – we still await our first market priestess. Also, and this may be to do with the scale of the domestic markets, with history and the important factor of regulation, they tend to be American.

At the risk of harping on about those twin major influences of computing power and bandwidth, one can readily see how the new technology has been an absolute boon for the gurus. One of the most powerful effects of the e-commerce environment has been to lower the barriers to entry for many businesses; this is true in spades in the world of financial information. It is now literally possible to run a global investment advisory business via the web, send email and even conduct web broadcasts from one's small bedroom at home. The gurus have seized this opportunity with a vengeance.

Finding a Guru

So how do we spot a guru? Well it's not very hard, they normally have lively advertising in the financial press, quoting staggering investment returns, and making a whole host of offers that usually include the words, 'secret, guaranteed, revolutionary, simple and please send your money to...'. One is instantly struck by an interesting thing here – gurus always seem to quote phenomenal performance records, and they nearly always stress preciseness and wallow in making seemingly direct and firm predictions. This is the opposite of the economists. Who has ever heard of a big name economist quoting the investment returns available from his advice?

The principle marketing line advanced by gurus is that the mainstream doesn't know what it's talking about and that they, standing aside from the bear pit of financial trading, are uniquely placed to offer high quality and very profitable advice and insight. This sales angle is undoubtedly aided by the fact that many of their customers have found, to their cost, that major institutions are frequently clueless about future moves in financial markets, but then we all are. But not apparently the gurus, who are in possession of the secret system, or the methodology handed down from an earlier genius, who – in good matinee style – was often overlooked or ignored.

Indeed there is something of a Horatio Alger story in this approach, the little guy from the poor background who takes on the big boys at their own game and wins, because he is smarter than them, and now we all have a chance to join with him in kicking sand in the faces of the so-called experts. There is a hint of a Samuel Smiles story as well, with the idea that independent self-disciplined analysis will overcome all obstacles in the marketplace. Certainly this second attribute is not a bad attitude in life, but here in the world of the guru we can cut through all that effort and self-sacrifice, it has been done for us and all we have to do is become subscribers.

Easy then – we clip the coupon, or more likely these days click on the website, and off we go. The variety of techniques and methods we are offered is eclectic to say the least; for example, and this is a very small selection, there are wave theories, special chart methods, time spirals, pattern recognition (this an area where the gurus have started encroaching on the chaos crowd) lunar cycles and astrologers!

At this point we can see that gurus split into two distinct groups (the iron rule of tribal splits in the ranks of seers remains as strong as ever). The first group targets the private small player who typically plays in either the futures market or the margin trading arena, with the second more polished and professional group attempting to sell to the financial institutions (the very people they accuse of being hopeless).

The undoubted doyen, or if you prefer, the Pontifex Maximus, of this group of predictive high priests was an American accountant called R.N. Elliott. A small-time cost accountant in the South West United States and Mexico in the 1930s, he is hailed as the greatest guru of them all and is credited with creating a hugely complex system called Elliott Wave Theory. This theory, developed apparently whilst Elliott was convalescing from an illness, seeks to break market price action into a series of waves that follow predetermined rules based around, yes you it guessed, Fibonacci relationships. Elliott developed a whole series of convoluted rules that centre around the idea that markets advance in a series moves of five up waves, and then are followed by three down waves. All the waves (of which there are a series of sub-divisions using the same ratios, in fact almost fractal like) are intricately linked to one another by certain proposed ratios and relationships, all invoking the golden mean and the Fibonacci series. At first glance this seems amazingly brave, armed with this theory you are supposed to be able to predict the future price moves in the market. Why brave? Well surely Elliott is forgetting the cardinal rule of prediction – be vague enough for an escape route if you are wrong. Surely all these precise projections are a straitjacket? Fear not, because conveniently in Elliott Wave Theory there is a whole section about alternative wave counts. In other words, if you said the stock would go up from point A to point B and it rather inconsiderately went down, no problem, it turns out that we should have used the alternative wave count!

Yes, but one is also tempted to look at Elliott Wave Theory and the foreign exchange market, which for all its excitability and sheen of global sophistication and technology is actually rather gullible. There are a number of Ellioticians, as the self-proclaimed disciples like to call themselves, who make a good living out of selling predictions about future currency exchange rates with Elliott Wave.

Interesting – the theory tells us to expect a series made up of five up waves followed by a three wave down series. Let's consider the US dollar/Swiss franc rate, with the dollar as the base currency, i.e. there being so many Swiss francs (and centimes) to one US dollar. So the dollar goes up in five waves and down in three right? Fine, but currencies can equally, and frequently are, quoted as an inverse, i.e. in this case what fraction of a dollar (US cents then) one Swiss franc will buy. Now applying wave theory to this form of essentially the same exchange rate market, something must be wrong. How can the first rules apply, it would mean the Swiss franc has to go down in five waves and up in three waves? Good point – agree the Elliott gurus, but for currencies it's a different special three wave structure for both the up and down waves. Elliott Wave does not appear to be the most consistent of theories then!

The Speculator's Plan B

Occasionally a well known market player turns guru, the best example of this being Jesse Livermore, who wrote a book called *Investing in Stocks* which interestingly has been recently re-issued. We could term this the speculator's Plan B – if all else fails sell your trading secrets to punters who will believe they can learn from you. There have been many other more modern examples of this faintly ludicrous spectacle. The whole idea is particularly depressing, because the inference is that the successful trader will reveal his secrets to the ever hungry public who will as a result of learning the secret be able to emulate him. The skill and knowledge to make a fortune is available to anyone willing to shell out a small amount of cash on a paperback and a few hours reading at the weekend. In Livermore's case the motive seems to have been driven by a desperate need for cash (an investment success you said?) and he cleverly put together a system that mimicked elements of Dow Theory, a method much followed (with little empirical evidence of success) by many during the inter-war years.

We could waste many hours ploughing through some of the other theories and sonorous sermons of other great gurus – but it would miss the point. The gurus fulfil a basic human need, that isn't in fact directly linked to financial markets and successful forecasting; they bring hope, comfort and confirmation to the investor battling away to try and make money. People dislike being alone, and like to think they can be privy to a secret idea or system that will give them an edge in the marketplace. As ever, any lack of success by the guru and his teachings is often faced with equanimity – the consumer continues to believe that next time the system or method will work (and thanks to the law of averages even truly dreadful ideas sometimes work) and all will be well. Funnily enough this mind set is similar to the lottery ticket holder who by getting three of the six numbers gets the minimum prize of £10 but feels they were close to winning the jackpot. (Remember getting three balls out of the six has odds of about 1 in 54; to get all six is above 13 million!) In truth people pay gurus to develop hope and nurture expectation, and like holders of the lottery ticket (it could be you!) gain a degree of economic utility from the misguided experience.

Needless to say there is precious little evidence that gurus have made much money from trading – though selling books, courses, software, and web subscriptions can be an enormously profitable undertaking. Supporters of gurus often trot out claims of huge coups and large fortunes made in the past. But where are the great banking houses and dynasties built on trading systems? Did J.P. Morgan make his money from wave theories? Did the founders of the trading and banking houses of say Baring, Rothschild, and Schroder rely on secret trading methods or theories? No major bank or broking company has the name of Elliott on the door – but when you look at the evidence it's not very surprising.

Pandora's Promise

Up until now we have only looked at forecasters and predictors of the future who have given their views and opinions. Now let's move to by far and away the most interesting, and possibly the most valid bunch, the traders who use black box systems. These guys trade with real money based on their models – this is heavy metal stuff compared with what has gone before. But why build a formal model or system to trade the market? It appears to be a response to the behavioural pressures we looked at earlier. Systems don't have emotions, and are not prone to the biases that humans suffer from, whilst these elements can be debilitating for us mere mortals, the hope is that the trading system route can neatly sidestep these pitfalls.

In many ways this group is a hybrid of the previous groups we have looked at. Some build trading models using econometric data, some are chart pattern based, others use technical analysis based systems and the high frequency data techniques described earlier are a natural area for these trading model types. Whatever methodology is used, they are all using rule based, or if you prefer heuristic systems, that seek to extract profit from the markets. Once again they are not a single homogenous group but can be characterised as two quite separate tribes. One group is really made up of developers who concentrate on building black box systems and then selling them to investors. Admittedly selling these systems is harder than selling advice and forecasting theories, because the prospective purchasers are usually very results orientated, and only make the purchase after careful assessment of performance statistics, but other than a more discriminating customer base this group is rather close to the gurus discussed before. Once again there is precious little evidence that off the shelf black boxes are consistently successful – the killer criticism being that if you really can develop a successful model then why sell the software to others?

The much more interesting group is comprised of the black box developers who build and then trade with their systems for themselves or their firm. Of course, like everyone else they are faced with the immutable fact that no one knows tomorrow – so how do they try to create predictive trading systems? Here we start to move away from the vague world of opinions and estimates of future market moves towards a very precise world where the designer seeks to control his investment strategy and is judged (indeed his job probably depends on it) by the consistency of his performance.

These are the two key themes: control and consistency. We have to be very careful how we define control in this environment; it means control of the investment strategy and process, not attempting to have some form of control over the market. The most dangerous illusion in markets is to believe one has some insight over what is controlling them; the markets do what they like, and for a myriad of reasons, one can no more control their day-to-day actions than King Canute could stop the tide. Given that much of the market action is totally unpredictable, the only way to survive is to have a strong, well thought out trading strategy. Black box builders essentially formalise such ideas into a system. Formalisation comes with an inherent and dangerous flaw, because the systems can lack flexibility. Consistency is even more difficult because many models and systems last for a year or two and then wither on the vine. Investors usually demand a three-year track record before considering a model, and this is a significant hurdle for many. Performance and attribution statistics are almost as complex as financial markets, but play an enormously important part in black box trading – we will turn to that area a little further on.

Just Enough Flexibility

So the real art of the trader who uses trading models is to develop a system with strong rules, but that is flexible enough to withstand the slings and arrows of the trading day. Indeed it is the lack of flexibility in off the shelf packages that tends to be their downfall – it is extremely unlikely that one standard set of parameters will work in all market conditions and time frames.

There are any number of approaches to building a black box, but let's walk through one possible route. First, the modeller has to pick a suitable market. One may be tempted to immediately pick equities, but they are not really the best market. In the stock market it is not always easy to go short – there are now more instruments that allow for bear positions, but they are all ultimately predicated on a willingness of the longs to lend stock. There is always a significant danger that the supply of lending stock will be restricted, and indeed this is a natural tactic employed by longs to try and squeeze a bear market. If choosing stocks the model developer has to be keenly aware of this potential problem – which may be quite difficult to integrate into the systems rules – though one could circumvent this by building a model that is only ever long or flat. The physical commodities markets come with similar restrictions in that at maturity of the contract one can be asked to deliver the goods, or equally distressingly have the commodity delivered to your doorstep! Commodity futures traders can also have the painful experience of limit days, where trading is suspended when the price hits a pre-determined limit during the day. There have been examples of commodity markets having five and more limit days in a row. If you are positioned the wrong way there is nothing you can do – the model may be signalling an exit but you can't execute an order in the market as it is shut. In such restricted liquidity environments, all the rules are thrown to the wind.

Some markets are cash settled, including the financial futures markets and currencies, so here there is pretty much symmetrical risk in being long or short and it is easier to build a model to trade the market. Unsurprisingly a large proportion of model trading is in these markets, though many developers have tried to conquer the equity markets as well. It's really an assessment of liquidity risk, which should not be dismissed lightly because the consequences of poor liquidity can be catastrophic.

Having picked the market, the developer then needs a period of market observation followed by some rule building, and then the all important stage, the testing phase. This is sometimes known as paper trading, as dummy trades are simulated on paper (well computer spreadsheets these days obviously) and the results carefully scrutinised. Once the developer is satisfied with the results, they bite the bullet and then use the model to trade for real in the markets, with real money.

Whilst the above methodology is straightforward, the real key to successful black box building is the testing and results assessment stage. As we have seen earlier the trading pitch is very much sloped against the investor/speculator, with the important costs of brokerage, slippage and the bid-offer spread weighing heavily on performance. This is equally true for those armed with a black box. Indeed the correct simulation of these costs is paramount when assessing potential models and the massive dangers of over-optimisation and curve fitting have to be carefully avoided. This is in fact the greatest trap in mechanical trading systems.

It is natural to comb through past data, create rules that would have most profited from the market activity seen in the historical data, write the appropriate trading rules and then set off confidently into the market. Natural, but usually wildly optimistic and nearly always wrong. Such curve fitting, which is looking for the best possible outcome in past data, can be disastrous. There is an enormous temptation to check all the possible combinations of the rules of the system and then plump for the most successful and profitable from the testing period. For example, imagine a system using a pair of moving averages (not exactly high flying stuff admittedly) as buy and sell signals. Computers make it extremely easy to back test all the possible combinations of the two averages to find the most profitable combination. The problem is such a result may be a freak or an outlier in the data, just as either side of the best selection may be truly awful combinations. Some modellers over come this by plotting all the results on a so-called heat map and then look for a cluster or bunched plateau of good results, rather than a sharp spike in the data. This makes sense but is still subject to unpleasant surprises once real world trading begins.

Perhaps the best and most conservative approach that helps avoid these problems is to use walk forward testing. Put simply this means first selecting a period of past data, say one year's worth of daily data, from two years ago. You then apply the rules of the system to that data set and find a reasonable fit that isn't a spike in the results. Then walking forward from the end of that initial test period, for the second year, up until the present date. This means you have fitted the system for the first test year, but are treating the second test year as a live period to see if the rules would have still worked. This is a very simple example, whereas the professionals build simulations with rolling test periods and highly complex measures of success. Obviously success is not just about overall profits – drawdown, periods of loss and peak to trough analysis of the returns curve are also very important. Consistency measures such as the Sharpe ratio and Sortino ratio are also normally used to assess performance.

All well and good, and certainly much more rigorous than the vagaries of chart and economic forecasters, but still no system, black box or mystic seer can tell us what will happen next in the marketplace. Interestingly some of the best trading systems, and there are those that publicly display their results, seem to adopt simple and rather coarse trading rules; building systems with large numbers of rules and parameters seems to increase the risk of failure. A broad brush approach coupled with rigorous money management rules is the best way forward. None of this need be complicated, and indeed a number of traders have produced successful systems that are simple and consistently make money. This is probably the best example and proof that the intelligent and skilful few can live very nicely off the insane gyrations of the herd-like majority.

One other group of black box operators that should also be mentioned is the non-commercial developers. This group who are nearly always econometricians in public institutions often build models to try and understand and perhaps predict future market moves. The best known example of this group is probably the US Federal Reserve model for valuing equities. This market model uses some quite simple ideas – it measures the gap between the earnings yield of the S&P 500 equity index (this is defined as the earnings per share divided by the share price) and the yield on the ten year US Treasury Bond. This model was very successful at predicting (perhaps they prefer "forecasting") when equities would be cheap or expensive in the past, but since the unfolding of the current bear market in US equities this fairly predictable relationship between the yield on equities and Treasury Bonds has gone off the rails. Now unfortunately the Fed Model has been signalling equities are cheap, only for them to get even cheaper. No doubt the developers make no great claims for the model, but once again in the dynamic environment of the market the static rules of a rigid model are eventually exposed and vulnerable.

It is important to remember that whilst any future market move is entirely unpredictable, that doesn't mean there aren't opportunities in markets to exploit mis-valuations or overlooked situations. The murky world of forecasting and prediction is not likely to bring forth fortune but there is value and profit to be made in exploiting market anomalies. This is really to adopt the vulture like quality that keeps markets efficient. Of all the forecasters, predictors and gurus, the only group that seems to have half a chance of getting the market right are the model traders who actually trade in the marketplace.

It's an old age saying that everything changes except change itself, but perhaps we can add that people's desire to know about the future also never changes, and neither does their gullibility in believing that others can tell them.

7

Quantum(ish) Finance

'Everything you can imagine is real.'

Pablo Picasso

Perhaps we are now getting closer to our goal of understanding financial markets. We have successfully shaken off the lure of gambling, taken a look at some past investment greats, considered risk, hopefully remembered to account for the costs (both visible and hidden) of trading and taken a pretty cold look at forecasts and their promoters.

One of the themes that runs through these elements is that of interacting agents, all watching and reacting to one another's behaviour. In a sense it is almost a derivative activity; the participant isn't just concerned with their own judgements and observations of the market price and particular stock price, but also avidly watches and reacts to the actions (or inactions) of their fellow players. So the fact that others are buying or selling is as important, if not more so, than the individual's own actions. This secondary behaviour seems to be the key to much of the activity in markets, and directly relates to the example Keynes gave regarding how to guess who the crowd will pick as the winner of a beauty contest.

As we touched upon earlier, many participants invoke the impersonal term "they" when trying to describe these factors. For example, 'They must be mad to sell the stock here,' or 'Don't they know oil is cheap?' This chapter tries to get behind the "they" factor in markets, and to do that we have to consider the effect of feedback in financial news and information.

Simplify And Exaggerate?

What is news? Why do we watch, listen and read about news? Is it a spectator sport or something that affects our daily actions? In financial markets is the news at the beginning or the end of a cycle of activity? What about the age old market advice of buy on the rumour and sell on the fact?

If you ask a journalist for a definition of news you are likely to get the answer that news is anything that is change. It may describe the cause of the change, the change itself or the follow on consequences. For the reporter who is seeking to tell his viewers or readers what the latest news is, the concept of change is the key idea. In fact to develop this a little further, news is actually how change is seen from the outside. An event happens that causes change, perhaps a terrorist attack, a natural disaster, or a political leader resigns. This information is then reported by a journalist who is an observer outside the event, reporting it to us, other outsiders who may or may not have an interest. The journalist seeks to maintain his professional credibility by faithfully reporting the news and not letting personal views or prejudices colour his report – in this he seeks to remain an outsider and not be part of the story itself. The report has to be brief and succinct, it is an iron rule of reporting that one should never underestimate the attention span of the general public. In this way news has been gathered and packaged for us outsiders who may or may not be interested. This view of news and reporting may in fact be termed the classical explanation, but it is certainly not the only way to describe the information process.

In addition to news, the market generates and then bombards its participants with endless amounts of data, and in fact we may term this raw data. (If you like the above description of change, this data is the very material that records and shows the change as it happens.) This data may be price information, company statistics, government statistics, company announcements, stock indices created by news organisations – the list is almost endless. There are other higher forms of facts as well; these can be classified as information, knowledge and wisdom.

There is no definitive description of these groupings, but in general we can classify them as follows:

- Data: Facts which can be used for reasoning, discussion or calculation.
- Information: Data with context, obtained from investigation, study or instruction.

- Knowledge: Information with meaning and understanding.

- Wisdom: This term can be ridiculed, but let's say it is knowledge with insight.

This model is popular in the world of information technology and seeks to explain where value gets added to information. It seems quite different from the outsider's view of news. Here everyone is a participant in the process rather than just a passive consumer. On the basis of this theory, we can all take data and facts and formulate plans, strategies and draw conclusions, and in doing so we enhance and build upon the original raw data.

Do either of these models describe financial markets adequately? No. The idea that news is generated by an inside event and then consumed by outsiders is superficially similar to market activity, but ignores the huge chain reaction within markets when a change or surprise takes place. The market reaction to the initial news can be newsworthy in itself and can cause a cascading effect in market price action. Equally, market participants are obviously constantly tinkering with data to produce higher forms of information, such as charts, forecasts, market strategies and econometric models, but none of this really describes the dynamics of the marketplace.

In the last chapter we mentioned the weather forecaster – this is an example of the outsider who reports on change, or more precisely in this case seeks to predict future change. This predictive element is a step along the road from the reporter who gathers and reports facts – the journalist is not supposed to make predictions. All of this is very blurred of course, as many journalists are now employed as commentators to give background and colour to events and inevitably this strays into prediction. Also PR agencies and government spin doctors seek to manage news. This doesn't necessarily mean they can effect or predict change, but they can try to minimise or highlight the various changes going on and get reporters to concentrate on the favoured areas. Although the weather forecaster is both describing current conditions (the journalistic function essentially) and then predicting the future outcomes, the critical point is that they have no influence on that outcome. The weather report may predict rain tomorrow – but the act of reporting this prediction can have no direct effect on the weather itself. The process remains closed where the weather forecaster is outside looking in. Financial markets are totally different.

In The Hall Of Mirrors

We tend to view ourselves as outsiders when viewing the financial markets and our language often reveals this stance. We talk about stepping in to the market and equally about getting out of the market. We fondly believe that we can sit on the sidelines, observe the market, make investment judgements and then enter and trade. Unfortunately reality is not so straightforward. In truth we are all within the market, and this inclusive state can be considered to manifest itself in a number of forms. The weakest form of this state is the very small player, who may have only a few thousand dollars to play with, so any influence they have on the market will be relatively small, but conversely the influence the market may have on them can still be great. In what we might term the stronger form of this concept are the big players; all their actions, news and rumours about them are constantly in the market and here is the paradox of liquidity – the larger your presence in a market the more reliant you are on others. If you are managing a large fund, maybe many hundreds of millions of dollars, even your inactivity is a factor in the marketplace. Many times we hear the phrase "A Wall of Money" where the market believes that there is a large amount of money outside the market waiting to enter. The money may well be outside, but the information about its possible intention is most definitely within the market. This situation is amplified in small and emerging markets – hence their volatility and proclivity to sudden vacuums of liquidity. Where the information or supposed information overwhelms a market liquidity usually vanishes because few if any want to expose themselves to risk in such situations.

So we have a world where reporters are also commentators and watchers are also investors. It is like being trapped in a hall of mirrors, where it is difficult to discern who else is in the hall with you. This is why objective judgements in financial markets are so difficult, it is impossible to break out of this constant positive feedback loop of information, rumour, action and reaction.

Of course market commentators and forecasters are always trying to see the next move, or discern the change that will cause news and market reaction. But in this sort of system they are doomed to fail. As soon as they publicly announce their views the market adjusts accordingly. This is equally true for the big fund manager because as soon as they start trading the market becomes aware and adjusts accordingly. This is also the reason why nobody has yet dominated a market successfully. There are a few examples in small markets where attempts have been made to corner a market, but they nearly always end in failure. Probably the most well known recent example was the Hunt Brothers' ill-fated foray into the silver market in the 1980s. Some may dream of dominating a market with a secret and powerful model or system – images of a James Bond type villain sitting on a yacht in the Mediterranean manipulating markets may come to mind – but the self-correcting mechanism of the market is always one step ahead. Why would anyone want to trade against you if you were always right?

We spent some time considering models in the last chapter but there is a coda to that topic that fits neatly in this area. As we saw, model builders spend enormous amounts of time and energy carefully back-testing their systems and trying to ensure against any obvious flaws. However, there is one overwhelming problem with the theory of model trading in that the past test data can not include the effects on the market had the model already been there. This may seem a slightly bizarre argument, but in fact is crucial. Imagine you develop a fantastically successful system that picks market tops and bottoms with ease, and identifies trends accurately and flawlessly. Well what would happen? Once you are using your model to trade the market would gradually change characteristics, and the rules and principles that drive the relevant buy and sell signals would start to fail. Over time the success rate would fall away as the market somehow rumbles the system. This factor cannot be back engineered into models and so they contain a fundamental flaw. All model builders have to face the fact that their testing cannot account for the impact of the model itself. So another mirror distorts all the hard work just at the point of seeming success. Interestingly, it is generally accepted that in live real-time trading, results from models are always less than the various testing periods, often by as much as 50% of the predicted outcome. Perhaps, almost inevitably, the market starts to gradually overcome the model, and any anticipated trading edge is swiftly eroded in the real world.

The Sticky Balance

So how can we gain any advantage, what hope is there to overcome the "they" factor? Well the information process is not smooth and continuous; new facts, opinions, rumour, and news usually enters the market in a haphazard manner, after which the market reacts. This usually happens in a rather jerky and ill-defined way, this is where the information inefficiencies lie; and from these inefficiencies the bright, well informed and the lucky, can profit.

One way to consider how information hits the market is to imagine a set of balance scales, with the pans holding piles of information. One pan holds any positive information about the market, the other holds anything negative. News, rumours and plain facts drop constantly into one or other of these pans, leading to an overall balancing position that represents the net emotion and thinking of the market. But there is a twist – our imaginary scales are sticky, so don't always react straightaway when a new piece of data is dropped into one of the pans. Then, quite suddenly, the scales may shift. This is pretty much what happens when markets try to digest news – there is no smooth information flow and the trick is to try and anticipate when the scales (i.e. the market realisation) will suddenly tip and change. The news and information is not important in itself, it is market reaction, or lack of, that is the key. Hence the title of this chapter – quanta are very tiny movements, in markets it is often the tiniest movement, the lightest of last straws on the camels back if you like, that sets forth the cascading market move.

Somewhere in this confusing world stand the regulators and in the past twenty years or so they have developed an idea called insider dealing. This seeks to penalise any participant who gains an unfair advantage through obtaining market sensitive (perhaps we should say relevant) information. When we say penalise this in fact can mean heavy fines, a criminal record and even a jail sentence in many jurisdictions. This leads to a world of endless shades of grey and at what point does the discovery of new news become an unfair advantage that can be subject to regulatory scrutiny? Whilst some instances may seem obvious (directors with access to internal company information) other cases are not always so easy. Interestingly of course, this scrutiny by the regulators creates actions that also become part of the equation – they themselves are within the system. They are not, as they may presume, outsiders drawing up the rules of the game and in fact their rule writing has a more complex outcome. The existence of their rules is just another mirror that reflects and sometimes distorts market activity. For example, the activity of government regulation in the California electricity market was a good if rather extreme example of the dangers of their involvement. Similar problems were also apparent in the UK insurance industry where the local regulator moved the goal posts a number of times on liquidity and solvency rules. Their actions in creating these rules in the first place has been to direct market attention to the insurance companies' investments. Naturally enough, the market has learnt the regulatory rules and then ruthlessly hunts down any company that may be close to the defined thresholds. (Curiously this has interesting parallels with the market attacks on stop loss orders.)

Top of the list though must be the Basel II Capital Adequacy rules that have had more than a passing role in the fall out from the credit crunch of 2008. The regulations seek to use market data, credit agency ratings and sophisticated models to assess and estimate credit defaults and possible recovery rates of bad debts. Based on these calculations banks can adjust their capital base up and down. This has had the unwanted (and potentially dangerous) effect of reducing capital requirements in good times, and increasing the need for capital in bad times. This can fuel speculative lending in booms (after all the models reflect these good times by using the benign data to keep signalling good times ahead) and will cause banks to slam on the brakes when things start to turn nasty (which is pretty much what is happening following the credit crunch). Even worse, this could have been predicted – the Russian Bond Crisis of August 1998 amply demonstrated that when left to their own devices, risk models produce perverse results and advice. Here, risk models made banks ditch perfectly good assets, and caused previously uncorrelated markets to be trapped into a lockstep of forced selling. Basel II is in danger of reinforcing this reaction during crisis periods.

All of these are magnificent examples of the self-fulfilling delusions of regulatory control. In extreme circumstances it might be that regulatory actions can cause more damage than if no rules were in place.

No discussion of this confusing and perpetually inchoate world would be complete without mentioning some ideas from particle physics. This is dangerous ground and often the source of much pointless discussion. Markets may or may not be subject to the rules of physics, but what is more certain is that some principles in physics offer a very useful metaphor to describe the seemingly confusing behaviour of the marketplace.

In particular Heisenberg's Uncertainty Principle, that says the more precisely the position is determined, the less precisely the momentum is known. This theory obviously applies to the world of quantum mechanics and sub-atomic particles, but also it does have echoes for the problem of understanding markets. This idea was originally known as the principle of indeterminacy, which quite neatly describes the conundrum of trying to fathom financial markets.

If we know where a market is at any point in time, can we really know its momentum and direction? Equally if we know the momentum and direction can we ever tell where it currently is? If this sounds obtuse consider the following real life slippage problem; how to execute a buy order in a bid market? Rest assured your fill will not be where you first thought it should be and once you have been filled and you know where the market is, suddenly you don't know where it is going next!

Trying to understand the motives of the market is hellishly difficult; the endless actions and reactions fuse together to provide a very complex picture. What is clear, however, is that our task is made more difficult by being within the system itself. In fact it may mean we are unable to fully understand the dynamics because we cannot get outside to look in and observe independently without affecting the system itself. Such complex arguments are rejected by the market of course. There the creed is to always look for the simple answer, so that is what we will do next.

Simple Explanations Sold Cheap

In Jane Austen's novel *Mansfield Park* one of the characters, Mary Crawford declares, 'If an opinion is generally held, it is probably true'. Clearly the fictitious Miss Crawford would have been an avid follower and believer in financial market news.

As was mentioned earlier, news is always edited, condensed and packaged. This is how we like our news; few people will bother to read a newspaper article of much more than a thousand words, and in fact many articles are barely five hundred words in length. Television news is a succession of very short sound bites, and little else. Is this because we are genuinely too busy to spend more time on news, or perhaps after the headlines the story itself and then the follow up background and facts tend to bore us? Certainly this is the case in financial markets, which are not known for their patience, and where few players have a long attention span. Intellectual myopia and a desire for quick answers are the ruling passions.

Earlier we spent considerable time looking at the perennial race for knowing the future. The headlong rush to know what's going to happen next also spawns an interesting phenomenon called the market story. Market logic states that everything happens for a reason but rather strangely, random behaviour is always dismissed as being far too outlandish an explanation. Market players always believe there is a motive behind every flutter in a share or commodity price, nobody believes that a lot of the time asset prices just fluctuate in a random and meaningless manner. (No wonder the statisticians have had such an uphill climb to get anyone to agree with their arguments that seek to demolish charts and show the futility of trying to make future price predictions.) With this set of beliefs the market always has to have a story to explain what's just happened, what's going on now and how it will be important or not in the future. Whatever the market, at any point in time there is an overarching reason given for why things are as they are. These stories are then recycled and packaged by business news reporters and TV programmes and often become business news. Obviously a lot of business news is about raw data and facts, such as company announcements, or factual data on share prices, but interspersed with that are the commentary pieces that originally started as the market story.

Often you see or hear journalistic pieces say 'The market thinks...', 'Traders believe further large buying interest may emerge from the Far East...' or 'Wall Street expects more falls in Latin American bonds because...' These comments may be true or they may be total nonsense, the truth is nobody knows. But as we now know the truth is of little importance in these matters, it's much more important to know the dominant story and how everyone is reacting to it.

Tell Me The Future Now!

Needless to say our old friends the forecasters are always willing to step into this particular arena. This ground is particularly fertile and attractive to the forecasters because it allows them to sound informed and authoritative and reinforce their air of knowing the future when in fact most of the time they are hunting around to give a plausible explanation for the present and occasionally even still trying to explain the past. All of this behaviour has got more prevalent (should that be manic?) with the explosion in media channels which blast the endless thoughts of these forecasters on a 24-hour global basis. There are sound commercial reasons for all this frenetic activity. The ability to show that your analysis was either faster or more incisive is seen as a key driver in the important battle of differentiation. If you can persuade your client base that your analysis is smarter, better informed or just plain faster than the competition this will hopefully persuade them to do that most important of things – trade with you.

Most market players are avaricious consumers of news – trading rooms are packed with television screens playing any number of news channels, and every market quotation system has a constant rolling headline news section. In addition there are huge numbers of specialist news and background briefing services – once again there is a tidal wave of information. Virtually all the large information vendors have their roots in news, and today the gathering and dissemination of business news is a multi-billion dollar industry. News is seen as the most vital source of information in the trading room. All of this has become a marketing man's paradise, with news reports and updates including fatuous titles such as 'Leading Edge', 'Breaking News', 'Power Analysis', 'Insider's Report' (is this one for the regulators, or perhaps just the advertising standards people if the regulators find no wrong-doing?) Often reporters do their piece to camera on a stock exchange trading floor, or on the trading floor of a large bank or brokerage house, to add to the sense of urgency and immediacy. As a result we have the bizarre spectacle of traders in trading rooms watching television programmes coming from other trading rooms – a close parody of the film *The Truman Show* perhaps? This is an almost perfect example of the closed loop of information that often circulates around the market.

The lifecycle of many market stories is extremely short, they can often be measured in hours rather than days, but are vital ammunition to the salesman, who can use it as a reason to call the customer. A bit like a hook in a popular song these news flashes offer a memorable tagline with which the salesman can push the bigger theme. They are nearly always vague: 'Have you seen the news from Russia? This could be bad for government bonds, did you get our latest research? Do you need a price in Treasuries?' You get the picture.

Once in a while though a theme just grows and grows, and a catch phrase or glib comment becomes a story that runs for weeks or even months. A good example of this was in early 2001 when, after the initial shock of the US economy hitting the buffers (which virtually the whole financial world failed to see coming), someone (in the best traditions of such phenomena nobody seems to know who) coined the phrase, the "V Shaped Recovery". The market really loved this phrase, it helped express hope for the distressed equity bulls who had failed to dump their tech stocks earlier in the year, it gave hope to the long-time bulls of the US dollar who wanted to believe the trend would just go on and on and it allowed the forecasters to wash away their failure to spot this setback, and to concentrate on the good times ahead. Of course it was all nonsense, but reams of research, endless TV interviews and newspaper articles hung on the premise that the "V" would take off at any minute. When this failed to materialise some even surmised that it would be a "U" shaped outcome and that the upturn was coming soon. Of course it never happened (more an "L" shape then?) and after a while everybody in the market got bored and moved on to the next story.

All harmless stuff you might say, and just normal market rumours, but there is a far greater intensity of experience thanks to global communications. Again more news, stories, and information but precious little knowledge. Given that our aim is to make money from markets it is very clear what dangerous and wealth destroying information is often pumped around the market. Occasionally it can be comic; let's recall that in 1986 the US dollar had a large fall one day on a rumour from Tokyo that the US President, Ronald Reagan, had had a massive heart attack. In fact Reagan was safely ensconced in the White House – whereas there was a true story that British 1960s singer Lonnie Donegan had had a heart attack in a Tokyo hotel! A misunderstanding or perhaps a Japanese accent mispronouncing the singer's name, so that it may have sounded like 'Ronnie Reagan', led to mayhem – well for a couple of hours or so.

A similar incident, though of a more serious nature, happened at the time of the attempted coup against the Soviet President Gorbachev in August 1991. A TV news report wrongly stated that Gorbachev, who was under house arrest, was continuing to be kept at his dacha in the Crimea (possibly a sign of a serious escalation and a deepening of the crisis) whereas the report should have said he was returning to the Kremlin from the Crimea (a completely different and much more peaceful outcome) – again there was frantic action in financial markets for a couple of hours. In this case the subsequent retraction and correction by the news organisation caused even more panic than the initial bad news, as the market scrambled to undo the positions it had taken on in response to the initial report. Of course there will be mistakes and errors in news reporting, and many market stories turn out to be pure fiction, but the scale of global communications has magnified their impact. We can now all make our mistakes faster and have them more easily transmitted than ever before.

On The Contrary

Why do we all listen to and often believe all of this stuff? Well it comes back to the problem of control. Human nature likes to feel in control, particularly where the circumstances can be unpredictable and potentially damaging. Randomness and the fell clutch of circumstance is not welcome, particularly in financial markets. We often hear the phrase that markets hate uncertainty. This is definitely true and if certainty cannot be easily found, the market often invents a story to take its place. The market story is yet another comfort blanket for those being tossed about in the financial storm.

Needless to say there is a counter culture to all of this – the contrarians, who may sound like a 17th century religious sect but are in fact people who seek to try and trade against the consensus. An admirable aim, but far easier said than done. Once again the consensus may take time to form and often flexes around in bouts of madness, and the critical element of timing often stymies the contrarian. For example, plenty of valuation indicators showed that high tech and internet stocks were massively overvalued as early as the end of 1998, but the rally sky-rocketed onwards until March 2000 when gravity suddenly took hold. Needless to say, very few players managed to trade out of their longs or go short at the top. So having a contrarian and sceptical view is extremely healthy – but in itself it will not be enough to make money. Indeed it seems the fate of many contrarians is to lose money by having the right idea but failing to finesse their timing sufficiently. This really feeds back into our earlier look at the "S" curve – in theory such curves are very obvious, but in practice it is extremely difficult to time contrarian trades.

Often one hears arguments from chartists and technical analysts that the reason their analysis and understanding of the market is superior is because they block out all the news and opinions that flood the market. Instead they only concentrate on their charts and indicators, but this means they fall into the trap discussed in the previous section. Any successful chart patterns or indicators become news themselves, and get fed into the same distorting machine. Being a chartist doesn't make you an outsider looking in. Indeed charts are now a major source of market stories. Any news that, for example, a 200-day moving average is under pressure, or that an oversold/overbought indicator is at supposedly extreme levels, this is flashed around the market almost instantly.

The lesson about market stories and all the hullabaloo that accompanies them is clear – remain sceptical and be slow to act. Again, psychological studies have shown that under stress humans usually react by being active and having a desire to do something. When market players feel stress from a rumour or story they feel they should act, buy or sell, or just do something. This action is often egged on by the bonus rewarded salesman – and is nearly always wrong. This is an interesting counterpoint to the massive issue of freezing when things are going wrong. Two sets of impulses seem to be at work here, we seem often compelled to trade in response to news or analysis, and then totally seize up when the position goes wrong. It would appear that absolute fortunes could be saved if we declined to seize the initiatives and opportunities that are on offer from fresh news.

Of course everyone wants and needs access to the facts, but it is vital for the investor to realise how these are often loaded with inaccurate or flawed interpretations. It is in fact very difficult to keep a level head given the megaphone volume of the research that is now pumped into the market on a constant basis. The advent of wall-to-wall news, research and instant emails is unlikely to help you become rich – a better start may be to just turn off the business TV programme.

Chaos, Correlation And Co-Incidence

Back in 2002 Brazil won the World Cup, which is exactly what was expected. Why, because they were the favourites? Well, no, actually they weren't, in fact there were other much more fancied teams, but all of these crashed out of the competition fairly early on. But Brazil were bound to win the cup – it was in the numbers. What? Well in the few weeks leading up to the competition in the Far East, somebody noticed the following little relationship:

- Brazil had previously won the World Cup in 1994, and before that in 1970. If you add 1994 to 1970 you have a total of 3964.

- Argentina won the World Cup last in 1986, and before that in 1978. If you add 1986 to 1978 you have a total of 3964.

- Germany last won the World Cup in 1990, and before that in 1974. Yes if you add those numbers together you once again get 3964.

Now for the clever (dare one say predictive) part. Applying this formula (which has been right three times before) we can take the total of 3964, deduct 2002 for this year's competition, and get the answer 1962. Clearly whoever were champions in 1962 would win in 2002. Well Brazil won in 1962 and did so again this time! All of this calculation (coincidence and wishful thinking more like) came crashing down with the results of the 2006 competition. Using our trusted system(!) we could have calculated that Brazil should have won again – but unfortunately Italy ruined things by lifting the trophy.

So what's going on with this little formula? Well in fact very little. It's just a very nice example of coincidence, nothing more; no supernatural force is guiding the destiny of World Cup winners, the results above may just be a fluke, but they are also extremely selective. It's hard not to be impressed by the initial run of success for this little formula, but in doing so we are forgetting some very important factors. The data above is a very narrow selection, there are plenty of examples where the formula just doesn't work, and as there have only been seventeen World Cup competitions, the data sample is just too small to be meaningful. Once again the human mind is impressed by statistics that are in fact insufficient and therefore probably unreliable – as was neatly demonstrated by the 2006 outcome.

Large amounts of academic research has shown time after time that we are over impressed by coincidences. We place too much faith in seemingly amazing coincidences when in fact many such events are far more commonplace than we imagine. Given the mindset of financial markets it is not surprising that many events are given undue attention because they are seen as significant when in fact they are merely coincidences. It is more interesting and impressive to reel off an amazing relationship in the marketplace than to coolly stand back and see that it was just a coincidence with no serious meaning. As we observed earlier the market is gripped by meaning and relevance; events are always supposed to have an underlying motive behind them. The term coincidence is rarely if ever heard in the market, it is simply not recognised as a legitimate explanation for any market move. Chance is given little house room in such an atmosphere.

There are numerous examples of market lore that are in fact only coincidences. One of the best known is the Super Bowl Theory of Wall Street that states rather incredibly that if a team from the old National League wins the Super Bowl competition, then equities will have a good year, and equally if a team from the old American Football League wins, equities will suffer. The fact that these two leagues have been reorganised hasn't stopped the pundits from invoking this indicator based on the old arrangements. Rather startlingly the success record is very good, with a current hit rate of approximately 80%. But it remains a coincidence and not a signal of future market moves. Another even more frivolous relationship was said to exist between the London stock market and the length of ladies skirts! The higher the market, the shorter the skirt. (Presumably dedicated followers of fashion were tending towards lower hemlines before the bursting of the internet bubble.) Slightly more serious is the so-called January barometer, this theory states that however a stock market performs in January this will set the tone for the rest of the year. This indicator has also had some success, but one hesitates to base an investment strategy upon it – though no doubt followers exclaim the powerful predictive qualities of the Barometer. Needless to say the availability of information and computing power to trawl through it is leading to more and more of these "amazing" facts.

Of course what's really going on here is back-engineering, or the fitting of facts. This being the classic trap of curve fitting that model traders strive so hard to avoid. Indeed the only real surprise is that there aren't more of these coincidences dressed up as important financial facts and indicators. The human mind has an enormous propensity for order, people seem to like nothing more than to flit around finding strange relationships and claiming the amazing fact that they exist. Again the reason is control, and the never ending desire to exercise it. It doesn't matter if you haven't a clue where the stock market is going; just watch the Super Bowl final or observe the length of girls' skirts, and by understanding the relevant relationship you will get the answer. Readers will once again detect another example of the almost palpable desperation of those attempting to know the future.

In contrast to coincidence, the term correlation is heard in the markets all the time. This is a powerful word, redolent with images of careful academic and rigorous study and as such many market participants often give too much weight to so called important correlations, but again they are frequently grabbing at the illusion of control. Certainly such work is much more scientific and mathematical in its approach to market relationships than any half-baked ideas based on single coincidence. Indeed a whole research industry has grown up to examine and test correlations in the financial markets. Some correlations are in fact common sense; one would expect major oil companies to have broadly similar share price activity and it would be entirely normal for their share prices to react in the same manner to any particular piece of news. Equally some currencies that have close economic links tend to track one another around in fairly stable orbits. Occasionally correlations appear that are not intuitive, but seem to be consistently working – these have usually been discovered by the economics teams within banks and brokers and are all part of the usual output of such departments. Many of these relationships break down soon after they become generally known, as the market's trading activity has the effect of destroying the happy relationship. Hence the feeling that things always correlate until one puts on the trade!

Of course some correlations are nothing of the sort, being just coincidences that have not been properly analysed, usually through too small or narrow a data set. A nice example being that after the war it was noticed that the growth of TV aerials and the increase in the incidence of cancer were expanding at very similar rates. So this correlation leads to the bizarre and totally wrong conclusion that more TV aerials meant more cancer! In fact one might say that correlations are in the eye of the beholder. In the herd-like and self-examining world of finance some false or bogus correlations can gain serious market support and end up as a self-fulfilling prophecy.

Unfortunately virtually all of the work on correlation analysis is by definition highly mathematical, and tends to put the market to sleep. Much of the analysis is soon bogged down in arcane arguments about normal and log normal distributions, GARCH modelling (Generalised Auto-Regressive Conditional Hetroskedasticity is the less than catchy full title!), fat distribution tails, extreme value theory and others. As a result much of it is either ignored, misused or misunderstood, and needless to say losses are sometimes incurred by those betting on dead certainties revealed by unexpected correlations. Whilst often very clever and perhaps giving new and interesting insights, correlations should come with the usual health warnings. Just because assets have had a strong correlation in the past, there is no guarantee that they will in the future. In that sense they are uncomfortably close to charts, once again we are drilling down into past results to try and find a meaningful and important relationship that otherwise would have remained hidden. Also, as soon as that relationship is revealed to market there is always a potential chance that it will breakdown. Hence the previously mentioned fear that correlations always work until you put a trade on.

Again at a very simplistic level there is quite a good analogy here with the physics theory of Schrödinger's Cat; this much quoted thought experiment does rather suit the maddening fact that profitable correlation trading is often just out of our grasp. (Also, whilst invoking the famous feline one could consider the following; I have known people buy lottery tickets and not look up the numbers to see if they have won until some days or even weeks after the draw. The reason being given that they feel good from having the ticket without having the almost certainty that it's a loser confirmed. This is a great example of utility theory but may also be an example of Schrödinger's experiment, for these people the ticket still has potential right up until they check the number and then reality washes away their vain hopes.)

Occasionally markets have what may be called government inspired correlations. One of the best examples of these being the so-called European convergence trade. In the run up to the European Monetary Union bond yields of the various participating countries were wide apart, but with the advent of the single currency they would converge as Euroland started to centre itself around one monetary and interest rate policy. So previously disparate markets started to move together, with many market players profiting from the appropriate bond spread trades. Again this is common sense, and totally unsurprising. But dangers still lurk even for this racing certainty, the whole idea is predicated on government policy not mathematical models, so the investor has to watch government actions not the maths. Interestingly as the euro celebrated its tenth birthday in January 2009 some of the credit spreads have actually started to show large deviations, in particular the smaller economies as against the core economy of Germany. This could be taken as a sign that the euro has a fatal weakness at its heart, in that the process of full integration and harmonising is flawed and failing to come to fruition. So the correlation effect may be breaking down for the same reasons it was first detected – politics.

Sometimes previous correlations breakdown in a spectacular manner – previously stable relationships blow up and market activity is often hysterical as investors try to unwind positions. This usually happens when many investors seem to draw the same conclusions, and seek comfort from correlations and therefore somehow believe their positions are safer with more predictable outcomes. These circumstances often lead to abnormally low volatility profiles, and when a blow up does occur, volatility typically explodes and liquidity disappears almost instantly. The resultant losses can be ruinous, and are often experienced by investors who had chosen the strategy as it looked a lower risk!

Blindfold Boxing

We shouldn't leave these topics without a few words about chaos – not the current fashion for non-linear mathematics, but just the sheer unpredictability of financial markets and all the news and information that swirls around them. In many ways being in financial markets is a little like blindfold boxing; occasionally you land a heavy punch and also from time to time you are hit from an unexpected quarter, in both cases they were often totally unpredictable. As we have seen the automatic response of human nature to such conditions is to seize at any pointers, and to rush around a lot and be active. In financial trading both these courses are unwise. There are commentators and market observers that are good at calling the market direction, but it is safer and wiser to try and develop this skill yourself. Equally it makes sense to be balanced and considered in any trading activity – there are large quantities of evidence that over-trading is a most damaging approach for an investor. As we have seen the costs of constantly trading can be extensive, and often the original financial motives for this frenetic activity are lost in a desire to be reacting or being seen to do something because of events around us. This chaos element, or at least perceived chaos, is a powerful agent that sucks people into unwise investment decisions. We cannot be outside the market and we cannot divorce ourselves from the "they" factor, but all sensible players seek to minimise the corrosive effects. In financial information less is truly more.

The Persistence Of Memory

Probably Salvador Dali's most famous and enduring image is the painting with the melting clocks. It is entitled *The Persistence of Memory* and is an ideal visual metaphor for this particular piece about market information and its interpretation.

Whilst trying to understand the present and figure out the future are extremely complex and difficult problems in financial trading, is there anything we need to consider about the past? The answer is definitely yes – we have already seen how the past is a major source of information for market players, but there are also other aspects to be considered.

For a business with a well-known disdain for old news and an often short attention span, the financial trading markets carry a lot of baggage about the past. Market history weighs on both the individual and the marketplace as a whole. As an extreme example the very number 1929 has become synonymous with the year of the Wall Street Crash and is known around the world by both market players and non-financial people. At a more personal level virtually all market players have past experiences that weigh on their current activities, as does the man in the street who often gets sucked into market fads and fashions just as they are peaking, indeed these people often have the most burning memories of the market. How each individual uses and learns, or in some cases fails to learn, from their trading experience is yet another reflecting mirror that helps make up the whole distorted information picture.

One effect of the past is to collect and recycle old market stories, some of which enter legend and others become the basis for sonorous advice that is often given but rarely followed. Virtually every market has myths and beliefs about certain past trading activities. As we saw earlier, the human mind is gripped by round numbers and when coupled with a huge capacity to believe that every market move has an underlying motive it is not surprising that myths grow on such fertile ground. It is common to hear that markets are ruled by fear and greed; though it seems more likely that the two dominant emotions are actually fear and hope, both spiced with an overwhelming desire not to miss out. It is an old saw that bull markets have to climb a wall of fear, and to that we can add the observation that bear markets slide down a slope of unfulfilled hope. Something holds back many people until a bull market is well and truly underway, and equally many cling to hope and their long positions well after a bear market has started. Investor's views and ideas about the past definitely colour their trading habits – though ironically few seem to have a truly big picture understanding of the market.

It was a common complaint of older and wiser(?) heads in the late 1990s that there were far too many in the equity market who had only experienced a bull market and had not even experienced the 1987 stock market crash. Instead of being bad news this should have been welcomed, in the mysterious world of "they" it is comforting at least to know some of the weaknesses of your potential trading adversaries. Equally the post-1987 "new boys" could have argued that missing out on that crash hadn't paralysed their view of the market – they were definitely all long during the great bull run of the 1990s. Needless to say the long period of very benign credit conditions up until the summer of 2007 led many astray – one needed to have experienced the financial hurricanes of the mid 1970s to have any idea what the resulting credit debacle could be like.

Occasionally this conditioning from the past adds to market inefficiency and investor irrationality. For many years large numbers of mainstream investors have shunned the commodity markets believing them to be too volatile. In fact studies show that they are no more volatile than major stocks, and are non-correlated with stocks so can add diversity and reduce portfolio risk. But conventional wisdom states commodities are dangerous and so many stay away. Undoubtedly commodity markets are relatively small, and there are some fearful stories about limit days and margin calls in the futures pits, but the facts show they are not as toxic as many believe. Indeed they are positively benign compared to some of the spectacular blow ups seen in split asset investment trusts, some Telecom debt issues etc. Clearly though commodities suffer from giving a dog a bad name.

So this is where perhaps we can invoke the imagery of Dali's clocks, in financial markets the past is a looming presence – and has different meanings and impacts for the different range of players, all with their own motives, risk appetites and investment horizons. The clocks seem to be running at vastly different speeds for different investors, for some the hands spin frantically as the latest figures hit the market, for others à la Dali, the clock faces can gently melt and slide almost as if time was running dead slow. Certainly the day trader and the treasurer of a large multinational have a vastly different view of both the future and the past; but they meet at that same point in the market – the present price. In simple economic terms the bid-offer price at any one time is the sum total of supply and demand, but it reveals little else. (What else do you need to work with, the price condenses and collapses everything to a single point, chartists would forcefully argue?) The price conceals motive, risk appetite and perhaps hope and fear. It is pregnant with the past, and charged with endless hopes for the future.

When we talk about the past we have to be careful. In theory the past is fixed and cannot be re-written, but it can be ignored, forgotten or misunderstood. In financial markets all of these happen, as market sentiment veers heavily towards the short term. The recent past is raked over endlessly by commentators, analysts and the market players themselves. Every piece of monthly economic data is religiously compared with the same data from the previous month, and occasionally from the same period the previous year. Chartists are big consumers of past data, and can possibly be criticised for only being able to successfully map these previous moves. The model builders and traders are also big users of past data. But in general beyond one year, the market's attention span seems to fall off a cliff. Somewhat like a mole that is constantly digging away to move forward, the market throws behind it all but the most recent data. In the push to move forward even a year ago is an age, and five or ten years ago can seem prehistoric.

That said, market price history is more valued these days and has some commercial attractions for the big data companies, who now religiously collect and store price data that can then be re-sold to chartists and modellers. (In a sense this business is a little bit like the record companies re-selling their back catalogues with Greatest Hits albums.) But still information is patchy beyond ten or certainly fifteen years ago. The exchange traded data series' are normally longer and more reliable, but the accuracy and depth of data – particularly for over-the-counter markets before the late 1970s – is sparse and sometimes non-existent. There are one or two extremely long and accurate series, for example the Dow Jones Industrial Average, with just over 100 years of history recorded and kept since its inception. For those wishing to study pure economic indicators, the economic time series for the United States and Great Britain are relatively good since the 1950s, but most other countries have poor records of such data.

So what? Does this really matter? After all markets are constantly evolving and so past data must be irrelevant to today's market conditions and characteristics. Well actually market history is important, and the more high quality past data the better. In our rush to see the future we often forget that the market has a tendency to follow similar paths to those taken in the past, even if it does not repeat itself exactly. The study of past market relationships can work well in a broad sense but such data can't and won't tell us about the precise future, though it can give us useful advice about potential outcomes.

This may seem to contradict the earlier observations about forecasters, and the assertion that you cannot use past data to predict the future. The earlier comments do hold true, but market history can tell us about market sentiment and psychology, particularly at extremes. There are problems in this idea in that it is difficult to know what is the extreme. This is the trap that contrarians can fall into because it's just impossible to know precisely when the extreme will topple over.

Whilst accepting all these very necessary caveats, probably one of the best uses of past data is the one least considered, studying very long-term trends and relationships. A certain amount of lip service is paid towards remembering the big picture but in truth most market participants are blissfully unaware of the long-term ebbs and flows in markets. There are undercurrents in financial markets that seem to stay in place over many years if not decades and here again one has to be alert to the correlation trap. Studying and understanding these moves and links between markets and indeed asset classes tends to be overlooked by the short-term crowd. This is the topic we will examine in the next chapter, but first there is one large group left to discuss and understand.

Meddling Princes

In this fog of information and misunderstanding the one remaining group we haven't examined are those who we may term the authorities, or perhaps the official sector – in other words I am referring to governments and politicians. We have already seen how regulators fade in and out of financial life, but there are a number of other official sector bodies that are often key players in financial markets, and can have enormous influence and sometimes control over the markets. In this sense they are just another distorting mirror in the equation, and as usual often mistakenly see themselves as outsiders rather than insiders within the trading process. For the investor or speculator they can be enormously important – though only the most naïve would believe they necessarily have the market's best interests at heart.

A variety of sources including at least two references in the Bible warn us not to put our trust in Princes, and this sage advice certainly holds true when examining the record of governments and politicians regarding financial markets. Aside from being prime movers in the ebbs and flows of the regulatory cycle, they are on occasion central to the workings of many markets. Clearly the most obvious of these are money markets, the control of the currency and the setting of interest rates. In many cases this responsibility has either partially or entirely been moved from government agencies to central banks with varying degrees of independence. However, no matter how much one is led to believe in the independence of such institutions, very close links to government and politics will always remain. From the perspective of the investor this matters because politically driven decisions are rarely based on sound financial principles – the domestic political calendar is always a significant input into any decision, and this frequently is not in line with market considerations or concerns.

Ill-Fated Interventions

As a result we frequently see government inspired moves in markets that are often ill-advised and poorly executed. Nothing illustrates this better than the fate of sterling since the Second World War. In 1967 Britain experienced a forced devaluation that Prime Minister Harold Wilson stated would not affect 'the pound in your pocket.' Perhaps "forced" is the wrong word here, what in fact happened was that reality caught up with British government policy, and Wilson's empty assurance was soon revealed for the arrant nonsense that it was. Following on from this supposed national humiliation the pound was allowed to float on the currency markets, though sink may have been the more appropriate description at the time. But no sooner had the government let go of trying to maintain a fixed currency rate against the US dollar than they decided to flirt, in 1973, with the first attempt at a European exchange rate system. This first British attempt at fixing the pound within a trading band of currencies with European currencies – descriptively named Snake – failed very rapidly, with sterling leaving within weeks of entry.

Free markets finally got on top of the government in the 1980s (fitting in nicely with the regulatory cycle described in Chapter Five) and the early years of the Thatcher administration saw the abolition of exchange controls and total freedom in currency trading. Politics and government interference soon came right back into vogue though, this time with Chancellor Nigel Lawson shadowing the Deutschmark as a precursor to entry into the European Exchange Rate Mechanism (ERM). By the autumn of 1992, sterling just couldn't hold within the ERM – or more precisely the market believed the government couldn't afford the political damage the ERM was thought to be doing to the UK economy. So along came Black Wednesday and Lawson's successor, Norman Lamont, singing in his bath. This was then followed by another period of uninterrupted free trading of sterling before the vexed question of entry into the euro came over the horizon. This time around the government has stood aside from any definitive action and has used masterful inactivity as its motto – this has suited both the economy and sterling. Clearly the merry-go-round of government involvement in the currency markets continues.

In all of this an important fact had been forgotten, or at least ignored by successive British governments. Exchange rates are prices, just like everything else and so they can be fixed or controlled like any other price, but there is a cost for this. We as investors have to remember that governments have no special access to knowledge and often ignore or fail to understand these costs. Almost inevitably these costs reassert themselves elsewhere in an economy and often with disastrous consequences. It was a proud boast of the Russian Communist party that a loaf of bread was the same cost in 1990 as it had been after the revolution in 1917. The Soviet authorities just froze the price, but the consequences of this and a number of other similar hare-brained command economy ideas was to lead to virtual national bankruptcy, a population that was getting steadily poorer and a falling life expectancy by the time the communists were finally thrown out. Indeed Russians used to ruefully joke that their country was Upper Volta with Inter-Continental Ballistic Missiles! The Russian experience was hardly an isolated example, nor are such situations confined to the distant past. The events in many Latin America currency markets over the past ten or fifteen years – for example the Brazilian Real Devaluation Crisis of 1999 – have shown the dangers of price fixing (trying to peg currencies again, which, interestingly, is often a favourite policy objective).

Government meddling is not restricted to just financial markets; the antics of European governments and the common agricultural policy are an object lesson in how such interference can have extremely bizarre consequences. Probably one of the saddest and most depressing statistics in the world today is that half the globe live on an income of less than US$1 a day whereas every cow in Europe (or at least their owners) receives a subsidy of US$2 a day. This seems to be a case of official "we know best" how to run the market gone mad.

As market players there is virtually nothing we can do about such government activities, and usually it can be difficult to profit from such situations. With currency blow ups in particular the rewards for being short of a currency prior to the inevitable correction can be spectacular, but the costs of maintaining short positions can be punishing through exchange controls and very high interest rates. But to successfully defend a currency a government needs a comprehensive strategy covering both the defined target exchange rate and domestic interest rates, together with a willingness to spend large amounts of hard cash in defending the currency in the markets. Unfortunately for the UK government in 1992 they only had half the structure in place. They quite happily tied sterling to an exchange rate trading band but the cost of shorting the currency was relatively cheap as domestic politics and the state of the UK economy made it impossible to raise interest rates to the levels required to dissuade speculators. When the explosion came many shrewd players had appropriate short positions at relatively low interest rates and cleaned up when the Bank of England and the government gave up trying to hold the exchange rate in the market; and all at the expense of the British taxpayer one might add.

Such government activities in the marketplace are very unlikely to ever go away, all we can do is to be extremely wary of them. It was a recurring theme of 1967 and then again in 1992 that British government ministers continued to give vocal public support to the currency fixing regimes when it was becoming increasingly clear that they were unsustainable. This also happened with similar vehemence in both Brazil – in 1989-90 – and Argentina – in 2001 – when they also had to face up to the truth that the costs of their policies had become demonstrably unsustainable. Government actions are not just statements from politicians and officials, they also use hard cash to try and contain markets, in effect they can find themselves trying to push water uphill. It is at this point they stop being spectators and find themselves as players on the pitch; and perhaps change the nature of the game more than they realise.

Paradoxically the entry of governments into the marketplace often triggers the very activity they are trying to suppress – the more politicians publicly decry speculation and speak-out against irresponsible markets the more they focus market attention on their difficulties. Attempts to influence market price action through intervention, or by rewriting the rules, seem at best to have limited success and at worst have led to serious financial difficulties for some countries. The act of drawing a line in the sand in a financial market to defend or protect a policy can in effect set up a target to be shot at, and this is frequently the outcome. It's as if the authorities extinguish one of their most powerful weapons – uncertainty.

At the beginning of this chapter that strange group "they" was mentioned; as we come to study how we absorb and analyse information, news and rumours, it becomes clearer that "they" do not exist – it is really us but through a fog of distortion and confusion. This will never change, and herein lays both a problem and an opportunity. The "us" problem as we should now call it, shows that we need to examine our own motives, how we filter information and news, and what psychological biases and tricks we play with ourselves to rationalise our market behaviour and performance. This is bound to be hard and problematical. Equally though, as everyone is suffering from the same problems, it might be that others' mistakes unfold nicely to offer up inconsistencies and inefficiencies that can be exploited.

8

This Is The First Time Since The Last Time

'History never repeats itself, but sometimes it rhymes.'

Mark Twain

The future is unknown, but some factors from the past seem to persist; is this really true and can we profit from such observations? As we have seen, believing that one can always accurately forecast the future is both naïve and usually unprofitable, unless one is selling the advice rather than taking it. However, there are one or two constants that seem to suggest that there may be loose relationships in financial markets that may repeat themselves, or at least vaguely resonate, and as such are worthy of some examination. This chapter sets out to look at some of these relationships and to investigate if they have any potential.

Ebbs And Flows

If we stand back from day-to-day banking, broking and trading, trends and themes seem to emerge. There is an immediate danger here, much of this picture can be distorted by our selectivity in looking at market data and asset prices, and so has to be treated with some caution. However, at the broadest and coarsest level there still appear to be certain financial relationships and interplay between markets. Indeed many believe there are underlying cycles that drive financial affairs – if so, what is the evidence?

Cycles and seasonal effects have long attracted attention in markets, and could at a stretch be labelled a constant factor in finance and business. Clearly certain agricultural commodities are seasonal and weather related, as is energy consumption, and commercial data as prosaic as beer and ice cream sales are closely tied to sunshine and warm weather. But can we claim that interest rates, currencies and perhaps stock markets display cyclical and seasonal behaviour characteristics as well?

The hunt for business and market cycles has been going on ever since economic and financial data has been collected, perhaps even beforehand. Indeed, wits may choose to quote the biblical story of Joseph telling the pharaoh that there would be seven fat years followed by seven lean years, and citing this as an early example! More seriously, and based on his business experiences, the leading English Victorian banker Samuel Jones-Loyd, later Lord Overstone, was an early exponent of the business cycle. He is credited by that early titan of modern economics Alfred Marshall with the observation that the state of trade 'revolves apparently in an established cycle. First we find it in a state of quiescence – next, improvement – growing confidence – prosperity – excitement – over-trading – convulsion – pressure – stagnation – distress – ending again in quiescence.' Although these sentiments are more than 150 years old they still have the ring of truth about them. The dotcom fiasco of 2000/2001 had all the feel of excitement, over-trading and then convulsion. In fact it could be said excitement is the most dangerous in finance – it seems to be always the prelude to disaster. The 2008/2009 cataclysm in the banking and credit markets was also preceded by a period of excitement and over-trading, (in fact a rocket-fuelled example with massive gearing and seemingly endless cheap credit) and it's certainly the case that the markets and the world economy suffered the consequences. The outlook is now very much described by the labels of stagnation and distress.

Since Overstone's time many economists and academics have sought to pin down the business cycle – these have included Kondratieff, Juglar and Joseph Schumpter – but problems have arisen, mainly because no precise cycle seems to exist. Then again, perhaps this is not surprising. It seems unlikely that a precise numeric cycle for anything as complex as an economy will be discovered because, as we have seen, economies and markets are far too complex and reactive to blindly repeat the same course in exactly the same time frame. Clearly flexibility, or perhaps more cynically to be very selective in our researches, is required in this type of analysis.

We should perhaps pause here to remember that these economists were trying to isolate and identify the business or economic cycle, which is definitely not the same as the financial market cycle. Financial markets seem to operate on a separate basis, though they are still closely linked to business and what is often termed the real economy. This bias, or perhaps timing difference, is because of the discounting element in financial trading – it is nearly always the case that markets are looking to the future not the present. Anything happening now has usually been absorbed into the market's calculations some time ago. The exception to this is if something totally unexpected happens, for example the September 11th attacks in America. Markets always hate shocks, and this is why price movements are so volatile when there is genuinely new news. Given this propensity to discount future possible news, one would expect to find that any market cycle, certainly in stocks, would lead business activity – and general observation tends to show that this is the case.

Our interest here is not specifically in business and economic cycles, but we should be aware of their potential influence on financial markets. We also ought to remember to look at another important relationship in finance – the way different asset classes relate to, and react with, one another – because market cycles are not the only game in town when looking at market phenomena. Far too many analysts and participants see the marketplace divided into vertical segments and frequently ignore the relationship between these segments; this is to miss some potentially important insights.

The Four Asset Classes

In general we can break financial markets down into four asset classes: Bonds and Interest Rates, Commodities, Currencies and Stocks. There is modest dispute by some who feel that currencies do not belong in this list, that they are not truly an asset in their own right, but instead are a vehicle sometimes used when moving in and out of the other three.

This is now a rather outmoded view, and the growth, liquidity and sheer trading volumes in currencies easily promote them into the first rank.

Looking at our four asset classes, what can we say? Well, our first observation is that most people will concentrate on equities and bonds, and there is a long tradition of looking at the relationship between the two. Pretty much since the 1950s equities have been in the driving seat – in most years their returns have been much better, though there have been strong bull markets in bonds on occasions. There have been notable crashes and bear markets in equities but they remain the market of first choice for most investors. In contrast, commodities have tended to be relegated to the sidelines, and this has been for two reasons. First, few investors wanted to get involved in the actual physical side of the business, and second, the associated futures markets were always considered (often unfairly) to be rather illiquid and volatile.

There have been times when commodities have attracted greater attention, most notably in the great inflation-induced bull run of the mid-1970s and the explosion in interest in the last few years fuelled by high expectations of the emerging markets, but these are the exception rather than the norm. Usually commodity markets have been very much smaller than either equity or bond markets. Both the bull runs mentioned attracted huge capital which led to a greatly expanded marketplace, though in the 1970s example the money didn't stay long, and since 2007 once again the same pattern seems to be repeating itself. It could well be that once more commodities will be relegated to a relatively small niche. That said the commodities markets, whatever the prevailing trend, have three very important and influential constituents; namely gold, oil and copper.

Despite some dispute as to whether currencies can ever be a truly proper investment class, the fact is that the foreign exchange markets have played, and are likely to continue to play, a pivotal role in the financial world. It is impossible to fully understand financial markets without watching and understanding activities in currency trading. Somewhat frustratingly currencies don't fit neatly into the cycle played out by the other three classes, but we can say that the dollar does appear to follow cycles linked to relative interest rate differentials with other major trading currencies. These cycles are not always easily discerned though, and it is possible we are falling into the trap that you can always find cycles if you look hard enough!

Perhaps the best way to consider these so called inter-market relationships is to illustrate things with a few of the linkages. In his interesting book *Inter-Market Technical Analysis*, John Murphy observes that three of them (Bonds, Stocks and Commodities) tend to move up and down in waves after one another. As mentioned, currencies seem to play a less predictable role, but on occasions can be very important. Despite the title of the book, much of Murphy's work looks purely at price relationships, and readers who feel jaded or unconvinced by technical indicators can easily avoid these references. Equally, if you feel that you will benefit from such comfort blankets then this book will work for you on more than one level.

Observation suggests that Bonds lead the dance, followed by Stocks, with Commodities bringing up the rear. This is a schematic view of markets, and we can't be certain that all moves will happen on cue, but there is a good body of evidence (researched and displayed at length in Murphy's work) that shows these relationships to be strong, and dare one say permanent. As we should expect, the moves in these three asset classes seem to lead activity in the underlying business cycle. For example, at the time a business cycle is still expanding but at a slower rate (another example of the "S" curve discussed in Chapter Four), these financial asset classes rollover and turn bearish. So, as an economy reaches towards its peak, first we see bonds fall (usually in anticipation of expected interest rate rises), then stocks start to fall (as the market, always looking forward, starts to pare back its company earnings expectations), and then finally commodities give up the ghost and decline as well (this is usually after the real economy has stalled and manufacturing and trade demand for physical goods starts to decline).

Equally when economies are bottoming and looking to turn up, financial markets are usually leading the way. Bonds typically turn up before an economy bottoms; there may still be quite a lot of pain to come in the general business environment, but bonds improve as the interest rate cycle always bottoms before economic activity finally finds a base. As things start to gently pick up, stocks often roar ahead (once again the market is discounting the future and sees jam just around the corner); then when the recovery properly takes hold commodities improve.

We have to be careful not to expect perfect results from these patterns, but history does bear out these relationships. The bear market in stocks that unfolded from mid-2000 onwards was dutifully followed by a bad time in base metals (copper as ever proving the important bellwether for this move) and bonds (with the notable and potentially excruciating exception of telecom and various other high-tech issues) did well as the business cycle started to reach the bottom.

A similar pattern was seen as the economy started to turn up in 2002/03 and the world equity markets came to life, bonds fell back and commodities had an explosive move up until mid-2008 as world growth looked set for great things. The slow motion car crash that was the credit crunch probably started in the summer of 2007, but it was some time before equities "noticed" that the world economy was going off the rails – though when they did wake up there was a bloodbath in 2008. Then, like clockwork, the bubble in commodities burst by mid-2008 with oil hurtling off 60% in six months and many base metals following in its wake. This has been followed by the inevitable "flight to quality" with investors piling into government bonds which have unsurprisingly done pretty well.

The Credit Clock

Another cycle that seems to have validity is the sequence of events that happens in the credit markets. I am indebted to the banking analyst Hank Calenti for the following clever illustration that shows the factors that seem to drive the cycle of credit. Basically, one follows the boxes around in a clockwise fashion and can place "hands" for each economy at the appropriate place. At the time of writing, early in 2009, it seems appropriate to suggest that the US and the UK are both at around 3 o'clock (Easy Money), with the euro zone just behind (probably around 2 o'clock at Panic, but moving towards Easy Money).

Figure 8.1: The Credit Clock

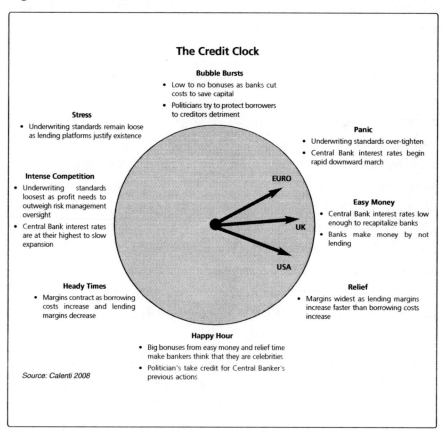

Readers who are looking forward to better times, big bonuses and stellar careers in credit trading will see that "Happy Hour" at 6 o'clock is some way off!

Gold, Oil And Copper

Whilst thinking about the moves between asset classes, what about some interesting moves within those groupings? Let's take a look at the commodities sector and in particular the big three of gold, oil and copper. With these three there are a number of angles to consider. First, there is the actual price of the commodity as quoted on various exchanges or through an over-the-counter market; second, there are shares in the companies that produce the commodity; and third, there are industry indices that group the shares of the leading producers together.

Interestingly the connections between the raw commodity, the index of key commodity stocks, and the individual stocks within the index seem to play out a fairly fixed pattern. Time and again the industry index leads the underlying commodity; so for example, the FT Gold Mines Index usually starts a new trend before the gold bullion price starts to move – in this particular case there is often only a short lag (this is an estimate – every new trend is always a little different). Also, within the FT Gold Mines Index there appear to be certain stocks that lead the way – they are what we might call in marketing speak "Early Adopters". So if you are interested in investing in bullion you can do worse than to watch the mining stocks; they usually give early warning signals of what is coming in the physical metal. This sort of relationship seems to work well for oil as well.

This troika of key commodities also make their influence felt in other ways: gold is a major guide to the currency markets, oil is an important determinant for the whole energy complex including gas and electricity prices, and copper still glories under the title Dr Copper as many believe it has a PhD in economics. Certainly most major moves in the US dollar (which may be tracked by following the US Dollar Index) are predicated by movements in the gold bullion price, and copper has a relatively good record of being an early warning sign for changes in overall economic activity. In the case of copper this may seem obtuse these days, after all there are whole blocks of the economy that don't use the stuff – but for whatever reason it seems to hold its role as an early warning system. Readers can discover plenty of other links with modest amounts of research. For example, gold and stock prices often move inversely, ideally unsurprisingly when there is an inflationary environment, and bonds and commodities are rarely moving in the same direction at the same time, though it is usually commodities that follow where bonds have been. Careful study can open up a number of interesting and potentially rewarding investment opportunities.

Persistent Inefficiency?

So, is cycle spotting and trading all too good to be true? Perhaps we need to stop and take on board a measure of salt at this point. Earlier we looked at the risks of coincidences and correlations. We have to be careful that we are not falling into some basic traps when looking at these inter-market ties. Our best defence is perspective because as we have seen it's extremely dangerous to fit patterns to small amounts of data. Certainly, inter-market information cannot be examined over two or three years of data and even ten years is not really long enough – we should try to look at the big ebbs and flows in assets over a twenty to thirty-year period. Paradoxically this might be why these relationships still work in the "must know now about tomorrow" culture of financial trading; most players can barely remember what happened the previous year and have little patience with the idea of looking even further back. Interestingly this is compounded by a data culture that often only retains information for the previous ten years (this is far too short –

after all it is already over twenty years since Black Monday and the stock crash of 1987) though there is some evidence that longer data histories are now being maintained.

Also, perhaps we should consider why these relationships persist; they are, in effect, inefficiencies that lie around for us to exploit. In an efficient market environment this shouldn't happen. Once again it may be that rational behaviour at the micro level in markets leads to slightly odd results at the macro level. Also, to repeat the important caveat from the start of this chapter, no relationship from the past is definitely fixed in the future – we can only say certain factors may be linked, and nothing more. Nothing is set in concrete and one of the biggest problems with racing certainties in market analysis is that as the market becomes aware of an idea its usefulness all but vanishes. That said, we have seen that human nature does seem to be pretty constant, our judgements, fears and hopes are pretty much the same as market players of, twenty, fifty and one hundred years ago. We all tend to approach markets with the same biases and erroneous beliefs and so in this way perhaps we are fated to repeat the mistakes of history.

Along with human behaviour there seem to be certain constants in institutional activity. We have already seen how there appears to be a cycle of regulation that comes and goes through financial markets, and in addition activity by governments and central banks often seems to repeat past patterns. Policies that have caused economic booms and busts – though always subsequently rejected and rebuffed with a familiar "never again" assurance from politicians and officials – do have a remarkable resilience and never quite go away.

Market Mice

In one sense this may seem a counsel of despair. Will we never learn from our mistakes? Are we condemned to be market mice running around the same old financial wheel? In quite another way it is extremely good news as it suggests that there may be large and worthwhile inefficiencies in markets, which if correct offers some potentially profitable trading opportunities. The puzzle with these issues is always the same; why should someone else in the marketplace allow me to profit from their actions or perhaps inactions? Well, human analysis can be hopelessly skewed, corporate strategy does not always seek to maximise every last penny, and governments and official organisations are notorious for bizarre spending and economic policy decisions.

To look at a micro situation that may cause inefficiencies to persist at the macro level, consider the example of the company hedging its future foreign currency earnings. Virtually all large companies have internal budgeted exchange rates, and it is the job of the finance officer or treasurer to try and ensure that any foreign earnings are converted at least at this target exchange rate. Sometimes this may prove impossible and other times, if the market moves are favourable, it may easily be achieved. But once that target rate is available in the marketplace the treasurer is likely to act. It may be that the market will continue on further, but there is little or no incentive for him to run the risk of not covering his company's currency requirements. By locking in the company's foreign earnings at the budgeted rate the treasurer has done his job. There may have been an opportunity cost in dealing at that rate, but the company has given up the potential opportunity to benefit further. So whilst the trading plan makes perfect sense to the company and its accountants, in market terms it has been an opportunity lost – or at least a profit potential that has not been maximised. This, in a small way, is a piece of inefficiency in the market price in the currency market.

There are many possible reasons for all these inter-market relationships. One could add that the activities of central banks in currency and interest rate markets are not motivated by the pursuit of profits and that their policy driven operations may well "leave money on the table" for others to collect. The presence of these opportunities seems to be testament to the fact that markets are not just populated by profit-maximising participants and that on occasions these relationships last for long periods of time – one could almost argue, with tongue in cheek, that there is a duty to exploit these advantages and help overall efficiency.

At the beginning we touched upon cycles and seasonality, and there are some additional aspects worth considering, so let's take a closer look at the supposed importance of certain times of the year.

Watch Out – It's October Again

By now it should be obvious that we all love patterns in life, whether real, imagined or more often than not, carefully constructed using selective pieces of data. This seems to creep into all our judgements, not just our financial ones. Scientists tells us that subconsciously we are strongly influenced by symmetry, that we are attracted to people who display perfect bodily symmetry, and that we often choose our mate on this basis. The theory behind this is that symmetry is a good proxy for health and strong genes. We like the comfort and reassurance that patterns seem to bring and psychologists may consider this a mechanism for building or reinforcing our beliefs and comfort zones. Also, even if patterns are not readily available the human mind is very adept at finding them – followers of Elliott Wave Theory have constructed a whole plethora of rules about the structures and patterns that they can see unfold in the marketplace, and this is disconcerting to those of us who see nothing but ordinary market price action.

Market players definitely seem to have comfort zones and seizing on any reassurance and hope that can be offered by cycles and patterns is eagerly sought in the markets. Any half-sensible cycle or pattern that appears to throw up critical periods is always considered good fare. As discussed earlier, one of the major problems is our inability to recognise coincidences for what they are – we always seem to prefer a reason or an explanation, and the more outlandish the better. Such material is also often used to try and help the second hardest problem in trading – timing. Whilst commentators and alike drone on and on about price direction, it soon becomes clear that the much bigger issue is timing (money management is the really hard one to master). We seem to believe that if we could get a firm grip on market timing everything else would be some easier – hence the hunt for cycles.

A fairly cursory study of financial and market history soon yields a fairly alarming picture – markets seem to suffer from a dreaded autumn meltdown effect. Figure 8.2 is a sample list that suggests the period between August and October (slipping into November to add another good example) is a nightmare time for investors.

Interestingly the five largest falls in the UK stock market have all been in October, as have the three largest in the US. To this we could add numerous political events that have had market-shaking consequences; both the start of the First and Second World Wars fall into this period, as do the terrorist attacks on the United States in 2001.

What does this list tell us? Well not a great deal really, it has a curiosity value, and it is intriguing that the August-October time period seems so crowded with disastrous market events, but it is hardly a guide to future trading. The human character does not rest so easy though, and numerous attempts have been made to suggest what may cause this autumn effect. It's the old trap of course; these coincidences provide no evidence of causation and whilst making for an interesting list, they have little other value.

If you look hard enough, and remain selective, cycles pop up all over the place. In the first half of the 19th century there was strong evidence of a 10-year boom and bust cycle, but this changed as time wore on. The Russian economist Kondratieff produced large amounts of research attempting to suggest that economic activity was determined by a long wave cycle of some sixty or so years. This cycle became suddenly fashionable in the mid-1980s as we were due the next disaster soon (some sixty years after the 1929 crash and resulting depression) but frustratingly for the bears nothing really happened.

Figure 8.2: Notable financial upheavals between August and November

23rd September 1720	The South Sea Bubble finally bursts. This was the end of the rampant stock speculation in the early days of trading in London, in a company with no revenues, but 'vast future potential'.
24th August 1857	US Railroad Mania ends as rail stocks plunge across Europe.
19th September 1873	Austrian and German land prices fall heavily as local banks collapse, precipitating the first world-wide crash, leading to Wall Street being closed for 10 days.
29th October 1929	The Wall Street Crash. You had to wait until 26th November 1954 before the Dow Jones Index regained the same level.
4th November 1967	Sterling devalues by 14% against the US$, to a new rate of US$2.40. Just outside our preferred danger zone, but a very significant event at the time.
19th October 1987	A much smaller affair than 1929 but still a 25% shakeout for most markets, and the Hong Kong stock market closed for 4 days.
17th September 1992	Sterling falls out of the ERM. The biggest event for the pound since the 1967 devaluation.
15th August 1993	Just one year later and the ERM falls apart, with new 15% trading bands having to be established.
17th August 1998	The Russian announcement of debt default, that led on to the Long-Term Capital debacle, and finally the massive 2-day collapse in USD/yen in October 1998.
9th August 2007	The first signs of trouble in the unfolding disaster that became the collapse of Northern Rock Bank.

Excitement was generated by the 1987 crash, but for cycle followers the 1990s were a disaster because it was one of the most successful periods for economies and markets on record. Then to cap it all – just when the whole thing looked totally discredited – technology stocks hit the buffers in March 2000. How inconvenient – as it should surely have happened in the autumn not the spring!

Cyclical Appeal

So cycles, whilst providing interesting market small talk and fodder to liven up dull presentations, can be difficult to actually trade. It's hard to organise one's portfolio entirely around these phenomena, not least because they often give signals and indications at the very point when investors are least willing to commit to the idea. This in a sense is central to the whole process that creates them in the first place. Ironically, cycle theory itself has a cyclical appeal. It seems to particularly appeal to bears and those who enjoy doom mongering and are looking forward to the next crash, and nearly always becomes popular during extended bull markets. One may be tempted here to claim some unintended success for these theories in that once they become widely discussed perhaps bull markets are in trouble? But in truth cycles are a very blunt weapon when seeking timing ideas.

Linked to the interest in cycles is the perennial talk of market crashes. It may be that the events of 1987 are still fixed in many minds, but in fact crashes are pretty rare, and should not be confused with bear markets. In fact, bear markets are usually much more punishing and draining than any short, sharp financial crash. Certainly it is easier to spot a bull and bear market cycle in equity markets than to try and discern some of the more obtuse business cycle suggestions.

Bulls And Bears

In fact, the shape of bull and bear patterns in equity markets is remarkably consistent – though as ever timing can be tortuous. We need to remember that there are two dominant emotions in trading; in bull markets the sentiment is fear, and in bear markets it is hope. At first glance this may seem the wrong way round, surely we are fearful of bear markets and keep hoping the rise will continue on a bull run? If we examine motivations and emotions closely we find that this is not the case.

During a bull run people are driven by the fear that they might be missing out on the move, after all it is the constant supply of fresh buyers and money that keep the whole thing going up. So the true characteristic of a bull market is to climb this wall of fear, and needless to say when fear subsides and becomes replaced with cocky assurance this is the first sign that the move is maturing and may ultimately falter. It is usually at this stage that observers talk about greed as the dominant emotion. Once the fear is totally extinguished the final stage of greed kicks in and disaster is only around the corner.

Equally, during a bear market we have a constant stream of dashed hopes. Distressed bulls who find themselves long and wrong are constantly hoping the cavalry will arrive. Occasionally hope flickers into life and we have short, sharp rallies that are a classic feature of bear markets. Unfortunately few longs appear to take the opportunity to get out but tend to believe that the much hoped for turn is finally arriving. Readers will recognise all the signs of the dreaded sunk-loss bias in this emotion. Naturally it is only when all hope is extinguished that bear markets come to an end.

Figure 8.3: Bull & Bear Sentiment

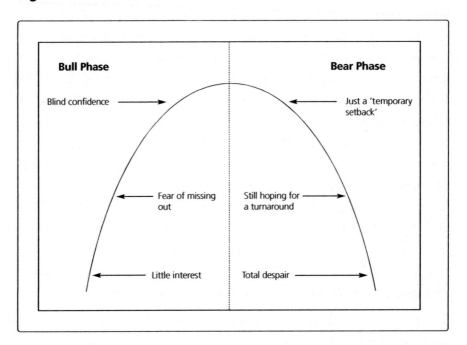

Another element of this familiar pattern is the way that cash and stocks alternate with one another. During bull markets, more stock is offered on to the market in the form of new issues, or as payment to executives via stock options; and much of the merger and acquisition activity associated with bull markets is paid for with stock. Again, judgement becomes less and less discerning and more and more paper offerings hit the market. The largest deals are nearly always close to the top of the market – a classic example being the merger of AOL and Time Warner, who announced their merger deal on the 11th January 2000 just eight weeks from what turned out to be the top in technology stocks with the NASDAQ peaking at a high of 5048 in March. Many stock analysts were ecstatic at the time of the merger announcement, with wild versions of the value of the deal being bandied around – figures ranged between US$150 billion and US$350 billion. Within two years, however, the market cap of the merged entity was below US$55 billion and the NASDAQ had lost over 80% of its value. This was blind optimism in spades.

Okay, this is easy to see after the event – but now in 2009 with bear market emotion ruling the roost in world equity markets, following the credit crunch, we can look forward to equally extraordinary tales on the downside. As the bull tide ebbs all sorts of frauds and crazy schemes are usually uncovered and come unstuck. In these circumstances, people will only take cash for their businesses, M&A deal activity shrivels to a fraction of its previous size, and former Masters of the Universe in banking and broking find themselves spending more time at home with their family and gardens. This is the world of the asset stripper, buying up undervalued companies, breaking them up and extracting more money than they paid for them. In the UK this was at its height in 1974 and 1975 and is usually seen towards the end of severe bear markets. It may well be that the return of the "vultures" will be the first positive sign that the despair phase of the current credit crunch bear market is over and things are starting to rebalance and grow again.

So trying to spot the next crash in equities, bonds or currencies is not really a worthwhile pursuit. Crashes are relatively rare, and far harder to spot than waning bull markets and developing bear markets. October may seem a dangerous month, and the autumn has thrown up some pretty awful market breaks, but there is precious little evidence to justify using these past examples as a good foundation for trading the future.

Leg In And Limp Out

As has been illustrated, one of the most dangerous parts about cycles and such like is the temptation to chase spurious accuracy. The most frustrating and potentially ruinous aspect of these cyclical relationships is that they are very difficult to predict with any degree of certainty. All sorts of gurus and sellers of software (will people never stop buying this stuff?) make all sorts of claims about uncovering precise cycles, but as ever, the evidence of their trading success is very slight. Of course we don't need to have pinpoint accuracy to take advantage of such big tidal changes in markets, but there is something in human nature that is gripped by supposed accuracy. We somehow believe that things are more professional and valuable the more accurate they appear to be. This is particularly true in finance where many of the participants come from a background in accounting, or science and maths, and are used to seeing precise and correct answers. In the endless shades of grey that is the world of trading there are no correct answers but this doesn't stop people looking for them or being impressed by claims that purport to show them. You will recall the very accurate claims of the ostrich investment promoters, whose potential returns were given to within a tenth of one per cent.

One of the consequences of this mindset is the dangerous manner in which many spread positions are traded. By spread positions we mean the relationship between two asset classes or instruments; for example being long of gold and short of oil, or perhaps a yield curve play by being short of the long end of the curve and long of the shorter maturities. These types of plays can be very profitable if carefully researched and properly undertaken but they have more risks than "plain vanilla" trading positions. Again this may not seem entirely intuitive, and in many cases such spread trades are undertaken by those looking for lower risks in the market.

So why is it that these positions may be more risky? Well, when you put on a spread trade you may feel you have one position, as represented by the net effect of your trades, but you actually have two underlying positions. So you have double the worries, in terms of bid-offer spread, liquidity and managing your loss and take profit strategy. This multiplies the potential points of failure, and many good spread trading ideas fall down in their execution.

Perhaps one of the worst crimes is trying to overly fine-tune the entry and exit of such positions. Far too often traders try to leg in to a position, by choosing to trade one leg of the spread first and then waiting for the most opportune moment to put on the other half of the strategy. Occasionally such activities can be disastrous, with very painful results, because a piece of news or event could move the markets when only half the trade is put on. It could be suggested that complicating the timing issue by splitting the spread trade into two separately timed legs in this way is not called for because the risk reward calculation for such behaviour is rarely that favourable. With these leg in, leg out strategies it is also difficult to execute stop loss strategies because you need to decide if you should have separate stops for each position, or a stop based on the spread? Can you get out of both markets at the same time? This is obviously a serious consideration for exchange traded instruments. Clearly these housekeeping elements are very important and once again illustrate that money management is more significant than picking direction. When thinking of fine-tuning strategies it might do well to remind ourselves of the possible consequences of such activity and perhaps we can paraphrase the Oliver Hardy catchphrase and say this is another fine finesse you have gotten me into!

Trailing around looking for exact cycles in predicting major turns in financial markets is fruitless; it is to succumb to that most dangerous of games, the illusion of control. There are no precise cycles in finance, though people constantly claim to be able to see all sorts of patterns, magic numbers, and waves, even square roots of moon cycles and planetary line-ups that affect markets. Life simply isn't that easy – it is naïve to think otherwise. That markets, and their constituent asset classes, do move in fairly reliable rhythms does seem true, but it is important not to be doctrinaire or stubborn about future possible outcomes. Many cycles happen because of government or official activities (movements in interest rates and how this affects other asset classes being the prime example). So it is quite possible that relationships will persist in the future and can be profited from but that is not the same as making the rather facile claim that they can be predicted.

9

The Divine Right Of Failure

'If we don't succeed, we run the risk of failure.'

Dan Quayle

We are getting close to the end of this tour around the world of investment and speculation, and hopefully we have covered virtually all the main topics and angles. There does, however, remain one very important subject to be addressed: performance measurement.

This is quite the most elusive part of the whole business and as we have seen with human behaviour and attitudes towards risk, one that investors often avoid looking at too closely. The French philosopher La Rochefoucauld commented that man couldn't stare too long at the sun or death; to this we can add investment performance. This may seem strange, as surely performance is what the whole business is about? Yes of course, but investors often want to hide from the real truth about their market performance, and fortunately there are a whole number of ways of viewing performance and risk-reward decisions – hiding from brutal facts can be achieved pretty easily.

So to finish our tour, let's concentrate on three areas: investment benchmarks, risk management using value at risk type measurement models, and that most difficult of financial topics, losses.

Never Mind The Benchmarks

How much money did you make? This may be the most commonly asked question in markets, but it is also one that is rarely answered in a totally straightforward manner. In fact, the first lesson of performance seems to be that it is somehow impolite to talk in terms of cash or monetary values; it is de rigueur to use percentage returns and a heap of other often arcane measurements. Performance is rarely spoken of in bald terms of profit and loss; instead a whole language for measurement has been invented. So along with percentage returns come comparisons to other investments or deposits, or perhaps specially selected baskets of investment instruments – welcome to the world of investment benchmarking.

Straightaway we have reached an important early crossroads; do we measure performance in absolute terms or in relative terms? Should we judge ourselves and our peers and competitors in terms of what they have made, or perhaps how they have fared when compared to everyone else? The vast majority of the investment management community have plumped for the relative route, and as we shall see this decision is steeped in self-interest.

Investment benchmarking has grown from simple beginnings into a huge industry in its own right, and is predicated on the idea that the indices and measuring tools provided give the investor a more detailed and accurate idea of performance and the risks being run. The whole business started with the humble stock index, of which the Dow Jones Industrial Average of 30 leading stocks is the first and still probably the best known. When Charles Dow set up the index in 1896 the idea was to create a measure that would show the market's overall performance. It gave a guide as to whether or not the stock market was in a bull or a bear phase. Naturally enough people started using this data in two ways: first to compare their own investments (am I beating the Dow?) and second as an analysis tool to try and predict (here we go again!) the future direction of the market.

Of course creating, calculating and selling index information could be a substantial business in it's own right, and this lesson was not lost on the publishers of the Dow Jones Index. Here was a chance to create a strong brand that everyone could use and rely upon. Such an attractive business model enticed other entrants to the field, and soon the world was awash with equity indices. In the United States alone there are at least five major indices; the Dow 30 (still going after over a hundred years), the S&P 500, the NASDAQ Composite, the Russell 2000 and the Wilshire 5000. Added to this, there are a whole host of sub-indices that track industry groups. For equity markets alone there are well over

100 indices around the world used by fund managers as measures for tracking markets, and constituent groupings. Needless to say the idea has proliferated into other asset classes with bonds being probably the next biggest grouping, and commodities lagging someway behind. Currency benchmarks and indices are far less common.

Interestingly a number of these indices have been produced within the industry, with many of the more specialised examples having been created by banks and stockbroking companies. Also the rating agencies have been active, as well as the originators of the idea in the first place, newspaper publishers. Creating a successful investment benchmark has become big business, with large-scale marketing and promotion by the creators to try and persuade the financial industry that their particular measure best reflects the market.

Why the growth in demand for these products? Well, investors felt they needed a way of judging manager performance, and were sold the idea that if a fund manager had outperformed an index this would be a fair and accurate way of judging their success. Superficially this is the case, but there have been a number of quite unwelcome consequences of this thinking.

If we look at equity investment first of all, the benchmark of choice tends to be the S&P 500, on the basis that the Dow 30 is far too narrow, and that the wider indices cover many stocks that are too small and illiquid. (There are similar indices elsewhere – for example in the UK there is the FTSE 100 and the FTSE 250.) So the fund manager sets themselves the task of outperforming the S&P index, and not worrying about total return. In theory they could range around the market and try and pick winners that will do well; in practice though they tend to invest the vast majority of a fund in a way that replicates the index, and only at the margins trim holdings in some shares to be underweight or overweight. This may be fairly sophisticated, in that they may use models or their good judgement to predict which sectors within the index will under and outperform and trim their positions accordingly. However, the scale of these adjustments is usually a marketing issue rather than just an investment management consideration. If a fund has been promoted as a steady, low-risk type of investment the fund will tend to cling quite closely to the index. Equally if it is more gung ho (a telltale phrase in the marketing literature is usually "opportunity") then there will be more latitude in the investment decisions. All fair enough and quite sensible you might think – but nowhere in this thinking is there any concern about returns. The aim is to beat the index, if money is made as well, great, but it's a secondary concern.

All of this is perfectly fine when markets are going well, and as we noted earlier, in bull markets the fear of missing out on the great times is a major driver in investment sentiment, but given that a fund is closely linked to a rising index the investor is likely to be feeling happy with things. As a result fewer people care about the nuances of outperforming the benchmark on the way up. In a bear market things should be different but the manager has a superb defence. Clearly the fund will be losing money but hopefully at no more than or at least close to the same rate as the index – this is deemed as success. Indeed the mantra seems to be don't look at any losses, just be grateful that we beat the index.

There is an interesting piece of thinking here, effectively the fund manager is saying, well you chose to be in equities, we have been following the equity market in our fund, what's your problem? The onus on the failure to make money is pushed back to the investor who made the decision to be in that asset class in the first place. This is a neat little argument, and has the massive benefit from the manager's point of view that they are not to blame for the negative return. Indeed one sometimes sees how the painful business of losses is dressed up to sound like success; 'Your fund declined by 8.9% but during the same period the index was down 11.4%.' No doubt they could claim to have added performance of 2.5%.

Another example of this thinking shows up in performance tables and peer comparisons. The retail investment industry in particular is swamped with comparative tables, even award ceremonies and other marketing "flim flam" to highlight supposed good performance. Investment companies make great play of how a fund was in the upper quartile, or how they won an award as Best Fund Manager in the Sector. The problem is that you can be in the upper quartile, even the top 5% on occasions, and still find that your investments have fallen off a cliff.

Okay so the message is caveat emptor, and we can all easily see how the performance game is played. But there are other important aspects to benchmarking that can have profound effects on market activity.

The really important decision is what should be in the index. For equity indices this is usually decided by an appointed independent Index Committee that meet regularly to consider who should stay and who should go. Typically these decisions are based on market capitalisation and index changes can happen fairly frequently – quarterly is about the shortest review period, though annually is more common. Going back to the analogy of the hall of mirrors these activities can have a significant distortion effect in markets. Clearly if stock ABC is a candidate to be thrown out of an index many fund managers have to be ready to ditch the stock (though quite a few will only do so once it is ejected). Equally if stock XYZ is due to be promoted into an index it will have to be bought by fund managers to once again keep their correct exposure to the benchmark.

For so-called tracker funds that set out to exactly replicate an index this has to be done at the exact time of the changes, but for other managers they may have some reasonable discretion in when to alter their holdings. Though timing is still an issue as stocks that have been ejected tend to fall due to the immediate activities of trackers, and equally those new arrivals tend to get bid up. For these reasons some managers may try to second-guess the index committees and trade ahead of any announcements, and as in general these committees produce few surprises, this should be a relatively low-risk decision. All of this seems quite a way from the traditional idea of investment, and analysis of individual companies and their prospects. Much of the business has been subsumed in to this benchmark trading game. As a result we can have herd-like behaviour in markets when the constituents change in benchmarks. Curiously this is a little like delta hedging of options where one is forced to buy more of something as it rises in price and sell more as it falls.

So far we have considered only equity benchmarks, but a very similar pattern seems to exist in bond markets. Here, the benchmarks are not usually so well known, at least outside the industry, though there are one or two large bond indices, particularly prominent are the Morgan Stanley Smith Barney World Government Bond Index and the JP Morgan Government Bond Index. Another factor here is the importance of rating agencies. In equity markets the decisions on suitable stocks for the index are left to committees and very much determined by market capitalisation, while in the bond markets there is a need for an independent credit assessment. This role is fulfilled by three or four major credit analysis and rating agencies who rate bonds according to various scales of creditworthiness. In addition, time horizon considerations – or more accurately investment portfolio average duration – is a factor as well. For professional investment groups there is much discussion about how long or short the average duration of a portfolio should be – but the fund manager will try to persuade the fund to adopt a reasonable benchmark.

The same benchmark games that go on in equity investing are also prevalent in bond markets, but the way constituent instruments move in and out of the index is somewhat different. Rather than the market price action that creates market capitalisation creating candidates as in equities, the bond markets are very reliant on the credit rating agencies' opinions and research – it is their rankings that decide the ultimate fate of a bond's creditworthiness. This is less than perfect, and on occasions the agencies have been royally criticised for being slow to act when credit conditions have changed. This was first seen in a large way with the post-bubble telecom debt in 2002 that created a notable fiasco amongst certain sectors of the debt market. This was only a precursor for the bigger disaster of 2008-2009, the credit crunch, where quite rightly commentators are now questioning whether the benchmarks and associated ratings system were of any use whatsoever. Once again it has been noteworthy that bond markets have suffered from liquidity problems when investment managers all head for the same exit door after a significant downgrade in a credit issue (the so-called German phrase of Torschlusspanik) – this bunching together is another unwelcome by-product of benchmarks.

Benchmarks are the perfect cover and alibi for fund managers, a good business for those who create and publish them, and the end users still fondly believe that they are useful tools, and they will not be going away. They do have some uses but also contain a dangerous flaw – they tend to anaesthetise people. Somehow the losses seem less painful if you have outperformed a recognised benchmark. This brings us back to our old enemy from behavioural finance, the sunk-loss bias. The benchmark comparison can give a good feeling to what may in fact be a disaster, and this can reinforce the sense of delusion that makes us stick with losses for far too long. In addition, benchmarks are part and parcel of the vertical dissection of markets. They help delineate the various asset classes and industry sectors, and trap people into this sort of thinking. Surely if investment is about making profits and good returns it makes sense to range across asset classes and sectors, not to be trapped in individual vertical silos that may be in a severe downturn?

Also, it is particularly ironic that the one group that markets itself and invests on the basis of total returns – hedge funds – is often pilloried for being too risky and not transparent in its activities. This is in fact a strange angle of attack; benchmarks may appear to make investment more transparent and to help assess the risk, but there is an argument that says they are in fact part of the problem, and certainly not the solution. At least with a hedge fund you have a management focused on total returns, not chasing an arbitrary goal.

So much for benchmarks and the measurement of performance. It's time now to consider the other side of the coin, the measurement of risk. It hardly needs saying that this is not as straightforward as one would imagine either.

Virtue At Risk

In medieval times it was standard practice for most businesses to only create a set of accounts, and very rudimentary ones at that, with the death of the proprietor or – in a larger concern – with the demise of one of the partners. Annual accounts were unheard of, and would have been thought very strange and unnecessary. The only exception to this rule was if the authorities tried to levy a specific tax, and proof of ownership and a business valuation had to be accounted for. So, although Luca Pacioli is credited with inventing double entry accounting in the 15th century, and we are encouraged to see him as the father of accounting (surely a slightly tarnished accolade these days?) his proposed methods were hardly in use. Indeed his work in this area was only one chapter of his much larger book on mathematics and he himself was a religious academic who never ran a business. However, with the emergence of business taxation and a growth in trade and related finance, more sophistication did slowly emerge. Annual accounting valuations gradually became the norm, and developed into early attempts at cost and management accounting so that by the 1880s, for example, the American steel tycoon Andrew Carnegie was receiving daily cost sheets detailing every expenditure at his steel works, which at the time was growing to become the biggest in the world. Banking and finance took a similar path, but as recently as the 1960s accounting and valuation time frames were pretty long with many bank's senior managements relying on weekly information about the institution's exposures and earnings. But as the business of banking and trading sped up, and the range of products handled exploded from the early 1980s onwards, the demand for more timely accounting and valuation grew with it. The financial business had entered the world of the daily revaluation, and a host of models emerged to analyse the current positions and to offer insights and tentative advice on possible future outcomes.

"What's our position? What risk do we have now?" were the familiar cries of senior bankers and brokers as their newly de-regulated world pushed them away from cosy, protected and well margined semi-cartels, into free competition with higher turnover, lower profits and often more principal risk-taking. Banking was no longer just a credit issue, balance sheets increasingly had a wide variety of instruments in them, and crucially these instruments were much more transparent in terms of valuation, and usually had far better liquidity than the traditional loan book. The trading element of the balance sheet grew, and the off-balance sheet items, which were mainly derivative-based, multiplied at a fantastic rate and soon overtook the traditional credit intermediation element. With all these trading instruments came a need and an ability to revalue and scrutinise them more closely. This led to the modern day risk management regimes that are currently so popular, and in many cases equally flawed.

A number of models emerged with fancy names, which in general we can lump together as Value at Risk models. Once again intermediaries saw the commercial potential in their own valuation models and quickly registered brand names and set up benchmark risk indices that they then promoted and tried, often quite successfully, to sell to others. In fact the parallels with performance benchmarking were even closer than the usual marketing bells and whistles and much of the underlying maths and thinking was very close to investment benchmarking. There were also similar flaws lurking within the carefully manicured reputations of these models.

So what exactly do these models seek to show us? In simple terms we are looking at risk in terms of a normal distribution, or bell curve. The risk software captures all of the outstanding positions, obtains relevant end of day revaluations and then calculates potential profit and loss profiles based on simple standard deviation mathematics. Managements are then provided with potential scenarios that show the institution's Value at Risk. These are normally shown in monetary terms to bring the impact home, so a VaR model may state that there is a 96% confidence level (that equates to approximately two standard deviations) that the investments or portfolio being analysed will not lose more than "X" dollars, pounds or whatever over the period.

For example, the model might say the portfolio will not lose more than US$5 million in more than 4 trading days out of 100 and as such it effectively gives a monetary snapshot of potential risk. On top of this analysts can "stress test" the portfolio to create "what if" scenarios that show how the portfolio is likely to perform under extreme or unusual market conditions.

For senior managements who feared losing touch with the huge potential risks being run by their institutions VaR seemed like a godsend. Here was a model that could distil the risks down into a straightforward number, and produce rapid reports as the market conditions and the portfolio of instruments changed. Unfortunately life isn't that simple and Value at Risk models come with a price. They make a large number of assumptions (not unlike the Black-Scholes option pricing model reviewed earlier), some of which may involve a suspension of market realities and more importantly that can have a potentially serious impact on the market itself. This is why we need to address the issue – if it was just another boring bit of financial software, who would care? Increasingly, and the events of the credit crunch have illustrated this, it has become clear that such models have dangerous implications for financial markets by actually adding risk through forcing unwise trading decisions.

So what and where are the problems with what looks like just another piece of accounting software? First, these models proved so popular that they exploded in usage and were soon being applied to a number of different areas, in particular, risk reporting and risk limits (including trading stop loss systems), and also regulatory capital and capital allocation within business units. Suddenly the middle office was born, sitting between the traders and the settlement clerks. These new operations soon started wielding a lot of say in many finance operations and usually had the ear of senior management, who in traditional market style grabbed at the simple answer these models provided. Readers will recall that it is an iron law of financial markets that there has to be a reason or an explanation for everything and that the simple answer is always the most readily seized upon and believed.

Second, the arrival of the regulators in this mix has been particularly important. They have equally quickly seized upon Value at Risk as a method that will accurately show an institution's risks. This has led to them issuing all sorts of recommendations that make the use of these models more and more central to the management of risk. It is at this point that the lurking dangers of these models started to emerge.

The principle danger is herding (pro-cyclicality is the more fancy term). In the same way that fund managers cling to benchmark-driven business, regulators and risk managers are now on a path that may, quite unintentionally, be increasing risks and not reducing them. This may seem far-fetched, surely closer monitoring and measurement of positions will help contain large exposures and risks? Well, it might do if the models only did measuring and monitoring the risk, but critically they are now also used to trigger trading responses as well. The models have more than just an advisory role in that they are increasingly considered as mandatory management tools for adjusting risk, and so they have now extended into the field of taking investment decisions. It is ironic to think that positions and risk, that have been priced and undertaken using the judgements and skills of bankers and brokers, are now often hastily unwound simply because of simple valuation algorithms.

Consider the following scenario. An unexpected crisis blows up (they usually are unexpected, though occasionally there are well known trouble spots that finally boil over, one thinks of various Emerging Market currency crises over the years), which causes higher volatility throughout global financial markets as the market starts to demand a higher risk premia. As volatility is one of the key inputs into these models, the higher levels create higher risk readings, and as a result the risk models trigger selling of assets as institutions seek to stay within their VaR limits. As everybody of any size is now running these models, they are all trying to sell assets into a market with few if any buyers. This leads to a liquidity crisis and a sell-off in what had been totally unrelated markets. Suddenly uncorrelated instruments and markets are funnelled together and start correlating in a most precise manner. The dangers here are obvious (and for sharp-eyed market vultures so are the opportunities). The VaR approach has caused herding of selling activity that often spills over into totally unrelated markets. The denouement of such activity could be the equivalent of a financial nervous breakdown.

A Warning From Recent History – August 1998

This scenario may seem overblown, but in fact we have already come quite close to this potential fiasco already. On Monday 17th August 1998 the Russian government defaulted on their external debt and the market reaction was savage. One would have expected bond markets to react, as investors sought comfort in better rated government paper, and probably sought to sell lower credits with higher risks. This certainly happened, but other markets also had substantial moves in the following three weeks; the Dow Jones Index lost some 1350 points (over 15%), the UK stock market (as measured by the FTSE 100 index) dropped over 12%, and bizarrely the initial reaction was for gold to fall by over $12 an ounce (only just over 4% but entirely in the unexpected direction) in the succeeding few days. Much of this movement was caused by a "sell everything" mentality that was significantly fuelled by risk models. Indeed this sudden and fierce set of moves may have been the first VaR inspired crisis.

To cap it all, within weeks we saw the near collapse, and subsequent rescue orchestrated by the Federal Reserve, of the American hedge fund Long-Term Capital Management. The fund had been using valuation models that sought to exploit arbitrage opportunities in the credit curve. Such strategies were blown away in the hurricane that followed the

Russian default, and the losses at LTCM threatened a serious domino effect across the markets, hence the much needed official action. One may compare this to the accusations that equity program trading enflamed the October stock market crashes of 1987. There are subtle differences, though the same thinking is clearly at work.

In the current mindset, the market risk models, benchmarking performance indices and stop loss programs are adding a new dimension to markets. Unlike program trading that may have impacted a single market or asset class, the new thinking ranges across all financial markets. This means that they are creating connectivities that simply weren't there before, or at least strengthening previously weak linkages. As a result the markets are losing diversification, and breaking one of the simplest rules in the risk book. As we saw when looking at the efficient frontier concept, it is prudent and actually more rewarding to run a portfolio made up of assets with low correlations, but the mania for modelling risk is in danger of reducing the possibilities for such prudent behaviour.

In addition to these consequences, the current flood tide in global regulation is causing these linkages and connections to get closer and we risk a world where everyone is bound together and – should one big player stumble – we all fall. Or if you prefer, one might observe that the gap between the financial dominoes is being reduced. So in what we might term normal trading conditions the models work fine, with individual institutions trimming their risk as appropriate, but in times of extreme crisis the models perversely draw everyone into the same liquidity trap. In simple terms, when markets are falling the only thing rising is correlation. In the first edition of this book in April 2003 I wrote: 'One is tempted to speculate that it is only a matter of time before we have a significant financial disaster because of these current risk management fashions.' The events of 2008 were dangerously close to this scenario.

Followers of behavioural finance may view all of this activity from a different angle. In one way VaR type models are very good, because they force the individual trader to take action on a losing position and so should help prevent the paralysis associated with positions under water. However, they can also create an air of over-confidence and breed that most fatal of market attitudes: a feeling of total control. This is a dangerous illusion that is only ever dispelled when low or non-existent liquidity forces one to look at the market and not just the model. (This is analogous to the observation that drivers tend to speed in their cars more often as vehicle safety improves.) Also, of course, the whole idea sets risk in aspic, as if it is static and can be measured and contained, which is plainly wrong because the dynamics of markets can constantly fool us and no amount of risk managers and fancy software can totally overcome this. This is perhaps one of the best examples of the concept of distorting mirrors in financial markets – risk managers are not only not external to the market looking in, they are increasingly directly embedded in its most vital structures. They are in danger of being part of the problem, not part of the solution.

Another Lovely Loss

The vast majority of books, courses, seminars and nowadays the inevitable websites, blogs and webcasts about investment and trading strategies all bleat on about success (gurus prefer the term investment secrets), and how by simply following a few rules anyone and everyone can reap the benefits of playing the markets. This is both true and also outrageously misleading. It is certainly true that a relatively few number of rules or methods can show us the way to profitable trading, and yes they are usually quite simple, after all investment is actually a very prosaic undertaking. These rules, methods and concepts are the straightforward bit, but, as has hopefully become clear, the execution is anything but.

Perhaps there is a nature versus nurture argument here; are investors born or made? How much success is down to chance and randomness? Is it just impossible to outperform the market, and so perhaps it makes sense to just pick a market and hug the benchmark?

Investment is in fact a skill which can be learned. The problem seems to be that the skills required are not usually those that are taught, and they are pretty hard to stick with. In fact the skills required need to be constantly relearned and revisited, particularly as the investment world and those who report on it are often "experts" who know little, and constantly perpetuate myths and utter nonsense about markets. This is accentuated by an atmosphere that believes investment and trading can be learnt quickly – it can't – and that by somehow following mystical rules, secrets and other arcane methods we will all be guaranteed successful results. (Once again one cannot overstress how significant the word "guaranteed" is in these cases; this is nearly always a major warning. It is a sure sign that things are not well when the "g" word is overly used in financial schemes.)

The traditional approach is to look at financial markets in terms of economics and business studies. All sensible stuff for learning the building blocks of the economy, and how business operates, but these areas are only one facet of financial trading. The attempts to predict the future by chartists are often no better than tossing a coin, and as we have seen, the current vogue is to try and apply mathematics to everything, from risk measurement, to performance statistics and even hunting down chaotic patterns in stock charts. But again maths is certainly not the whole answer, and in fact it may be a dangerous blind alley.

The keystone to trading is in fact personal responsibility and self-control. The skills and disciplines that we can use to avoid over-indulgence in other areas of our lives are exactly the same as we need to control ourselves in the markets. Just like keeping to a sensible diet, or avoiding drug addiction and alcoholism, we can be taught all sorts of rules to avoid this behaviour, but we still have to be disciplined enough to follow them.

There is a Zen Buddhist proverb that says, paths cannot be taught only taken, which is a nice little way of saying that it's experience that counts in life. This may seem trite, but it is very true in financial trading where no amount of outside help will definitely provide the investor or speculator with success. One has to tame and control one's own inner thoughts and decisions. To try and illuminate further on this we need to concentrate on the most important and often very frequent part of the business – losses.

The first and most important thing to say about losses is learn to love them. Far too much money is lost by investors and speculators who try to avoid losses. What? This seems a very strange comment. But if you think about it, once a trade has gone wrong, why should you hope or expect it to return to your entry level? Why should you be allowed to escape scot-free? What exactly are your motives here; trying to make money or just trying to look good? Followers of behavioural finance will recognise this as trying to "get back" to the reference point as defined in Cumulative Prospect Theory. In plain terms we are often willing to risk more and more to try and get back to breakeven. This is rogue trader territory where bigger and bigger bets are placed in an effort to get to breakeven. The very interesting work by Kahneman & Tversky shows we actually become more risk-seeking when in these situations, i.e. we pile on more risk as we run our losses – or more precisely as they run us and then often overwhelm us.

It is probably true to say that more money has been lost by people trying to save face than in any other cause. This doesn't just affect individuals – institutions often fall prey to this vice, for example the seemingly never ending disaster of the British government's expenditure on the Millennium Dome was an object lesson in failing to face up to unpalatable facts. (It has always amused me that the dome was billed as an attraction when in fact nowhere near enough of us were attracted to go and visit it.)

Somewhat perversely a string of small but contained losses is in fact probably a sign of trading success. (Perfect trading records are always a serious warning sign – the recent events concerning Madoff illustrate this rather neatly – unfortunately such consistency is frequently not picked up by many risk models!) So losses are a continuous feature of trading and investment, and any record that shows they have been contained and accepted is very positive. Equally, trouble always lurks with the unrealised monster of face-saving investment decisions, which are usually driven by hope and prayer rather than rational thought.

Investment should be seen as a percentage game and we should realise that we can afford quite a high percentage of losers provided we can contain them. So the vast majority of our time and effort should be directed to money management. This means considering capital allocation, loss strategy (this may or may not involve stop/loss orders), profit targets and levels of activity. All of this implies a great deal of discipline, which is extremely difficult to attain.

Prospecting Risk

One other and final aspect of losses that is often overlooked is what we may term prospecting risk. Drilling for oil, mining for metals or for that matter producing theatre shows and films all have the same risk profile, and also have some lessons for financial investment. Typically, prospecting risk has two main characteristics: first, the risk should be spread over a number of ventures, for example a number of theatre shows. This is just normal common sense and simple portfolio diversification, and helps guard against the fact that a high proportion of them are likely to be failures. Indeed in the film industry in any ten projects it is likely that there will be five or six total failures, three or four that barely cover costs and hopefully one or two big successes (though not necessarily blockbusters) that cover all the costs of all the films plus a healthy profit margin. Second, the timing of where the successful 10% or 20% comes in the run of projects can be vital. This may seem irrelevant, after all if say you have divided your capital up into ten equal portions and allocated it accordingly to say ten drilling project; it shouldn't matter whether the pay dirt strike is first or last. True but there is a very large caveat. It is vital that you stick to only using the allocated capital for each project, if you overrun your resources you may run out at, say, drilling attempt number eight, and there is a chance that the big winner would have been number nine or ten. With these types of risks containing your costs is vital, and cost overruns are the nightmare of any mining prospector, movie producer or theatre impresario. The parallel in trading is our trading losses. If we fail to exercise sufficient discipline whilst experiencing losses there will be no chance to stay in the game to catch the big winner.

Unfortunately the world is full of romanticised stories of how down on their luck business heroes conquered all by betting their last cent on the one project. (The early oil prospecting experiences of J. Paul Getty make an interesting read in this respect.) But we only hear of the great successes while the silent majority of failures disappear into the land of losers anonymous. This survivorship bias plagues the investment world. So the lesson of losses is learn to accept them as a normal part of the investment business, but be ruthless in containing them because if you don't the market will be ruthless with you.

10

Signposts

'It is not the strongest of species that survive, nor the most intelligent, but the one most adaptable to change.'

Charles Darwin

There is an old Irish joke, at least it's Irish in the version I know, about the tourist who stops the local policeman in a small remote country village and asks the way to Dublin. After much pondering and chin rubbing the policeman volunteers 'If I were you Sir, I wouldn't start from here!' This is my advice to any reader who has skipped most of the book and hopes that here they will find earth-shattering investment tips, and the hidden secrets of profitable trading. Sorry to disappoint you, but if that's your aim the following ideas are unlikely to help you that much.

As this chapter title implies I have put together some ideas that are signposts towards hopefully worthwhile and profitable destinations. Such things are very personal, for as we have seen much of the business of investing is about personal preferences, risk appetites and biases. What works for some can be a real wealth killer for others. Anyway here are a dozen or so thoughts, they may be of help or you may consider them blind alleys. The fact that no two investors always agree is one of the primary engines that drives the whole financial business.

Don't Pray – Get Out

Things don't always go well in speculation: how many times has the old phrase speculate to accumulate turned out to be wrong? In fact seasoned and experienced investors expect a high rate of failures, a fifty-fifty split of winners and losers is probably on the very optimistic side. Indeed it's normally a certain sign of a newcomer when somebody underestimates the number of their likely losses. We have to get used to losses, even the most successful investor experiences them on a frequent basis. Given this, the key is clearly keeping those losses screwed down to the minimum, or at least to manageable levels. As the old market saying goes, the first cut is the cheapest cut. The game is about making money and you can only do that if you protect your capital. As we have seen there are a host of capital killers out there: brokerage, spread, slippage etc., even before any losses. And the profit/loss equation is asymmetric; when losses come (as they will) they are hard to recover from. Remember the rule about percentage gains and losses. Obviously keeping the losses small is vital, if you fail in this respect you will lose your capital and be out of the game.

Your own internal thoughts are the greatest demons in this situation; some find it almost impossible to take a loss. There are a number of psychological reasons for this, which all really come down two factors: being unable to admit that we were wrong, and facing the consequences of taking the loss. Many people become quite wedded to their speculative or investment positions, and believe they are still right even when faced with the daily decline in their fortunes. Far too many of us hang on hoping that the cavalry will arrive any minute. Of course on occasions we can have a lucky escape, but in the end such a cavalier attitude towards losses will be punished. In the string of losses we all have to accept there will be one real blockbuster that will floor us unless we can control ourselves. The sunk-loss bias in people's judgement systems can be very hard to overcome and we often go to extraordinary lengths to avoid or postpone the accompanying pain when faced with a loss. What can be done about this?

There is no easy answer, but a common technique is to leave a stop loss order. This is not as simple and straightforward as it may first appear. For the small player the stop loss has only one risk, you fear that you will get stopped out of a position only for it to then come good. Somewhat like a piece of jetsam, your investment is washed up on a beach before the market swiftly reverses, but you are beached and you miss out on the turning tide. This is the central fear that usually stops some people from leaving stop loss orders. Again it's part of that hoping against hope emotion that the cavalry will arrive, and not wanting to miss out when they eventually turn up.

For the large player these fears are also present but there is an even bigger problem – liquidity. The placing of a stop loss order to protect a large investment is tantamount to giving the market inside information on your investment strategy. For the big player the real worry is that the stop loss order gets known in the general market and other players hunt it down, get the order filled and acquire the position at what may be a favourable price and time. So trusting your counterparty, broker or whoever with the order becomes paramount. The big boys often insist on the use of code words, and the executing broker or bank usually has elaborate security to keep the details quiet, but the fear is always there. Sometimes, if the order is really substantial, it is impossible to leave a meaningful order anyway because the lack of liquidity will make it impossible to fulfil. Only the greenest of new boys ever leaves an at best order. (After all, one wonders at best for whom?)

For larger players, one idea might be to give the order to a trusted third party – this way you divorce yourself from the emotion of a stop loss order, and you don't actually leave an order in the marketplace. For some markets this is more practical than for others. It's fine for a market that is only open for limited periods, but in a 24-hour market like foreign exchange it is hardly a practical solution. In the professional world of banks and fund mangers many of them have strict VaR limits that effectively act as a third party constraint. One of the problems with this approach is that the valuation levels at which VaR limits are triggered often make no sense in market terms and can create forced liquidations that are not grounded in good market strategy.

Some players try to avoid all of this by having their broker call them if a certain level is hit – but that doesn't really help either. You receive a call to say your worst fears have been fulfilled and the broker asks you for instructions – are you going to deal or not? Once again the hobgoblins of fear and hope will almost certainly cause you to freeze, do nothing and pray that things get better.

A number of players use the fifty-fifty rule, they set a pretty tight stop (this is a very black art, dependent on market conditions, deal size, etc.) and automatically cut half the position on this level being hit. The remaining half of the position is protected by a stop further away than the first level. This seems to work for quite a lot of people because it reduces your exposure as things start to drift away, and it gives you a second bite at the cherry if the much hoped for cavalry does arrive and rescue the price action. This may seem like mental game playing, and avoiding taking proper action. But as avoidance is the default response to losses some form of action that seems to satisfy our emotions (however cock-eyed in its logic) is far better than no action at all.

So no great comfort from this first signpost other than the extremely practical – when things start to go wrong Don't Pray, Get Out!

Always Take the Cash

Virtually all successful businesses are ultimately built on a foundation of cash, without it they are reliant on credit, and by extension, valuation levels. All valuation levels are subject to the myriad of market forces we have examined throughout this book and as such can turn very nasty, very quickly, and often at the worst time. Warren Buffett put it rather nicely when he said 'Cash is a fact, everything else is an opinion.' Of course no business or individual can rely totally on cash but during any crisis or market meltdown, given the choice between having cash, other assets or uncommitted lines of credit, cash wins every time. The investor often has to make this choice, and as events after the end of the last great bull market in stocks have shown (will this be called the Millennium Bull?) it can be extremely risky to accept anything other than cash.

In fact the popularity of cash seems to ebb and flow with the fortunes of the stock market. In bullish times people will take increasingly dubious and ultimately worthless assets, but with a bear market, cash is the only currency. The late 1990s saw all sorts of non-cash inducements, payments and offerings. Chief amongst these were stock options, convoluted vendor financing schemes (giving credit to your customers so that they can buy your goods) and mergers and acquisitions financed with ever-increasing avalanches of stock. None of this was new of course, but the intense levels of activity belied the underlying truth that in mature (and therefore consequently vulnerable) bull markets, whilst stock becomes a powerful currency in its own right, its value can vanish very quickly the moment the market turns. This was particularly true as the final stages of the e-commerce bubble came to a head in the late 1990s.

At that time newspapers were full of stories of senior executives leaving well-paid secure jobs in mainstream companies to join new fledgling operations that hoped to be winners in the e-commerce gold rush. Typically these individuals were paid small(ish) salaries topped up with large amounts of deep out-of-the-money options. Why did they accept this? There were two reasons. First, they had become sucked into the greater fool thinking of bull markets. Just as an investor keeps buying stock well beyond any reasonable valuation (remember the Palm and 3Com example) so these business managers must have imagined that everything would just keeping rising and that their options would soon convert into hard assets with a cash value. Second, they fell into the classic options trap (more on which later) that out-of-the-money options are a good thing with fantastic gearing when (not if in this case) they come good.

For the new operations trying to lure management talent to their new exciting but commercially untried fields, the acceptance of just paper promises must have seen almost too good to be true. Effectively these companies were issuing their own non-convertible, non-cash currency. To add to the fun many tax regimes gave the companies very generous tax treatment of such schemes, so that they were almost cost free to the company. No wonder things quickly spiralled and ultimately ended in tears.

In some ways the beleaguered managers (well that's what they became in pretty short order – though naturally the media initially concentrated on the "huge fortunes" that had been supposedly generated) were no better than serfs in a peasant society where only the ruling class had opportunity to gain and keep the real wealth. It is the oldest trick in the book of totalitarian regimes to issue worthless paper currency to the general populous whilst the ruling elite have access to the real wealth via genuine currency. (You will recall from the recent past that in the Soviet Union only the elite had access to US dollars or other hard currencies that could be used in special shops to buy luxury goods.)

So the bull market had turned perfectly sane and often intelligent business managers into "internet peasants" armed with worthless options deals in place of solid cash. Investors in the M&A blitz at the time fell for the same trick, only to find the real bid for their investments was often well below their effective entry levels after the endless deals done by the managers of their company.

In a bear market sentiment slams heavily the other way; sometimes cash becomes overly revered and investors are not willing to buy any assets at all, preferring to hang on to cash in all cases. In fact there comes a point where price is no longer relevant because investors become just too scared to move away from cash. If this sounds like a fantasy then take a look at the last fifteen years in the savings market in Japan, where the ordinary saver has become so disillusioned if not downright scared of keeping money in precarious banks that private hoarding of cash is quite common. Of course, eventually the self-correcting nature of finance will overcome these fears as an initial brave few decide assets are so cheap it's worth spending their cash on acquisitions. For those who think such conditions are somehow special to Japan and would not happen in Western markets, we should recall the boast of the late J. Paul Getty that during his career he considered some of the cheapest oil he had found had been "drilled" on Wall Street during the depression years of the 1930s.

Cash is also an important indicator in equity valuations. It is common for most stock analysts to concentrate their efforts on price-earnings ratios. These have a very mixed record of assessing future company profitability and consequently share price performance. A much better indicator is to look at company cash flow as a return on capital. This seems to work because it is far harder to play around with cash values in a company's accounts than valuations on other assets such as stocks. Far too often companies book profits on items that haven't even been sold – marking up the valuation of stock or work-in-progress is a favourite trick. By assessing the cash flow of a business we can cut through the creative accounting and window dressing that pervades so many published accounts.

It was the ruling ethos of the London Stock Exchange that the market worked on the basis of 'My word is my bond'. This statement was the cornerstone of a market that felt it would develop and prosper only if there was complete trust and confidence in its operations. Fair enough – but wags used to twist the motto by saying 'Your word is your bond? I'll take the bond then please!' Okay a cheap jibe – but still there is a grain of truth. Don't take companies' or individuals' promises as payment, take the cash.

Options – Confusing Price With Value

At some point we all fall under the spell of traded options. They satisfy so many of the emotions and desires that speculators feel in the marketplace. They are pretty simple to understand, but have a sufficiently convincing gloss of sophistication to sound clever, and come with the fantastic promise that you can limit your losses whilst still having the possibility of large profits. The message is clear: the sky's the limit and you have a known fixed cost – buy an option and the world is your oyster. Well not exactly! Needless to say this happy state of affairs is rather more complicated than the marketing and sales people would have us believe, and in fact the buying of options is one of the hardest ways to try and make money in financial markets.

What are we buying when we buy an option? It is a mix of elements with time and volatility being the most important. So, whereas the novice player who buys an option thinks that they only have to get the direction right, the truth is that they must also correctly predict the implied volatility as it unfolds over the life of the option, and also suffer the salami slicing of their investment through the inexorable shrinking of time value. Juggling these three elements successfully is very much harder than most newcomers imagine, and it is no wonder that around 80% of exchange traded options (the figures from various exchanges regularly record this dismal state of affairs) expire worthless. A lot of premium money is clearly washed away into the grateful hands of option writers.

With three factors to get right, plus the usual enemies of brokerage, spread, slippage etc., the seemingly "easy" route to riches through buying options suddenly starts to look like a very hard uphill climb. One of the most common mistakes made is to buy low delta, i.e. far out-of-the-money options, on the basis they are cheap and the gearing is spectacular if they come good. This is rather like saying it's always a good idea to put money on a horse at fifty-to-one. We must remember why the odds are fifty-to-one in the first place – the nag's not likely to win!

Low delta options are often considered cheap as the premium payable is low, but this is to confuse price with value. In fact these options are normally more expensive in their valuations than buying the more highly priced at-the-money, or fifty delta, variety. As in all markets, supply and demand is a driving force in option pricing, and demand for the out-of-the-money instruments tends to drive up their costs. This is rather neatly illustrated by something called the volatility smile.

The following diagram shows implied volatility on the Y axis and the strike price of an option on the X axis (i.e. ranging from deep in-the-money through to deep out-of-the money options). In theory one might expect the implied volatility to be uniform across the range of strike prices, but in fact there is a definite pricing bias, or smile, causing a curve on the graph, in place of the expected horizontal line. Of course, option writers mark up the cost in response to the market demand, and punters who lack full information happily pay up, still believing they have bought a cheap entry ticket into the market.

Figure 10.1: The Volatility Smile

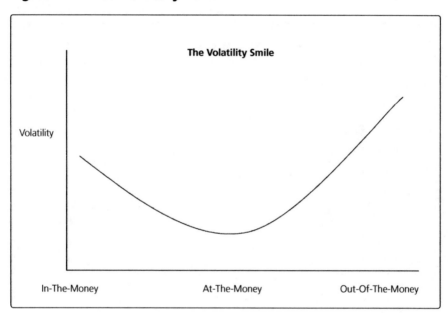

Option writers rely on the fact that buyers lack information on implied volatility and are also price insensitive. One might imagine that the option smile only exists in retail pricing, but the wholesale or professional market also displays this bias, where the same myopia about valuation is also exhibited.

The other factor, time, is more visible but is still an extremely invidious cost to deal with on a long options position. Time value also does not follow its expected path; it does not tick down in a nice straight line, amortising over the life of the option, but rather falls off in the shape of an arc, dropping faster and faster as the expiry date looms. As a general rule of thumb the first half of the life of an option sees the time value decline by one-third, with the other two-thirds melting away in the second half of the time period. This can be seen in the next illustration.

Figure 10.2: The evolution of time decay

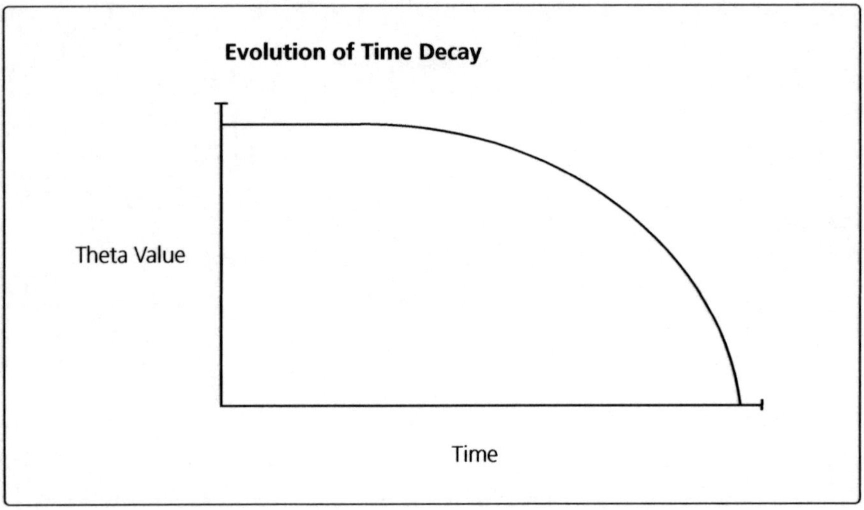

general rule of thumb the first half of the life of an option sees the time value decline by one-third, with the other two-thirds melting away in the second half of the time period. This can be seen in the next illustration.

So because of the cost of time value, you need to allow for more time in your option than your anticipated investment horizon. In an extreme case, you may buy an out-of-the-money option for little money, only to find the underlying market does in fact just get to your strike price right at the expiry date. So you would have been right about the direction, correctly predicted the time needed for the move, but made no money and in fact lost your premium. In general it is usually sensible to buy an option that is twice as long as your investment horizon, so at least the cost of time is being held in check (or more precisely ebbing at a slower rate) whilst you hold the option.

All of this begs the question – rather than buy options why not sell them? Earlier we examined the career of Russell Sage and it was exactly this strategy that worked well for him. As with any activity that is profitable, some work and effort is usually required in return. To successfully run a short options book demands two things: a diversified portfolio, because naturally it's easier to run a large number of short options which effectively then spreads the risk of exercise, and second it's important to have a clear idea of implied volatilities and the characteristics of that market. The small player may well lack the resources to obtain and analyse implied volatility data, but without it there is no hope of running a successful short options book. Sage did manage to price his book without this data, but in its place he had flow information, as he was a big enough player to see a sizeable part of the entire market. Also, the market Sage operated in was relatively illiquid with relatively few competitors, creating keener prices. Finally, remember implied volatilities move around in response to supply and demand. They are not some magic conjured up by a computer. So Sage's demand data from his customers was a pretty accurate proxy for the unavailable implied volatilities information.

There will be times when speculators may consider the risk-reward of buying options to be worthwhile, and they can be a valid and powerful investment tool, but remember to be careful when buying such instruments. The price is not the issue, it's important to understand whether you have obtained good value.

Gold – Currency Or Commodity?

What is it about gold? Why all the mystique and myth about the stuff? Gold often seems to bring out the worst in people – indeed quite a few of us seem unable to treat it as just another investment instrument. The yellow metal divides many observers into two quite extreme camps; one which believes it is the only unsullied asset left in the world, somehow a beacon for freedom and individualism whilst the second group consider it an unwelcome old-fashioned curiosity, harking back to less sophisticated times before the design and implementation of proper global monetary systems.

For the vast lump of us in neither camp, gold is still something of a mystery, perhaps it's all the glossy images from James Bond films, or more prosaically the fact it has often been banned, restricted or heavily taxed as a form of investment. As a result few people seem to able to view gold unemotionally – this is a shame because the gold market is the single best asset class with which to understand most other markets. Such a statement is bound to be a generalisation, but gold does come close to fulfilling many helpful market roles.

Naturally enough we tend to think of gold as a commodity, albeit a very rare one. It does have some industrial uses, and there is major demand as jewellery; but because of its rarity it has an intrinsic value that seems to make it stand above ordinary metals and transforms it into money. So it can be argued that it is better to think of gold as a currency rather than a commodity – it certainly has the main attributes of money in that it is a store of value and a medium of exchange. As a currency it also has some very special qualities because it cannot be printed (though passing off debased metal and coinage has been the traditional way to try and sidestep this) and therefore is not easily manipulated by governments. Furthermore, one could say that it has its own internal rate of inflation, which is really any new supply that is mined every year. It also is an excellent independent reference point for valuing other markets, in particular the US dollar.

A set of newspaper and financial magazine advertisements some years back proclaimed that the US dollar had never been devalued. These ads set out to promote the launch of a new high security version of the dollar bill and to reassure the public about their quality and security. However, players in the gold market knew differently. When the price of gold was no longer pegged at $32 an ounce the price soared, in fact within ten years it had briefly touched $800 an ounce, a pretty staggering devaluation of a kind. When the gold price was decoupled from the US dollar by President Nixon in 1971 as the financial realties of the Vietnam War finally hit the US economy after the massive bullishness of the 1960s, the true vulnerability of the almighty dollar was quickly revealed by the gold market.

Throughout history there have been different benchmark currencies, and these days we live in an age where the US dollar is the dominant global currency, while before that it was sterling. Further back in history various currencies have come and gone, but the one constant that has remained is gold bullion. For this reason gold has an independence and trust that is simply not found in other assets, though as with all assets it has bull and bear markets. In recent years it has enjoyed a bull market that saw the price almost quadruple, but there have also been long bear periods for the yellow metal. So for the speculator, gold is just another instrument to trade, and also makes a useful independent reference point. It is particularly useful as a benchmark for other prices; one of my favourites being the ratio between gold and oil. It is always interesting and instructive to see how many barrels of oil one ounce of gold will buy. This relationship tends to trade in broad terms between 10 and 30 and is an extremely good indicator for understanding global inflationary pressures.

So gold is really a hybrid, being both a commodity and a currency, the market price action is very similar to currencies, but its settlement characteristics can subject it to commodity-like delivery and settlement problems. These settlement issues are not trivial, for the player with a short position access to deliverable metal is vital, and in common with other commodity markets delivery squeezes can be painful.

For the general investor gold has two uses, it's a good reference point for other markets with a key role in the financial markets cycle, and it's a perfectly good trading instrument, with an active futures market to trade in. We should not be blinded by all the myths and mysteries of gold, it's just a good trading market. Whilst small investors can find access to the market difficult, as purchases of gold coins are a very poor way into the market (with retail profit margins and taxation on top of the actual bullion cost); a better way is probably the futures market. Alternatively, it is now possible to buy shares in an Exchange Traded Fund that invests directly in gold with the share price mirroring the spot gold price.

Money, Martingales And Pyramids

There are three main elements to a successful investment: direction, timing and money management. Each of these is progressively more difficult to master. Many market players (though not usually the most successful) seem to think that correctly anticipating market direction is the key to success, but in fact this is a relatively small part of the trading experience. Undoubtedly timing is important, but again not as vital as one may at first believe. By far and away the most important element in trading is money management. One can be excellent at direction and timing, but if you fail to follow prudent money management rules you will come unstuck. Equally, and this may seem somewhat perverse, one can be relatively poor at direction and timing but disciplined money management rules will at least reduce your problems and may even keep you profitable.

Needless to say money management and risk rules are a very personal decision; we all have different ideas of acceptable risk. As we have seen earlier, the dangers of rationalising away losses can be fatal, and so strict adherence to any rules is important. This can be far harder than one may imagine – it is one thing to have rules, and quite another to follow them. Institutions also have money management regimes, with VaR type structures, but these tend to concentrate only on potential losses. Ideally a comprehensive money management regime should also address the profits side of the equation.

Most money management is plain common sense, and is about creating a realistic structure that you can and will strictly follow. The first basic step is usually to divide your trading capital into a number of equal amounts with which to trade – ten is usually thought to be a sensible number. With this you never commit more than 10% of your capital to any single trade. Many speculators play in geared markets (so-called margin trading or via futures contracts) and here any gearing or leverage of more than five times your initial capital is courting disaster because at this level your P&L account is effectively moving five times as fast as the underlying market. In fact it may be more prudent to limit one's gearing to no more than three times.

So for an account size of US$100,000, three times gearing gives a total exposure of US$300,000, with no more than US$30,000 committed to any single trade. When you trade, one of two things can happen: you either make money or lose it. Either of these outcomes causes a dilemma – is it right to keep the same trading size, or increase or decrease it?

Starting with losses there is a school of thought that says you should increase your stake after a loss, in an effort to re-coup the previous setback. This has echoes of a well-known gambling strategy called a Martingale which involves doubling your stake on each successive bet, and is particularly popular amongst roulette players betting on a colour or on the odd or even series. This strategy is superficially attractive, but assumes the gambler has an extremely large amount of betting capital. To restrict such strategies, casinos habitually impose table limits that prevent gamblers with very deep pockets from constantly doubling up. Some investors have tried similar tactics to recoup trading losses, but this strategy has the horrific quality that you double your gearing on a reduced capital base. As such it makes no sense at all, and increases your exposure at an alarming and probably unsustainable rate.

On a more positive note, what about the more pleasing problem of how should we react after a string of wins? Some would argue that we should increase the investment size (after all each trade is now a smaller proportion of the increased capital pot), though there is a counter-argument that says after a run of successes you should in fact reduce your activity as it is likely that losses will be bound to be coming your way. The problem with the first idea is that you have chosen to gear up after your wins, and so any subsequent loss will be correspondingly greater. Equally, not increasing your deal size means you are no longer keeping each trade at the same proportion of your capital, and arguably you are not maximising your profit potential.

My preference in both the case of losses and profits (I put losses first just to reinforce the dismal fact that losses are a constant part of the investment scene, and so we should accord them due prominence) is to only re-adjust the trade size once a year. Admittedly, if during the year you experience a string of losses then your bets are getting proportionately bigger (because of the reduced capital base) but at a far lower rate than actually increasing their size. Equally, in a period of success, you are now effectively under-investing but that may be prudent after a string of winners. All of this is rather subjective and depends on the scale of your winners and losers – an alternative idea instead of the annual review is to re-base your deal sizes every time your capital base increases or decreases by a fixed amount or percentage.

These issues, whilst simple, hide quite a degree of complexity. Apart from closed out winning and losing trades, some investors choose to adjust the deal size whilst still in the trade. The most common strategy here is called the pyramid or reverse pyramid trade. Here investors refine their trade rules by sub-dividing the individual capital amounts per trade. For example, going back to our original figure of US$30,000 per trade, they then divide that into three amounts of say US$15,000, US$10,000 and US$5,000. The idea being that they commit half of the allocated capital at the initiation of the trade and then feed the other two amounts into the market at the appropriate time. Then when closing the position they sell the entire amount in one go. This sounds a good idea, in that you are buying into a rising market and you will achieve an attractive average in-rate. However, in practice it's extremely difficult to execute. What, for example, are the appropriate levels to add the second and third portions?

The reverse pyramid idea merely reverses this idea, suggesting that you should commit only a small proportion (say US$5,000) in the initial part of the trade, so that if it goes wrong early on, you have only committed a small part of your capital. If the market does continue to go your way you can add the other two larger lumps. The obvious problem here is that the average in-rate of the trade is pretty poor, and you may have effectively put the trade on too late or at an unfavourable overall rate.

On balance I think pyramiding and its various derivations should be avoided because it adds a number of subtle complexities to what is already a complicated decision process. It may also sow all sorts of seeds of indiscipline regarding actually cutting loss-making positions.

As I said earlier money management is an extremely personal and subjective topic – I find that the best rules are clear and simple and that you must discipline yourselves to follow them. There are a large number of books on the topic that often have a strong statistical bias and attempt to discuss optimum solutions. That is all fine and well but when you are trading it's your discipline that counts, not just the most elegant mathematical solution. It's likely you will find simple rules the easiest to execute, so stick with them

To summarise then, I find dividing my capital into ten portions, keeping my gearing low and reviewing my rules annually a happy medium. One final tip – keep a trade diary recording all the details of the trade; the simple act of writing down your investment strategies seems to help keep focus.

Yesterday's Papers

'Who wants yesterday's papers?' opined the Rolling Stones. Indeed, but in fact what use are today's newspapers? They were written yesterday anyway and let's be honest how many journalists have ever made a fortune out of financial markets? No doubt regulators, given half a chance, will want to stop any financial market activity by journalists and in fact this may turn out be an unplanned act of kindness – why risk being in the markets when you can write about yesterday's events?

In the world of investment and speculation news is an illusory commodity, and unfortunately thanks to global communications we are bombarded constantly by the stuff. News occupies a world where the suppliers confidently believe we the consumers have an unending appetite but the truth is that the sheer quantity of output has jaded even the most enthusiastic. In fact we suffer from a form of "news inflation" where increasing supply has devalued the content. It is extremely difficult to decide what to read, listen to and watch, let alone who or what to believe. Financial intermediaries spend an absolute fortune on live news feeds, specialist websites and pay TV services. Do we need to do the same? Well probably not, though that is not to say news should be dismissed out of hand.

When we examined news in the Hall of Mirrors chapter we touched upon the hierarchy of information often adopted in the Information Technology industry. This hierarchy tries to define various states, such as facts, information and knowledge. It is the received wisdom these days that the higher up this knowledge tree the greater the value of the commentary and so-called expert opinion; information and analysis is thought to be worth more than plain facts. Indeed, plain facts are often given away free or sold very cheaply, it is the commentary and analysis that usually commands the premium.

At first glance it makes perfect sense that an expert, economist or analyst should be able to charge for his skills. Unfortunately, as we have seen, there seem to be precious few that are successful in speculation or investment. So there seems little point in subscribing to their material. Equally, investment tips or ideas in the financial press and business TV are ten a penny and generally can be ignored (though as with all forecasting, occasional successes can be put down to random luck).

All very cynical then? No not really – it's just good to remind ourselves to be careful when reading and watching the highly edited versions of events we see called business news. Chartists always affect withering disdain of news and fundamental data, but in truth there is value in the facts; it's up to you to do your own analysis and donkey work. Many will also point out that when a piece of information is in the news, it is far too late to act. Indeed markets often seem to act perversely on news – it's the iron rule of trading to buy on the rumour and sell on the fact. Also, some observers have pointed out that when a big business story hits the general press the reported trend is almost certainly near its end. Screaming headlines about the strength of a bull market, or how the whole financial world is in despair and misery, nearly always mark the end of the trend, with a "surprise" reversal often soon upon us. So when do we know the news is relevant and when can we just switch off and read a good novel?

As ever we have to fall back on watching our competitors in the marketplace – in other words everyone else. Understanding the mood of a market and its participants is much more useful than most of the commentary that is available. Also, studying market history is likely to be more informative and rewarding than manically staring at news all day. In the headlong rush to instantly analyse and understand everything immediately, much useful and profitable information is either discarded or forgotten. Of course, as per the Gorbachev story related earlier, the first instant reaction to news is frequently totally wrong. Such is the capacity to transmit information quickly and globally that financial markets are now littered with these potential trading death traps.

The publication of US economic data is probably the most acute example of this disease. At least four times a month vital US data is published over the newswires (usually at 8.30 am Eastern Standard Time and 1.30 pm London Time), almost without exception the hours before the publication (i.e. the trading morning in Europe and the afternoon session in Asia) are very quiet, and upon their release there is a frenzy of activity. By the end of the day normal trading patterns return. This fluctuation in volatility is often cited by investors who consider such news releases to be important. In truth, however, they are more often than not just a source of more instant analysis. Probably more money is lost through trading decisions based on these data series than anything else. Readers in the London market can note with some satisfaction that this information coincides with their lunchtime, and probably can save themselves a lot of money by staying at their lunch tables and ignoring the bear pit atmosphere at 1.30 pm.

News has some importance, but it is far more important to understand its context, and also to be able to gauge the reaction of the marketplace. As such it can be viewed at a distance and in a leisurely manner. Both of these thoughts are counter-intuitive to the dominant credo of grabbing at all the latest news, that's why I try to follow this alternative view.

No Flags In Sight

The celebrated and highly successful American speculator Bernard Baruch once wryly commented that 'They don't put out flags at tops and bottoms in the market'.

It's everyone's dream to hit tops and bottoms, but chasing these rainbows is usually an expensive mistake, so is there any hope of getting on at least most of a move?

Follow the trend, or don't fight the tape, is considered sound investment advice, but what about the conflicting advice which says the consensus is always wrong and follow your own instincts?

Well needless to say there is often a neat aphorism that can be found to suit your investment views at any one time. But is there any way we can get ahead of the investment crowd?

As we have seen, it's wrongheaded to believe that one can be outside looking in on the investment process, but that doesn't mean that we have to follow the dominant sentiment within the game. The real problem with trying to decide when to be with the crowd and when to trade against them is timing. Timing is closely linked to risk appetite. Broadly speaking, the less your capacity for losses the more crucial the timing element in your trading style. This relationship is often magnified by gearing – the small player who has geared up can only afford to trade against the crowd if he manages to pick almost exactly the top or bottom and needless to say failure is the usual result. With a geared position this failure is often a painful if not ruinous experience.

Of course, much of the market advice, tools and trading systems offered to investors concentrate on trying to pinpoint precise market turns.

There are endless offers of systems, technical trading ideas and market timing packages that all try to find the mythical flags at the tops and bottoms of the market. This is a waste of time and money, but amazingly people are still attracted to this stuff. Why? Well the desire for control is usually the underlying driver – we all love the idea of being "in" on a secret system that will make everyone else in the market look foolish. The aim is ostensibly to make money, but so much of market behaviour is geared towards looking sharper than the next man.

A less exciting but usually more profitable way to time market positions is to eschew the bogus claims of pinpoint accuracy offered by various trading experts and instead look for the long pull of a new trend. This inevitably means either being too soon, and being exposed to mark-to-market losses, or being late and fretting that you have joined the party too far behind to get the benefit. Also, this broad brush approach assumes deep pockets and by definition low or zero gearing.

Interestingly, many market speculators reject this approach and seem to think making "only" 10% is not worth their while. In the same way that newcomers find it difficult to accept or expect losses, so it is with returns. Experienced players know and understand that very large returns are virtually impossible. Simple risk theory teaches us higher rewards entail higher risks, but the highly geared small player still chases these impossible goals. They seem to forget that 10% pa compounded doubles your money in just over seven years, and if you manage 20% pa compounded you reach the same target in under four years. For many, such pay back horizons seem far too long but such thinking is shallow. To repeat an old cliché, investment is a marathon not a sprint.

Of course we still have to identify the trend, or decide when a new trend is starting, but as ever there is no definitive approach. Chartists employ moving averages, trend lines and other paraphernalia, economists tend to talk in very broad macro economic terms, and most professional players resort to a mixture of everything including the all-important market gossip. One hesitates to recommend any charting technique, but there are certainly a whole host of trend-following ideas, together with over-bought/over-sold indicators, to choose from. Many people swear by some of these techniques, but of themselves they are unlikely to be very profitable. A more successful approach is to use strict money management rules.

One area I have experimented with is to toss a coin as the method for choosing the market direction. This may seem hare-brained but with careful application and thought it can be quite successful. The model (a rather pompous term for coin tossing!) is always invested in the market (so there is always either a long or short position in the asset), so timing is no longer an issue. The key then becomes to build a money management system that concentrates on cutting losses and trying to run profits.

At first glance, such an approach must seem mad, but there are some interesting elements to this idea. First, by using the coin we are getting away from the whole direction guessing game. We must remember that successfully predicting market direction is not the same as trading profitably. The harder issue of timing is side-stepped by always being in the market. Once an existing position has been exited by a money management rule, the coin is tossed again and a new position immediately established. This leaves us to concentrate totally on profit and loss rules. This is the hardest part of trading. As we have seen, how to calculate and execute stops is a complex business, as indeed is how to set take-profit rules, but these are at the core of trading, not the off-the-shelf magic systems that claim they can predict where the flags are at tops and bottoms. Such a money management regime, if properly constructed, will in fact allow you to run your profits on favourable trends and cut your losses. Of course, that word "if" is a very big one in this case. We all have to study and understand markets very well before we can successfully implement such a model. In an ideal world one would end up with a block of capital divided into ten parts, each being money managed with the coin as the decision engine!

Perhaps mad, but I suspect this has more chance of being successful than some of the advice and tactics being suggested to investors and would-be plungers.

What's The Score?

One of the most misleading and confusing parts of the investment process is performance measurement and attribution. This is puzzling because in many ways it should be very straightforward – you trade, you make or lose money and there can be no argument about how much you have at the end in your account. True, but there are a few more complications than that simple description. Let's start by considering some of the factors that blur the outcome.

The oldest trick in the book is to talk about relative rather than absolute performance. Financial advisors love benchmarks, and they aggressively market them as the true way to measure performance. At best this is only partially true, and in some cases it is wildly misleading. Fund managers, technical trading types and all sorts of model promoters always talk about how their performance has beaten an index or benchmark. Typically fund mangers claim they have outperformed the index, or are in the top quartile of fund managers in their sector. So what?

What sort of success is it if the index is down 10% and your fund has only lost 8%? Well according to the fund management industry this is a successful outcome! One could counter that it is no different from committing suicide by jumping out of the 8th floor rather than the 10th floor! Amazingly, many investors swallow all this benchmark nonsense, and it allows often lacklustre managers to stay in business. The benchmark industry has become an enormous focus of market attention with endless references to outperformance, tracking errors, and higher and lower quartiles. All of this analysis and introspection neatly circumvents the only important question – did you make any money?

The second great misleading investment statistic is the prediction success rate. Typical of this are adverts for technical trading systems that claim they were right 84% of the time, gurus who claim four out of five trades are winners, and pundits who have unrivalled accuracy in their predictions. As has become plain, prediction or forecasting (or even lucky guessing) has very little to do with trading and investment. Simply predicting a trend is not the same as making money out of it. It is not uncommon to discover that the sweeping generalisations usually miss out that although four out of five trades were winners, the fifth trade wiped out all the gains on the other four!

For anyone looking to place money with managers what are the sorts of performance information we should be looking for? The main three indicators to ask about are percentage return, drawdown and gearing. The percentage return is pretty clear, the actual profit or loss made over the year. The drawdown relates to the troughs in performance. If over a twelve-month period the fund had periods of losing money what was the worst trough in its performance or so-called equity curve? This is the drawdown. This is important because we need to know what potential pain there will be in investing with the fund manager. Of course we may be unlucky and invest in a fund that then has a subsequently worse drawdown than previous results, but at least this data gives us some reference point for potential exposures. The investor should also be aware of whether the fund or investment is geared or not – often the stellar returns that are quoted by some funds involve high gearing that may well mean the fund is also prone to very large losses.

Much of this information is rather opaque, indeed many investment funds produce monthly performance statistics, but ideally this is what an investor should receive. As a rule of thumb the drawdown on a fund should never be more than a third of the total annual return, and geared funds that are over five times geared are likely to be extremely risky. Indeed it is probably prudent to select a fund that is only three times geared.

In addition to these measures one should also be able to get so-called peak to trough figures. After any peak in performance there is an inevitable trough – this data tells the investor how long it is before the previous peak is exceeded. Also, measures of consistency of returns such as the Sharpe ratio and the Sortino ratio, together with the standard deviation of returns, should be scrutinised. It should also be possible to see results in terms of ratios of winning trades to losing trades, winning months to losing months and how much of the profits were attributable to the five best investments. Such information is extremely revealing in explaining the investment style of a fund manager, and as such should be crucial in any selection process.

In general funds that can show ungeared returns of more than 20% per annum are highly unlikely to be able to consistently produce such returns. Any fund or investment that can consistently make between 10% and 15% every year on an ungeared basis is very good. We should consider then a geared fund making around 30% consistently to be extremely good, and we should expect the associated drawdown to be no more than 10%. It is easy to forget that returns of 20% pa mean that you double your money in a little over four years – this is spectacular and any fund that claims consistent performance above this level should be treated with caution. After all, above these levels we are starting to venture down a thin tail on the distribution curve of returns, and we don't want to end up like the poor souls who sunk their cash into ostrich farming!

Finally, we must learn to ignore all the rubbish and marketing hype about quartiles of performance, pointless comparisons with benchmarks and the increasing use of surveys and polls where fund managers pick up rather tacky awards such as "Best Fund Manager in XYZ Sector" because none of that counts for anything. Unfortunately the retail investor has little chance to get any of the hard data metrics suggested, and has to make do with asinine stuff from marketing departments. In contrast, the more professional end of the market, and indeed the much maligned hedge fund community, normally provides extremely detailed performance data.

When selecting a fund manager, or even trying to assess our own trading results, the only thing that counts is hard statistical data. It is no surprise that many hide behind misleading and vague performance statistics – you have been warned.

The Far Horizon

Much of this book has been about time and market timing, and perhaps we should take one final look at this investment component. Obviously time is central to finance, and is also a factor in the more mundane money matters of our everyday existence. Most importantly it is never neutral in finance – time is either working for you or against you.

First, the concept of a risk-free return, which is normally associated with investment in high credit worthy government bonds, has a time element. The yield on such bonds gives us a minimum level that we should be able to attain on our investment over time. This return is usually termed the positive carry and is really the only benchmark that counts (and perhaps the only time we should countenance this over-used term). We should be able to earn more than this from our trading, if not we should give up and just buy the bonds.

Also, at a personal level we have costs. Living on the planet is not free, every day we either spend income or capital to maintain our lifestyle. This burn rate or negative carry is also true for companies, and of course, many financial instruments have a built-in negative carry, two of the best examples being long option positions, and shorting a high interest rate currency in the foreign exchange market.

As well as being embedded in our income and cost calculations, time is closely linked to volatility. As we have seen the greater our time or investment horizon the lower the effect of market volatility. This is why day trading is an extremely risky proposition and just to compound things most day traders usually trade on margin, or in geared futures products. This is not usually the path to great fortune, and unsurprisingly the day trading arena is littered with failure.

Keynes (that man again!) famously said that in the long run we are all dead – this was a riposte to the rather Micawberish attitude of some investors that everything will be alright in the long run. This attitude is just as dangerous and unrealistic as expecting to make a fortune in a few weeks from day trading. Many investors are crushed by unrealised losses, for example the so-called sunk-loss bias described in Chapter Four, and are terminally unable to cut a loss-making position. Time does not always heal a poor investment, and it is a well worn investment saying that long-term investments are short-term positions gone wrong. In normal life persistence is a much touted virtue, in trading it can lead to ruin.

In addition, the markets have increasingly adopted what are in effect artificial time constraints – the use of daily benchmark fixings, VaR calculations and alike all increase the telescoping of time at certain periods of the day, and on occasions can seriously distort investors' investment horizons. Effectively, false volatility has been added into the marketplace – often by the very people who are most risk-averse and are trying to avoid violent moves!

We also find that time creeps up in other areas, notably technical trading systems where the time element is a basic calculating ingredient for many indicators. Obviously moving averages, relative strength indicators and momentum studies are all wrapped up in ideas about time. Various investment gurus not satisfied with trying to predict future price moves often try to impress their audiences with forecasts of the timing of future moves. It has to be said their record is poor – but they keep trying as the investment community is gripped by the idea of "when" as well as "what" in the marketplace.

Time in financial markets is not linear. While we have already noted that the dealing room clocks tick around the dial like everywhere else, there are periods of intense activity (wide time perhaps) and equally periods of numbing inactivity (narrow time). These time patterns seem to have a fractal quality as well – some investment instruments and even whole asset classes often "go to sleep" for large periods of time. Of course the investor can take advantage of such inactivity by selling volatility, so quiet periods need not mean a lack of trading opportunities.

Perhaps the most telling effect of time on investment is compounding. Compound interest is pretty boring and low level stuff for the first few years, but after around fifty years or so it starts to warm up and eventually becomes a huge rolling behemoth. Of course few of us are likely to live to see the great pot of money that can grow from small beginnings, for example a US$1,000 at 8% pa compounded becomes approximately US$ 321,000 after 75 years, and approximately US$ 2.2 million after a hundred years. But the compound growth of profits can be a good way to build up capital, and also shows that wealth is often built with modest returns. Consistency of results is far more important than trying to get big winners. To use a cricketing analogy (though American readers can see the same idea in baseball terms) it is better to score quick singles than try to smash the ball out of the ground.

In an investment world that is gripped by market direction and thoughts of what will happen next, the nuances of time are often lost. I would still maintain that money management remains the most vital discipline in trading, but also to me it is clear that time is more important than direction. Timing of a trade has a very subtle effect on its subsequent management and the setting of risk parameters so we have to consider time a close neighbour of money management. In contrast the market direction is a rather subsidiary topic. We must learn how time can work in our favour and against us, and to try to shape our trading strategies accordingly.

Well They Worked Last Time

The renowned British economist Charles Goodhart shrewdly noted that as soon as you focus your attention or rely on any particular economic indicator or set of statistics it immediately starts to give false signals and fails to live up to its reputation as a sound guide. Whilst bearing this caveat in mind, I thought I would put forward a couple of trading ideas that have worked quite well in the past. Needless to say I can give no hope that they will always do the trick in the future.

First let's re-visit some inter-market ideas and take a look at the Financial Times Gold Mines Index. This is the premier index for gold mining shares and as such is a pretty accurate barometer of mining stocks, and more importantly market sentiment about gold bullion. In many parts of the world there are restrictions or sales taxes associated with dealing in bullion, as a result much of the market's interest is directed towards the mining stocks. Consequently, early and speculative trading activity often shows up in mining stocks before, or at least coincident with, any bullion price move.

For example, the gold bullion price made a significant high at the start of February 1996 with a high of US$418 per ounce. This was important because almost exactly to the day the FT Gold Mines Index also put in a high at 2515. Now, we could not have known that these highs were in place immediately, however by June 1996 sentiment was evidently faltering in the mining sector and by the year end the index stood at 1824 (a decline of over 27%). This was only a precursor to an overall move that would see a fall to the 570 level by 2000. The gold bullion price soon followed suit; by the end of 1996 it was trading at US$369 (off nearly 12%) and proceeded to make lows in 1999 and 2000 at just a shade over US$252 an ounce, an overall decline of nearly 40%. Here two things are clear, the gold mines index was the more geared market play (this makes sense as mining stocks are extremely volatile, particularly if they begin to trade near or around their gold production cost levels – which was definitely the case for many when the bullion price stood in the 250s) and second, if you missed the mining play, or were frightened by its higher volatility, you could still take it as a good signal to play in the bullion futures market.

The signals for an upturn in the gold market were pretty clear as well, and in this case with an interesting twist. In late August 1999 the bullion price hit a low of US$252.50 and was accompanied by demonstrations in London's Trafalgar Square by South African miners protesting at the British government's decision to auction some of the UK's gold reserves via the Bank of England. For the seasoned market observer a number of thoughts came to mind – protesting in the streets and follow up newspaper and press coverage is normally the sign of the end of a move, *not* the beginning. Second, there was something wearily inevitable that government selling would be after a 40% decline – there was no sign that the British government were looking to exit at above US$400 in early 1996. Then suddenly in early September 1999 there was a major shock to the market – a group of the largest central banks with significant gold holdings announced to the world that they would adopt a self-denying ordinance and restrict themselves regarding future sales. The bullion price immediately went ballistic, briefly touching US$330 within a few days of the announcement, but – most importantly – the FT Gold Mines made a far less enthusiastic move and soon both mining stocks and bullion were continuing down into 2000. Although the bullion market had made a valiant attempt to start a new bull market, price action in the gold mines was half-hearted at best. So in this case we failed to see either mining stocks lead or reinforce a bullion price move.

Things finally got moving nearly a year later, in November 2000, when the Gold Mines Index made what turned out to be a low, and within six months it was clear a new trend was underway. Needless to say the bullion market took much more notice of this price action than the cartel-like antics of some major governments, and right on cue gold made a low of US$254 in February 2001 and was challenging the US$330 zone by June 2002. On this occasion the bull move had been stable and sustained rather than a knee-jerk reaction to a bit of opportunism amongst official (and no doubt somewhat distressed) holders of the precious metal. So it would appear we can learn a lot by watching the inter-play of mining stocks and bullion. This is hardly rocket science but a profitable relationship if carefully (and slowly – these markets tend to grind along) studied.

Another relationship that works pretty well is the link between economic recessions, the dollar and US interest rates. The inter-market cycle shows that when the business cycle turns down the authorities react by cutting interest rates, and it is this action that in time causes the bond markets to first stabilise and then rise as long-term rates usually fall, as do the short-term rates set by central banks. In general the dollar suffers when US interest rates are falling, so one would expect this to be the case in recessions with authorities slashing rates, however in fact the dollar is usually strong in the early parts of a recession. This has once again happened in the period after August 2008 with the sudden and fierce move in the dollar with its trade-weighted value soaring by 15% or so in five months. Why?

The basic reason is the US money supply and its reaction to the business cycle. As business activity peaks Fed action usually starts to restrict credit and tighten the money supply, as the economy begins to cool and head towards recession banks cut back on lending and as a result the supply of dollars in the marketplace is reduced. This invariably causes the dollar to rise against most major currencies in the early part of the downturn. As the economy slows the Fed naturally eases credit, reduces rates and increases the supply of dollars into the market and this effectively devalues the dollar against its major trading partners. The credit crunch that unfolded throughout 2008 hit the currency markets in early August and the immediate (and to some quite puzzling reaction) was very strong buying. At some point probably around a year later the position will be reversed as more dollars flood onto the market and currency markets slam the dollar into reverse. The pattern has happened in every single US recession since World War II and is probably one of the easier market moves to predict and exploit.

One final long-term relationship worth pondering involves an asset class that we have not considered up until now – domestic property. At the time of writing this edition (early 2009) UK house prices are tanking, with some of the worst declines seen since the early 1990s and dire predictions for the future. The picture is similar if not worse in the US.

Once again we are seeing that property market collapses follow bear markets in stock markets like night follows day. Here's some evidence from past sequences. In the early 1970s property was the great inflation protector – 'Put your money in bricks and mortar' was the advice – but when stocks hit the skids in 1974 property hung on for a couple of years before falling (certainly in real terms). Equally, after the crash of 1987 we had a two-year gap before the music stopped, and this time property prices were slammed. Papers were full of negative equity disasters and house owners just handing in their keys to banks rather than trying to keep up with their debts.

Well, I would venture that here we go again. The year 2008 was calamitous for stocks, indeed a significant bear market emerged, accompanied by a bloodbath in the bubbles in emerging markets and commodities. This time many would argue that the credit crunch was caused by a bubble in property and that it was this that fed the fall in stocks. In this case the falls have almost been simultaneous, but what is not in doubt is how closely these two asset classes seem to be correlated.

This time perhaps past form will let me down, and maybe all the above examples of the past are just that – anchored in the past. In particular we may be tempted to recall the coincidence described regarding the Brazilian football team in the World Cup, which singly failed to work for the 2006 tournament. There is, however, a difference in these cases – here there is some underlying causation that should give us some hope that we can trade profitably. On balance I would rather have money on a falling property market than a bet that the World Cup formula might come good in 2010!

So despite all the traps and hedging in with various warnings, it is clear that diligent study of market history can still turn up interesting links, many of which can be traded very profitably, at least for a while before everyone gets in on the act.

Yeah I Know...But

In this concluding section I want to restate some of the major themes of this book. First, and most importantly, finance is simple but not easy. There is a fashion these days to believe that finance is complicated and wrapped up in complex maths and arcane terminology. This need not be the case because the basics of finance are simplicity itself. The whole business can be seen in terms of three basic actions: buying or selling, borrowing or lending, and executing the transaction now or at a future date. The idea that much of financial activity is based on accruals and annuities, and the fact that financial risk can easily be understood in terms of four simple graphs, should not be forgotten.

The hard part is in the execution of financial business. The vagaries of the inner self, the imponderables caused by time, the nature of volatility, all conspire to make financial speculation a difficult endeavour. On top of this the megaphone advice, research and sales patter that engulf us all is extremely difficult to survive. Experts, gurus and pundits have an answer for everything and an instant view about the future for every likely paying customer. To be able to shut yourself off from these sirens is perhaps the hardest part of the business.

We also live in an age that worships information technology, the computer and the ability to communicate globally on a very cheap basis. All very worthy achievements, but secondary to the business of speculation and finance. The market is not primarily about technology, it is not just about software packages and the latest developments in global bandwidth, it is still a business about judgement and skill.

History is another overlooked area within financial markets – in the manic atmosphere of always wanting to know what's next, we are in danger of forgetting the bigger picture. In finance there truly is nothing new under the sun. Markets have become more sophisticated, the pricing of risk has probably become more accurate, and trading volumes and activity have exploded in the last twenty-five years, but the basic themes and underlying cycles are still in place. Their amplitude and frequency may change but the core characteristics still hold true. Much money can be made by studying long-term relationships and understanding the linkages between various asset classes. The prevailing orthodoxy that markets should be analysed and traded in narrow vertical sectors is myopic.

Magic solutions don't exist; econometric models, technical analysis, high frequency data analysis, genetic algorithms, kernel regression systems et al, will not give you the perfect answer. They may be right some of the time, but we must remember that markets are dynamic and not static. By this we don't just mean the prices move constantly, but that the characteristics and emotions of a market are in constant flux. It's virtually impossible that a static system can capture all of this activity on a consistent, on-going basis. Flexibility is a key attribute in investment, and systems by definition are usually too rigid.

Performance claims by others must be viewed with a particularly critical eye – ignore the marketing drivel about fund manager's league tables, industry awards and surveys, and outperforming pointless benchmarks. The only test is how much money you or your investment manager made. Is it consistent? Is it sustainable? Does the manager understand the market or have they just been lucky in a bull market? Much is made of transparency in today's markets, but the case for clearer and more accurate investment information still remains unanswered.

Perhaps one of the best ways forward is in the realm of behavioural finance. This has grown in popularity in recent years as more research has been done into the decision-making processes of market participants, and on trying to understand their motives and rationale for their actions. It may be a cliché but understanding ourselves may in fact be more important than understanding the markets. How we act under pressure is perhaps more vital than trying to predict any sudden move or surprise. Learning to control ourselves is much more attainable than trying to learn how to control markets.

Because we are all different in our approach and our capacity for risk we will find that different ideas and angles suit us best in trading; that is why it is pointless to get hung up on one idea that seems to work for someone else.

Costs are, as we have seen, another overlooked but dangerously toxic area. The costs of constantly trading can be vast; in trading; less is often more. Constantly trading is not advisable. Your broker will love you, but your bank manager may be very concerned. Small costs such as brokerage, spread and the hidden factor of slippage are potentially fatal, and only the greenest of newcomers fail to understand this. Also, losses are natural, it is hard to say that we should welcome them, but we have to get used to them because they are constant visitors in this world.

Finally, remember that speculation and investment is about understanding the difference between price and value. Fashions come and go, pet theories, big market names and high finance ideas ebb and flow, but correctly understanding the relationships between price and value remains the key. Every investor or speculator has to find that out for themselves and for many of us it remains a hard battle. Don't believe anyone who says it is easy – they are misleading you. As I said earlier it's simple to understand but not easy to do.

I will leave the very last comment to that titan amongst American bankers J.P. Morgan who, when buttonholed by an anxious journalist outside the New York Stock Exchange during a period of anxiety, was asked what the market would do next. Morgan fixed the journalist with a calm stare and coolly replied 'Fluctuate!'

Bibliography

Books and reference works on finance, trading and markets are legion, and so I have tried to keep the following list to relevant sources and references. In many ways it is impossible to make a definitive list, but I hope that the following will be helpful for those who wish to pursue the topic of investment and speculation further. Hopefully readers will find that all the listed works have value, but I would like to particularly highlight four works which I think are informative and thought provoking; *Butterfly Economics*, and *Why Most Things Fail* both by Paul Ormerod, *From Here to Infinity* by Ian Stewart, and *A Mathematician Plays the Market*, by John Allen Paulos. Full details of these are in the following list.

References

Bachelier, Louis, *Théorie de la Spéculation* (Paris, 1900).

Ball, Philip, *Critical Mass: How One Thing Leads to Another* (Arrow Books, 2005).

Beinhocker, Eric D, *The Origin of Wealth: Evolution, Complexity, and the Radical Remaking of Economics* (Random House, 2007).

Cooper, George, *The Origin of Financial Crises: Central Banks, Credit Bubbles & the Efficient Market Fallacy* (Harriman House, 2008).

Elliott, Geoffrey, *The Mystery of Overend & Gurney: Adventures in the Victorian Underworld* (Methuen, 2006).

Gallwey, W. Timothy, *The Inner Game of Tennis* (Jonathan Cape, London, 1975).

Keynes, John Maynard, *The General Theory of Employment, Money and Interest* (Palgrave Macmillan, 1936).

Marshall, Alfred & Marshall, Mary Paley, *Economics of Industry* (Original Edition 1879) (Thoemmes Press, Bristol, 1998).

Murphy, John J., *Inter-market Technical Analysis: Trading Strategies for the Global Stock, Bond, Commodity and Currency Markets* (John Wiley & Sons, New York, 1992).

Ormerod, Paul, *Butterfly Economics* (Faber & Faber, 1999).

Paulos, John Allen, *Innumeracy: Mathematical Illiteracy and its Consequences* (Penguin, 1997).

Schwed Jr, Fred, *Where are the Customers' Yachts?* (John Wiley Sons, New York, 1995).

Shaw, George Bernard, *Everybody's Political What's What* (Constable and Company, 1944).

Stewart, Ian, *From Here to Infinity: A Guide to Today's Mathematics* (Oxford University Press, 1996).

Further Reading

Berlinski, David, *A Tour of the Calculus: The Philosophy of Mathematics* (William Heinemann, London, 1995).

Chancellor, Edward, *Devil Take The Hindmost: A History of Financial Speculation* (Macmillan, 1999).

Davies, Glyn, *A History of Money: From Ancient Times to the Present Day* (University of Wales Press, Cardiff, 1995).

Douglas, Mark, *The Disciplined Trader* (Prentice Hall, 1990).

Eastaway, Rob & Wyndham, Jeremy, *Why Do Buses Come in Threes? – The Hidden Mathematics of Everyday Life* (Robson Books, 1998).

Galbraith, John Kenneth, *A Short History of Financial Euphoria* (Penguin, 1994).

Geisst, Charles R., *Wall Street: A History* (Oxford University Press, London, 1997).

Getty, J. Paul, *As I See It – My Life As I Lived It* (Prentice-Hall, 1976).

Harrison, Fred, *Boom Bust: House prices, Banking and the Depression of 2010* (Shepheard-Walwyn, 2007).

Josephson, Matthew, *The Robber Barons* (Harcourt, Brace and Company, New York, 1934).

Kelly, Fred C., *Why You Win or Lose: The Psychology of Speculation* (Fraser Publishing, Burlington, 2000).

Kindleberger, Charles P., *Manias, Panics and Crashes* (John Wiley & Sons, 2005).

Lefevre, Edwin, *Reminiscences of a Stock Operator* (John Wiley & Sons, New York, 1994).

Livermore, Jesse, *How to Trade in Stocks* (Traders Press, Greenville N.C, 1991).

Mackay, Charles, *Extraordinary Popular Delusions and The Madness of Crowds* (Harriman House, 2003).

Ormerod, Paul, *Why Most Things Fail: Evolution, Extinction & Economics* (Faber & Faber, 2005).

Paulos, John Allen, *A Mathematician Reads the Newspaper* (Penguin, 1996).

Paulos, John Allen, *A Mathematician Plays the Market* (Penguin, 2004).

Redmond, George, *Stock Market Operators* (Financial Times Prentice Hall, London, 1999).

Rothchild, John, *A Fool and His Money: Odyssey of An Average Investor* (John Wiley & Sons, 1998).

Sarnoff, Paul, *Russell Sage: The Money King* (Ivan Oblensky Inc., New York, 1965).

Sarnoff, Paul, *Jesse Livermore Speculator-King* (Investors' Press, New Jersey, 1967).

Skidelsky, Robert, *John Maynard Keynes, Volume Two: The Economist as Saviour, 1920-1937* (Viking Penguin, 1994).

Smitten, Richard, *Jesse Livermore World's Greatest Stock Trader* (John Wiley & Sons, 2001).

Stewart, Ian, *Does God Play Dice? The Mathematics of Chaos* (Basil Blackwell, Oxford, 1999).

Index

3Com 17-19

A

absolute return objectives 5

Allen, Woody 3

AOL 215

asset backed securities 49, 59-60

autumn effect 211

B

Babbage, Charles 15

Bachelier, Louis 133

back-engineering 184

Baring 158

barrier options 49, 118

Baruch, Bernard 34, 260

bear markets 79, 88, 112, 137, 189, 213-216, 246

behavioural finance 100-101, 104, 115, 234-236

bell curve 90-91, 229

benchmark currencies 253

benchmarking performance indices 233

benchmarking 80

Benoulli, Jakob 4

beta valuation 68

Big Bang 49, 110

Black Wednesday 70, 194

black-boxes (trading models) 112-114, 158-163

Black-Scholes formula 30, 93-96

Black-Scholes options pricing model 230

bonds 201-204, 207, 223, 266

Boneparte, Napoleon ix, 7

Botvinnik, Mikhail 15

Bowie Bond 59

Bowie, David 59

bull markets 189, 202, 213-216, 224, 245

burn rate 61-62, 266

business and economic cycles 199-206

butterfly effect 142

Byron, Lord 16

C

candlestick charts 130

capital gains taxation 5, 58, 121

Carlyle, Thomas 147

Carnegie, Andrew 228

carry 62, 266

cash 244-247

Chaos Theory 64, 131, 142, 144

charts and charting 67, 130-136, 190-191, 258

chess 14-16

Chest Endowment Fund 39

Chesterfield, Lord 152

coincidences 183-185

commodities 161, 189-190, 202-207

compounding 268

computers 15-16, 147

    charts and 131

    impact of 48-49, 129, 141-142

confirmation bias 102-103, 117

contrarians 180, 191

copper 202, 206-207

correlation 184-187

    government-inspired 186

coupon strips 49

credit risk 78, 79, 80

creditworthiness 60, 226

crowd following behaviour 22

currencies 144, 161, 184, 193-194, 202-203

Cutten, Arthur 36-38

cycles 199-206